D1598060

Sergey Volkov

A Concise History of Imperial Russia

Maps and cover

by

Alexander Krishchyunas

This book presents a concise history of Imperial Russia from the perspectives of geopolitics, system of government, social structure, and military history. Many original maps in Plate Carrée projection help the reader follow the story of imperial expansion

CONTENTS

Maps

iv

Chapter 1

Russia at the cusp between the 17th and 18th centuries

Russia's geopolitical and economic situation in the late 17th century was extremely dire. The climate and environment of East European plain (where the core area of Russian state-building was located) was hardly favorable for agriculture, which was central to the economies of those times. Compared to most European countries, growing season for crops was relatively short. That, along with frequent freezing weather spells (both in spring and fall), poor soils across most of the country's land area, and a number of other factors made harvests poor. In turn, low productivity of farming made it difficult to accumulate sufficient surplus resources required to build up defense capabilities and support cultural growth.

Dramatically lower population density than in the rest of Europe made it impossible to have a comparable level of national infrastructure. That handicap was further compounded by the fact that during catastrophic Mongol invasion of the 13th century it was the most densely settled and economically productive areas of medieval Kievan Rus' that suffered the worst devastation. Russian statehood fell into decline. Peripheral North-Eastern Russia came under the vassalage of Mongol-founded state of Golden Horde, while the core areas of old Rus' became part of first the Grand Duchy of Lithuania (Lithuanian-Russian state) and then of Polish-Lithuanian state. While in pre-Mongol period Rus' was an integral part of a wider European community, it now became culturally and politically isolated.

The whole history of ascendancy of the principality of Moscow (or the Muscovy state period of Russian history) was one of the struggles to revive the lost meaning of Russian statehood. Those struggles were long, but ultimately met with little success. It took Moscow over two centuries to reunite even the lands that remained under sovereign Russian rulers, that is to say the principalities not ruled by foreign powers (principalities of Tver and Ryazan, and the states of Novgorod and Pskov were annexed only at the end of 15th and early 16th century).

Even as newly strengthened Russian state adopted a more assertive foreign policy in mid-16th century, it won no gains along the western frontier. Mopping-up successor khanates of decrepit and broken-up Golden Horde was successful, but clashes with European neighbors essentially brought no gains. While in the eastern direction Russia's boundaries advanced by thousands of kilometers, along the western frontiers there was no advance to speak of. Moreover, in the early 17th century, the very continued existence of the Russian state hang in the balance under concerted onslaught by Poland and Sweden. By the end of the period of so-called 'gathering' (or unification) of lands of Central Russia (in the first third of 16th century, or at the start of Ivan the Terrible's reign), Russia's western border ran close to Smolensk and Chernigov, but a century later (and even into mid-17th century) it was pushed back even closer to Moscow itself as Muscovy lost some earlier

1

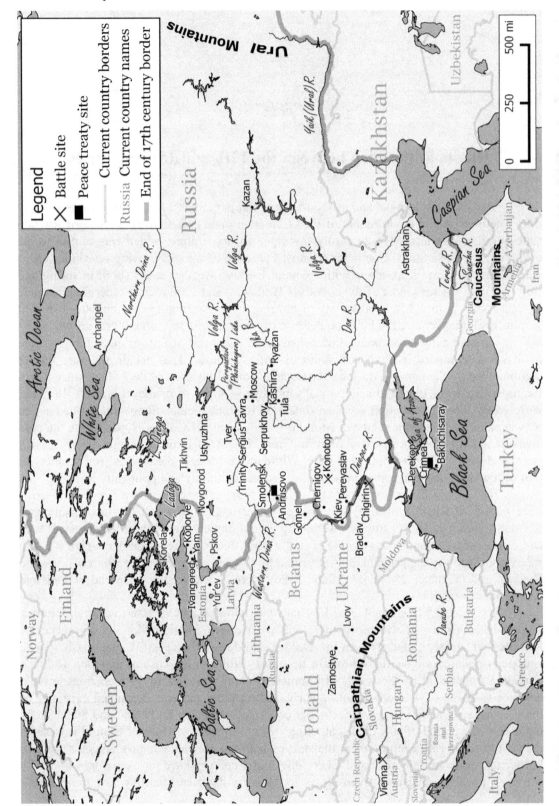

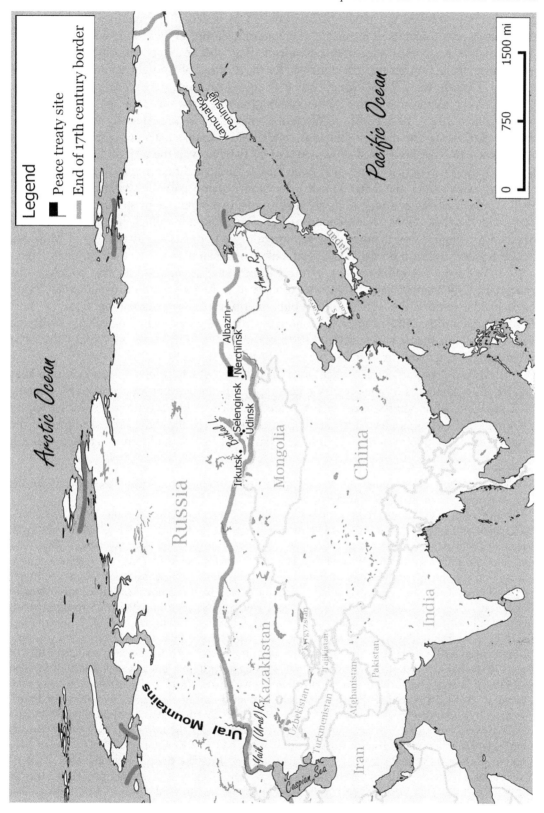

gains. Having imbibed too much 'Asianness'[1] in its successful struggle with foes to the east, Russia now found itself incapable of countering European foes to the west.

Some temporary successes notwithstanding, the absolute majority of wars with adversaries from European West either ended in a draw, or brought additional losses of territory. In those wars, Russia sought advance along two strategically important directions. One was to break through to the Baltic coast and return erstwhile Baltic possessions (prior to German conquest, both banks of Western Dvina River were owned by Russian princes receiving tribute from the Liv and Lett tribes, while native Estonian population was in dependency to Novgorod and Pskov, and part of Estland with the city of Yur'ev (Tartu in Estonia today) was actually part of Kievan Rus'). Another thrust sought to regain lands in the west, which after the Tatar-Mongol invasion became part of Lithuania and later of Polish-Lithuanian state. Along both of those fronts, two centuries of struggles brought less than modest gains.[2] With the exception of Left Bank Ukraine (which was annexed not by Moscow's conquest, but thanks to the sentiment of its population), by the end of Muscovy period Russia's western border was less advantageous than before Ivan the Terrible's reign.

With poor conditions for farming, economic weakness of the country was exacerbated by another factor that was directly due to its geopolitical situation. Being landlocked excluded the country from bulk maritime trade – something open to most European countries. Of all forms of economic activity then available, maritime commerce was the most profitable and beneficial for economy at large. It served as the key driver of economic development for the most successful powers of that time.

By contrast, in Russia even overland trade (which brings fewer benefits) was significantly hampered by the country's geography. Its huge expanses accounted for sparse road network, while long winters and extended periods of impassable roads during spring snowmelt and fall rains pushed transportation costs through the roof. That said, even if the country had agricultural surpluses, inherent limitations of animal-drawn haulage make it

---

[1] In Russian, the word connotes all the bad traits that westerners historically associated with the Orient: tyranny, sloth, and overall backwardness.

[2] The only wars to prove rewarding for Russia were those with Lithuania in 1500–1503 (which won back lands of Severia) and in 1513–1522 (which won back Smolensk). All the other wars (with Livonian Order in 1480–1482 and in 1501, with Lithuania in 1507–1508, with Sweden in 1496–1497 and in 1554–1556) booted Russia nothing. The war with Lithuania in 1534–1537 actually made Russia lose previously regained city of Gomel. Livonian War of 1558–1583 lasted a quarter-century and bled Russia dry, but not only failed to give it access to the Baltic Sea but cost the loss of Ivangorod, Yam, and Koporye to Sweden (a later war with Sweden in 1590–1595 restored status quo). Finally, during wars with Poland in the so-called Time of Troubles (1604–1618), Russia lost lands regained from Lithuania a century earlier. War with Sweden in 1614–1617 brought a new loss of lands regained in 1595, but also of a major part of Karelia with Korela, and complete loss of access to the Baltic Sea. Polish War of 1632–1634 brought negligible gains. A new war with Sweden in 1656–1658 was also futile. Even initially impressive successes of Russian troops in wars with Poland in 1654–1656 and 1658–1667, which happened under the most favorable conditions (wrecked by Ukrainian revolt of 1648–1654 and subsequent Swedish invasion of 1656–1660, Poland barely survived as a state), turned into very modest gains under the terms of Peace of Andrusovo (1667), which followed the rout of Russian army at the battle of Konotop (1659). That peace gave back to Russia only lands lost in 1618 (even though Russian troops occupied almost all of Byelorussia), while the only part of Ukraine (from which Poland was driven entirely all the way to the cities of Lvov and Zamostye during the war) to be annexed to Russia was its Left Bank (under the terms of Union of Pereyaslav (1654)).

4

fundamentally unsuitable for exporting perishable products. Russia had only one seaport to support maritime trade, Archangel, but conditions in the White Sea, brutal climate of Northern Russia, and that port's remoteness from the country's core and its more productive farming areas severely curtailed its potential as a port of export.

Strictly speaking, being landlocked was in itself sufficient to rule out successful progress of the country. Staying within those boundaries would have doomed it to stagnation, decline, and eventual carving-up by its western and southern neighbors.

While Russia's boundaries in the west after the Peace of Andrusovo (1667) and Treaty of Eternal Peace with Poland (1686) were quite disadvantageous, they enjoyed peace and faced little threat of invasion. By contrast, southern parts of the country lived under constant threat from predatory Crimean Khanate and its overlord, the Ottoman Empire. In the second part of 17th century, tremendous effort went into fortification of southern borders: the construction of defensive lines made of felled trees and numerous forts (that needed to be manned). Situation in southern Ukraine remained quite tense.

After the second half of 16th century (when it suffered a number of defeats from European states), Turkey no longer posed an existential threat to the world of Christian Europe. Yet, its military potential was far from exhausted, and its principal efforts in the second half of 17th century focused on Eastern Europe. In 1672, it wrestled from Poland the region of Podolia and strove to establish itself in Right Bank Ukraine. This led to Russian-Turkish war of 1676–1681, when Ottoman and Crimean-Tatar troops attempted to seize Kiev and Chigirin. After pitched battles near Chigirin in 1677 and 1678 they were stopped, and under the terms of 1681 Peace of Bakhchisaray Turkey and Crimea recognized Russian sovereignty over Left Bank Ukraine and Kiev, yet lands south of Kiev, around Braclav, and in Podolia remained under the rule of Turkey and Ukrainian Hetman (ruler) Yuri Khmelnytsky (allied with Turkey).

That state of affairs, which did not significantly relieve the threat posed by Crimea and Turkey to Russia's southern borders, was not satisfactory to Russia, and it sought any opportunity to remove that threat. Such an opportunity came along with the emergence of anti-Turkish alliance between Austria and Poland, and the crushing defeat dealt to Turkey by Polish king Yan Sobiesky in 1683 at the walls of Vienna (one consequence was the return of Right Bank Ukraine to Poland). The year 1684 saw the conclusion of anti-Turkish 'Holy League' of Austria, Poland, and Venice. Russia joined that alliance in 1686 following its own Eternal Peace with Poland and dissolution of peace treaty with the Turks. So-called Crimean expeditions led by Prince V. Golitsyn were undertaken as part of that coalition's war efforts. The first one took place in May–June 1687, and the second in February–May 1689. The objective of destroying Crimean Khanate was never met. Even though the troops numbered in tens of thousands (even over a 100 thousand in the second expedition), they suffered heavy losses due to the heat, disease, and lack of forage. During the first expedition, the troops never reached Crimea as they were stopped by burning steppe grasses set afire by the Tatars, while during the second one they reached the Isthmus of Perekop, but stopped shy of entering the peninsula.

In summary, by the late 17th century Russia had a calm (even if extremely disadvantageous) border in the west and a rather fraught one in the south. Up to the year 1700, Russia had to pay annual tribute to Crimean Khanate to buy protection from raids by Crimean Tatars. In the Northern Caucasus, Russian possessions were bounded by rivers Terek and Sunzha and protected by a number of forts. Kabarda (then the most organized of many local societies in the Caucasus) was a vassal of Russia, and provided assistance to expeditions against Crimean Tatars and the Smaller Nogai Horde, while often taking arms against them at its own initiative. In the south-east, the border followed Ural River (then known as Yaik). Major revolts by the Bashkirs in the region east of the Volga River (in 1662–1664 and 1681–1683) were by then suppressed. Siberia, where Russian settlement started at the end of 15th century, was as yet very sparsely populated (Russian population counted no more than 25 thousand families), while in the lands along the Amur River in the Far East, which the Russians reached by mid-17th century, they came into contact with Qing China. War with China in the 1680s led to the loss of Russian settlement of Albazin (today's Albazino in Russia) and posed immediate threat to Selenginsk, Udinsk, Nerchinsk, and Irkutsk. Nerchinsk treaty of 1689 left Russia with the bulk of previously occupied lands, but stopped its further advance along that vector.

Domestic situation

By the late 17th century, Russian monarchy of Romanov dynasty (which was established in 1613 following the Time of Troubles) maintained the same essential features that distinguished it at its inception, even if ideologically it sought to erase collective memory of the circumstances of its assumption of the throne (through election at Assembly of the Land), and emphasized instead its connection with the Rurik dynasty and its divine mandate. The tradition of convening Assemblies of the Land (*Zemsky Sobor* in Russian) was done away with: while in the first third of 17th century they were convened fairly often, by the end of 17th century that institution was dormant (the latest assembly was convened in 1653).

The tsar's power knew no legal constraints. Advisory council of high nobility, or *boyars* known as *Boyar Duma* (from *dumat'* – 'to think' in Russian) had no legally defined status, and served as a purely deliberative body. Its members were appointed entirely at the tsar's discretion. The only individuals capable of influencing policy-making were the tsar's relatives and members of his immediate circle. The whole political elite of the country was confined to the Sovereign's Court (*Gosudarev Dvor*), while the executive power operated through the system of chancelleries known as *prikaze* (from Russian word for command – *prikaz*).

The Sovereign's Court was a pool of individuals from which appointees were chosen to fill all positions of importance in both the central and provincial governments, as well as for special missions. Members of this corporation were arranged into a hierarchy of 'ranks', and listed in periodically updated 'boyar lists'.

The highest-ranking group consisted of *Duma ranks*, i.e. members of the Boyar Council: boyars, okolnichyis (junior boyars), so-called *Duma* nobility, and *Duma dyaks* (clerks). The same status was enjoyed by persons occupying senior positions at court (senior equerry, major domo, armorer, treasurer, royal meat-carver, keeper of the seal, equerry, master of the chamber, master of the hunt, falconer, and chamberlain) who counted just a few people all told and could be members of the boyar council at the same time. The next step in the hierarchy was the so-called *Moscow ranks* (that is to say the ranks unique to the capital city). That group included such ranks as *stolniks*, *stryapchyis* (servants of the royal household), Moscow nobility, and *zhil'tsy* (residents bound to defensive duty). The lowest rank was known as *deti boyarskie* (literally 'boyar children'), who were in effect the mass of petty nobility serving the state whenever they lived (in the 16th and 17th centuries, there also existed a subgroup of 'selected nobility' who also ranked as members of the Sovereign's Court but were excluded from it by the end of 17th century).

By the end of 17th century, the court had conclusively detached itself from provincial nobility corporations, and the structure of the serving class assumed the following shape: 1) *Duma ranks* (boyars, junior boyars, Duma nobility, and Duma clerks) plus holders of senior positions at court; 2) *Moscow ranks* (servants of the royal household, Muscovite nobility, and residents bound to defensive duty); 3) provincial nobility or *city ranks* ('selected nobility' and petty nobility performing military duties). By the late 17th century, the Sovereign's Court had ballooned. As of 1692, there were 182 members of the top rank (versus 73 in 1667), and the sum total for the Court (excluding residents in defensive duty) stood at 7068 persons (compared to only 1656 in 1667).

Central government operated through the system of 55 agencies (as of 1698), 36 of which were *prikaze* (main chancelleries). Of that number, 27 had jurisdiction over matters of the state, 6 over court matters, and 3 over church matters. Personnel of those agencies totaled 2762 individuals, including 23 judges (that was the title of a *prikaz* head), 5 Duma clerks (who were also *prikaz* heads), 86 clerks, and 2648 assistant clerks. Clerks (*dyaks* in Russian) were the pivotal group in government machinery. In terms of their political status, they ranked with (and occasionally above) *stolniks* and *stryapchyis* (servants of the royal household), while in terms of social origins they were closer to the lower strata of the Sovereign's Court (a third or more did not belong to the nobility, and their children had to enter service at lower ranks). As to the assistant clerks, their social standing was below that of petty nobility (in later times, a forefather's service as an assistant clerk was not regarded proof of noble origins).

Razryadnyi prikaz was considered the most important one and bore responsibility for the service of the state system. Its remit included maintaining the record of servicemen classes and making appointments to all court, civilian, and military positions. This *prikaz* maintained lists of all provincial nobility and periodically compiled so-called 'boyar lists' of all the ranks included in the Sovereign's Court. It also decided how much acreage of a landed estate every serving member of the nobility qualified for. *Pomestnyi prikaz* (Landed Estate chancellery) managed government-owned lands, maintained a registry of both the government lands available to be awarded as estates and of hereditary (patrimonial) lands. It allocated lands to the serving nobility.

Three of the *prikaze* dealt with matters financial. So-called *Prikaz of Great Revenue* collected customs fees and was responsible for maintaining the system of weights and measures. *Prikaz of Great Treasury* had oversight of industry and commerce, and was in charge of the mint and coinage. Another special *prikaz* was responsible for collection of excise duties on sales of tobacco and alcohol.

A number of *prikaze* shared judicial and law enforcement functions. *Razboynyi Prikaz* handled all criminal offences committed outside Moscow, while *Zemskyi Prikaz* handled the same offences in the capital city and maintained law and order there. *Chelobitnyi Prikaz* (or Office of Petitions) occupied a special place. It investigated cases involving government officials and also functioned as the highest court of appeal.

A whole group of *prikaze* dealt with military matters. Those partly fell under the jurisdiction of *Razryadnyi Prikaz*, which was not only in charge of personnel, but also directed military operations. Special-purpose *prikaze* dealt with specific categories of the service class: *Streletzkyi* (Rifle Guardsmen Office), *Cossack Prikaz*, *Pushkarskyi* (Artillery

Office), *Reitarskyi* (Cavalry Troops Office), and *Inozemskyi* (in charge of foreigners in Russian service).

Posolskyi Prikaz (literally 'ambassadorial', i.e. Foreign Affairs Office) was in charge of receiving and sending diplomatic missions and of all other dealings with foreigners (including merchants). It also managed a special fund earmarked for ransoming captives. *Yamskoyi Prikaz* performed the functions of a post office. Finally, a whole group of *prikaze* was in charge of governing peripheral areas of the country. *Kazanskyi Palace Prikaz* was responsible for the lands of former Khanates of Kazan and Astrakhan. Similarly, dedicated *prikaze* existed for Siberia, Little Russia (i.e. Ukraine), and lands of former Principality of Smolensk.

Although the system of *prikaze* covered all aspects of governance, it was not sufficiently specialized and often had redundancies since the jurisdictions of individual offices overlapped. Judicial system was not separated from the executive. Most petty offences fell under the jurisdiction of landowners, while the rest were tried by provincial governors, or by various *prikaze*. In major cases, the final judgment belonged to the Boyar Council and the tsar, who were the highest court of the land.

The principal administrative unit was *uezd* (county). Those were about 250 in number. Counties evolved from former appanage (or patrimonial) domains, and therefore differed widely in land area and population.[3]

Legal system of that time was based on the Law Code of 1649, which in turn was based on the Law Code of 1550 with incorporation of all subsequent decrees and rulings. The Code was a compendium of 967 articles arranged into 25 chapters. Its content was dominated with issues relating to the tsar's powers and service of the state system, and with definitions of status and duties of various social groups, the serving class in particular.

As in all European countries, the highest social categories were the serving class and the clergy. The clergy (which following the convocation of 1667 was outside the jurisdiction of secular courts) gradually evolved into a distinct autonomous corporation. Through its senior hierarchs – archbishops, bishops and abbots – it played a noticeable political role, even though the church's claim of primacy over the power of tsars (as pursued by patriarch Nikon) was decisively suppressed in 1666 by Tsar Alexey Mikhailovich. In their role as princes of the church, metropolitans and bishops (there were 15 dioceses) were large landowners with several thousand households of bonded peasants each. Large land areas (that were legally defined as patrimonies) were bonded to monasteries as well. While the Law Code of 1649 banned acquisition of new patrimonial lands by monasteries, by mid-17th century they already owned 83 thousand peasant households. Parish clergy was elected by parishioners and confirmed by bishops. Although in formal terms the clergy could be joined by people from any other social class, as a

---

[3] *Uezd* was further broken down into units known as *volost* and *stan* (rough equivalents of a borough). The largest *uezd* towns (or county seats) had *prikaze houses* with one to ten scriveners (sometimes more). By 1698, there existed 302 such *prikaze houses* employing a total of 1918 civil servants, including 28 clerks, 17 senior assistant clerks, and 1873 junior assistant clerks. A county seat was ruled by a governor (known as *voevoda*) appointed by Moscow and chosen from the ranks of Sovereign's Court. Governors' remit included military, administrative, judicial, and fiscal matters. Smaller districts – *gubas* (rough equivalent of a township) were headed by elected officials. *Guba elders* were elected by free population from the ranks of local nobility, while their assistants came from the ranks of tradesmen and free peasants. Elders were in charge of maintaining public order and of criminal justice.

practical matter it was an exclusive corporation. Candidates coming from clerical families were always preferred as better prepared to perform ministry (besides, the community of parishioners had little enthusiasm for continued payment of collective taxes for a member who left it). Church convocation of 1667 expressly condemned ordaining people from outside the clerical estate as priests and deacons.

By that time, the nobility was not yet legally defined as a single estate, but the question of whether an individual belonged to it could be answered quite unambiguously. That was a community of all the servicemen who served 'by patrimony', that is to say their service was hereditary, and their estates were given them as land grants for service. Other than the church, they were the only class allowed to own land with peasants. Such land grants were conditional on service, and an estate had to be returned to the treasury upon completion of service to the state. If a son continued to serve following his father, he could inherit the estate; widows and orphaned children of noblemen who died while serving also qualified for small estates. Members of the serving class could also have patrimonial estates, which were unconditionally owned and inherited, and freely disposed of by their owners. As a rule, those were owned by heirs of former appanage princes, or in general, by the highest nobility. Since all nobility were bound to serve, there was no dramatic difference between owners of granted versus patrimonial estates (frequently one person could own both). All male offspring of the nobility were duty bound to serve (sometimes starting at a rather tender age), and they were the only ones with the right to enter service 'by patrimony'. By 1678, estate owners numbered 20.8 thousand, of whom 9.7 thousand (47%) had fewer than twenty peasants, 8 thousand (38%) owned between twenty and a hundred, and 3.1 thousand (15%) over a hundred. The total noble estate (with all family members) then stood at 158 thousand (1.7% of the population).

Twice a year all servicemen had to show up for muster. They had to be ready to answer the call to arms immediately "with horses, people, and armaments", which is to say they had to be outfitted out of their own money and bring along a number of armed and mounted men depending on the size of their estate. Dodging service was punishable by the whip and full or partial confiscation of the estate. Members of the Sovereign's Court served in rotation: initially for 4 months a year, and by late 17th century (as the Court expanded) for 3 months a year.

A class below servicemen 'by patrimony' consisted of servicemen 'by selection'. That category included *streltzy* (rifle guardsmen), city Cossacks, artillery soldiers, and other petty servicemen. Those were typically recruited from relatives of people already in that class and among other free persons. Although their service was in fact frequently hereditary, it was not officially recognized as such and therefore did not entail the same privileges. There was an impermeable wall between this class and servicemen 'by patrimony'. In isolated cases (such as for distinguished service) they could be rewarded with an estate, and their sons would then go on to serve 'by patrimony' (that actually happened on a large scale during and in the aftermath of the Time of Troubles when the greater part of Russian nobility perished), but there was no established channel for them to become servicemen 'by patrimony'. In peacetime, businesses and trades of these servicemen were taxed just as those of common tradesmen.

Town tradesmen consisted of craftsmen (who had the Russian equivalent of guilds) and petty merchants (divided into three ranks depending on revenue and owned property). A significant proportion of craftsmen served the needs of the state. Town tradesmen were not numerous (by the mid-17th century this group counted 40 thousand households, with over half of them in Moscow). Tradesmen were taxed and bound to carry certain other obligations. A privileged position was enjoyed by large merchants (known as 'guests'), who were consulted by the court on matters of economic life and could perform certain administrative functions (collection of various taxes and duties).

Peasants made up the absolute majority of population and were the largest of groups subject to taxation and performance of specific obligations. Most peasants were bonded to various landowners. By 1678, 67% of peasant households were owned by the serving nobility, 13.3% by the church, and 9.3% by the crown. In other words, about 90% were serfs, while the rest (so-called 'black-plough' peasants) were free peasants subject directly to the state. Peasants' obligations included labor duty (working at their landowner's estate for 2 to 4 days a week) and rents in kind and in money. They also had obligations towards the state.

Manufacturing of the time was dominated by cottage industry, as the absolute majority of manufactured goods came from peasant and craftsman households. That said, there existed about thirty large manufacturing works. Those were both government-owned (serving the needs of the court, but most importantly of the military) and privately-owned by Russian and foreign merchants in industries like copper-smelting, iron-making, leather-tanning, rope-making, salt-making, cloth-making, glass-making, etc. Principal areas of metal-working historically evolved south of Moscow (Tula, Serpukhov, Kashira, and others) and in northwest Russia (Ustyuzhna, Tikhvin, Lake Onega northern peninsula). Russia significantly lagged behind European countries in large-scale manufacturing, which had a direct impact on its military capabilities.

Noblemen militia made up the largest part of Russian armed forces. As in all European (and not only European) countries, cavalry troops were traditionally formed of landowning servicemen and mounted soldiers that they were obligated to bring along. The number of nobility fit for military duty stood at 15–20 thousand, which allowed for fielding up to 40 thousand (or even more) cavalrymen. *Streltzy* (rifle guards, 'shooters' in Russian) units emerged as early as mid-16th century. Those troops were organized into regiments commanded by colonels. Regiments consisted of ten *sotnias* (hundreds) commanded by a *sotnik*. For the most part, *streltzy*, so-called city Cossacks, and artillerymen made up city garrisons. At times of war, additional cavalry units with their own commanders were raised among native non-Russian minorities of the country (Tatars, Bashkirs, etc.). Additionally, members of obligation-bearing lower classes could be mobilized for auxiliary military roles. Total strength of Russia's army at war could reach or exceed a hundred thousand, but its fighting capacity in a clash with Western neighbors remained rather low (as demonstrated by the wars in preceding centuries).

The authorities were well aware of the need to have a standing infantry, which by late 17th century formed the core of all European armies, and they made efforts to address that weakness. *Streltzy* were permanent troops, but not a regular standing army (they lived in their own allocated city quarters or suburbs and in peacetime pursued various trades). As early as in 1630, during Smolensk war, the first attempt was made to create so-called 'new order regiments' (at that time formed out of foreign mercenaries) of infantry, reiters, and dragoons. But in peacetime those regiments were disbanded. From mid-17th century, such regiments began recruitment among peasants and tradesmen, yet almost all officer commissions still went to foreigners. Service in those regiments was unpopular with Russian nobility since it meant serving alongside foreigners, who, according to the notions of the time, were the ultimate 'ignoble' people of unknown parentage, and therefore serving with them impugned family honor. By 1692, only 8.6% of officer positions were filled by servicemen of *Moscow ranks*. Nonetheless, those infantry and cavalry regiments gradually expanded, and during the reign of Feodor Alexeyevich there were 48 regiments of the infantry and 26 of reiters and lancers.

An important aspect of Russian society of that time that affected efficiency of both government and the military was its aristocratic nature, whereas the nobility of one's family was a principal consideration in all appointments and career advancements. Precedence system brings that aspect of society into high relief. Its logic suggested that a person whose forefathers occupied a higher position in service could not possibly serve under someone whose forefathers occupied a lower position. Anyone to agree to such an appointment would lower the future status of all his kin and descendants. At the time when considerations of family honor dominated the worldview of serving classes, appointments inevitably gave rise to numerous disputes, quarrels, and litigation. Such prejudice was so deeply ingrained in the public opinion that even a tsar had to take it into account. He could not appoint into a position of importance someone more gifted, but less noble than alternative candidates. In particularly crucial cases, a pronouncement would be issued that during a particular campaign everyone will "serve without precedence" (which meant that appointments during such a campaign would not count toward future calculations of precedence).

Even though precedence system first and foremost constrained freedom of action of supreme power itself, it was abolished only in 1682, but even after that one's family origins remained the key to career growth. Opportunities available to those entering government service were also extremely unequal. In theory, the tsars could elevate any member of the nobility to the highest rank (that of a boyar). But prior to that, someone of humbler origins had to climb through all the ranks below, which happened quite infrequently. At the same time, members of about 20 highest-born family clans became boyars by default (skipping even the preceding rank of *okolnichyi* (junior boyar)). Those from the next lower tier of noble clans entered service as junior boyars, and those from an even wider group of noble clans started out as *stolniks* and *stryapchyis* (servants of the royal household).

While an impenetrable wall separated those who served 'by selection' from those who served 'by patrimony', the latter group was also divided by informal but quite tangible partitions. The highest two, *Duma* and *Moscow* ranks, were mostly self-replenished, as the majority of their membership had ancestors who served with the same rank. The overwhelming majority of rank-and-file nobility (*deti boyarskie,* or petty nobility) inherited their parents' status and position with no prospect of career advancement. All of that made it most difficult to promote gifted people into senior government and military positions.

Political situation at the beginning of Peter the Great's reign

Tsar Alexey Mikhailovich (the second Romanov) died in 1676. His youngest child was Peter, born on May 30, 1672 by the tsar's second wife. That second marriage of Alexey Mikhailovich brought about a bitter strife between numerous relatives of his first wife, the Miloslavsky clan, and a smaller clan of Naryshkins, to which Peter's mother belonged. The Naryshkins had the backing of the most influential public figure of that time, boyar A. Matveyev, but their attempt to elevate underage Peter to the throne failed. The oldest son, 14-year old Feodor Alexeyevich became the new tsar. His rule was completely dominated by influence-peddling of his kin from the Miloslavsky clan. Being of feeble health, Feodor died in only 6 years, in 1682.

After that, the Naryshkins gained ground because of the two remaining sons the older one, Ivan (from Miloslavskaya) was sickly and feeble-minded, and Peter clearly made a much more promising successor to the throne. Yet in anticipation of that a cabal formed at the court that staked its hopes on one of Alexey Mikhailovich daughters, Princess Sophia. That cabal included Prince V. Golitsyn, Prince I. Khovansky, and I. Miloslavsky. When clear preference for Peter emerged (the boyars and Patriarch Joachim leaned in his favor, and crowds in the Kremlin square shouted their acclamation) the cabal resolved to drastic measures by instigating a revolt of Moscow's *streltzy* troops.

The Naryshkins and A. Matveyev (who just returned from exile), had no time to act. On May 15, 1682, *streltzy* (enraged by planted rumor that the tsar's heir Ivan has been murdered) stormed the Kremlin and summarily dispatched some Naryshkin supporters[4], while others of that circle were exiled. Power passed to Princess Sophia, who was installed as regent for underage Ivan and Peter. Yet, the *streltzy* (led by Prince I. Khovansky) slipped out of control of Sophia's circle and presented the threat of turning into a force of their own capable of dictating terms to Sophia. Sophia hastened to wipe out that threat through an abrupt execution of Prince Khovansky and his son. That left the revolt without leadership, and by year's end Sophia disposed of its principal instigators. The most prominent figure of Sophia's 7-year long reign was Prince V. Golitsyn, one of the best-educated people of his time and well familiar with European culture.

Although Peter took part in court ceremonies required by the protocol, he seldom stayed at court, and mostly lived in Preobrazhenskoye village in the environs of Moscow. During Sophia's reign, he was not considered to be the first in line to the throne, and no particular attention was given to his education. To a large degree he was left to himself. That gave him the opportunity to indulge freely in his favorite pursuits, which were quite diverse and rather uncommon for someone in his position. Since childhood, Peter had an interest in various crafts, machinery, and devices, which he had access to through meeting members of German colony[5] in Moscow. Besides, his direct exposure to a diverse and large group of people from unprivileged classes (especially playmates and peers in age) gave him a good notion of what their interests, habits, ways of thinking, and attitudes were. His greatest passions were the art of war and seafaring. Two 'amusement' regiments trained along European lines were formed for his games and eventually grew into a real fighting force. Interests of that kind and the broad outlook he had developed could not help but give Peter a good idea of the ambiguity of his position at court. In 1689, he turned 17 and got married, which paved the way for him to remove Sophia and rule in his own right. That was equally well understood by Sophia who had no intention of surrendering her position.

An open conflict became unavoidable and came to a head on the night of August 8, 1689. Just as she did seven years earlier, Sophia decided to rely on *streltzy*. They were commanded by F. Shaklovity. A rumor was circulated that Peter's 'amusement' regiments were on the march from Preobrazhenskoye to Kremlin. *Streltzy* were alerted and prepared

---

[4] A. Matveyev, Prince M. Dolgoruky, I. Yazykov, F. Saltykov, and two brothers of dowager Tsarina Natalia Kirillovna.

[5] In those times, 'Germans' (*nemtsy* in Russian, meaning 'mute') was Muscovy's generic label for all North European Protestant people: the Swedes, Danes, Hollanders, Englishmen, Scots, and French Huguenots, who had quite a few churches clustered in the 'German Quarter'.

for combat. Upon learning about *streltzy* moves, Peter (who was rousted out of bed) and a small group of his confidants raced to Trinity-Sergius Lavra (a great monastery close to Moscow), where he was soon joined by his two 'amusement' regiments (Preobrazhensky and Semyonovsky) and some other units. Thus, an openly rival power center opposed to Kremlin emerged, and the gauntlet was thrown. The Kremlin and the Lavra started to exchange messages and jockey for supporters. The face-off lasted about a month. Initially, Sophia had greater forces, but they gradually melted away. As a legitimate and no longer minor ruler, Peter attracted more followers. Sensing the precariousness of her position Sophia traveled to the Lavra for parley, but Peter ordered her to go back to Moscow, where she faced loss of support from *streltzy* as well. *Streltzy* demanded that F. Shaklovity be surrendered. He was sent to the Lavra and soon after executed, while Sophia was confined to Novodevichyi nunnery.

Following Sophia's ouster, the business of daily government was entrusted to a circle close to Tsarina Natalia Kirillovna. Lead roles were played by her brother L. Naryshkin, Prince B. Golitsyn (Peter's closest confidant during his stay at Preobrazhenskoye), and some others[6]. Preoccupied with military maneuvers on ever-expanding scale and with construction of ships at Pereyaslavl' (Pleshcheyevo) Lake, Peter did not involve himself in daily governance. In 1693, he visited Archangel where he studied foreign-built ships and laid the keel for his first seagoing vessel. It was in those years that the circle of close associates crystallized around Peter, the people who in future would lead Russia's government and military.[7] After his brother Ivan died in January 1696, Peter became the sole ruler.

---

[6] P. Lopukhin, T. Streshnev, Prince P. Prozorovsky, P. Sheremetev, Prince I. Troekurov, and Prince Ya. Odoevsky.

[7] They included F. Apraksin, Ya. Bruce, I. Buturlin, A. Vinius, F. Golovin, G. Golovkin, P. Gordon, F. Lefort, A. Menshikov, Prince A. Repnin, Prince F. Romodanovsky, P. Shafirov, and P. Yaguzhinsky.

Chapter 2

Russia under Peter the Great

The new tsar, who found himself ruling a vast but landlocked country virtually isolated from Europe, faced formidable foreign policy challenges, which he was fully aware of. Yet he had only the same means and resources that were available even before his reign to address those challenges. Out of two strategic theaters, the northern (the Baltic Sea) and the southern one (the Black Sea), he chose to deal with the latter first. By that time, Sweden, which dominated the Baltic Sea, was a first-rate European country that joined the club of great powers following the Thirty Years' War (1618–1648) and essentially transformed the Baltic into its inland lake. Although it had enemies in Europe, it also enjoyed the support of first-rate naval powers of the time, England and Holland. It seemed unpromising to begin the struggle for access to the seas with a war against Sweden.

By contrast, in the southern direction the Ottoman Empire remained at war with anti-Turkish 'Holy League', and was noticeably weakened by battles against Austrian and Polish forces. The Ottoman Empire included Orthodox peoples who were beginning to see co-religionist Russia as a potential deliverer from the Ottoman yoke (at that time, their church hierarchs were in active negotiations with Moscow Patriarchate and secular authorities). Finally, Russia continued to remain a member of the 'Holy League', and following its Crimean campaigns it remained in a state of war with Turkey. Therefore, in 1694 the choice was made, and Azov campaigns became a direct extension of the earlier Crimean ones.

The fortress of Azov that controlled access to the Sea of Azov was selected as the immediate campaign objective. Forces mustered for the campaign were very substantial. A force of over 30 thousand commanded by F. Lefort, P. Gordon and A. Golovin marched off straight for Azov, and its advance units reached Azov in late June of 1695. At the same time, an even greater force of over 100 thousand men (mostly cavalry regiments raised from the nobility) led by B. Sheremetev and augmented with units of Zaporozhye Cossacks, was sent to the lower reaches of River Dnieper. Peter and the remaining troops sailed to Azov by rivers. The siege lasted almost three months. Even though the campaign was fairly well organized and the forces amassed considerable, it failed. General assault staged on August 6 ended in failure. After being encamped near Azov for about two months more, Peter decided to relieve the siege on September 27.

However, Peter didn't lose heart. In fact, he started even more diligent preparations for a new campaign. Over a thousand-and-a-half different watercraft were built in the area of Voronezh, and about two dozen ships built in Moscow were brought to the Don River disassembled. In April 1696, the second Azov campaign began. By blocking the mouth of Don River, Russian ships left Azov without food supplies. After the siege and bombardment started, the Turks surrendered ahead of the general assault on the fortress

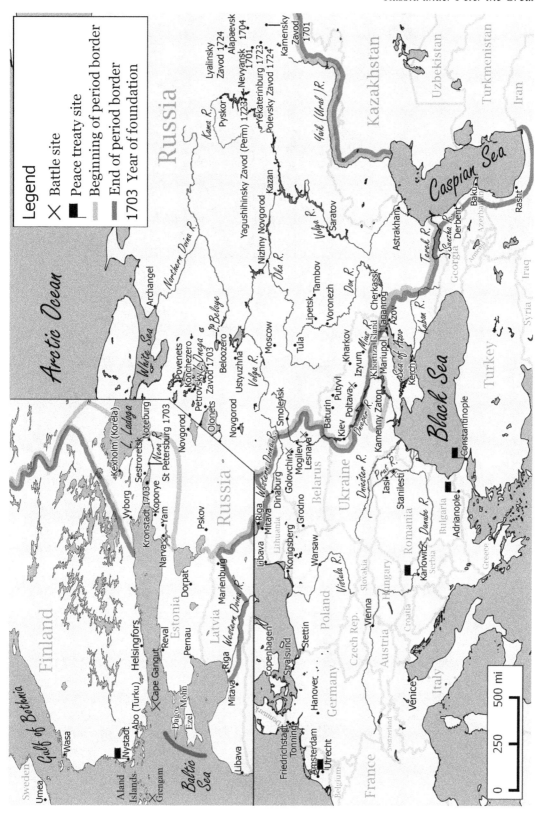

15

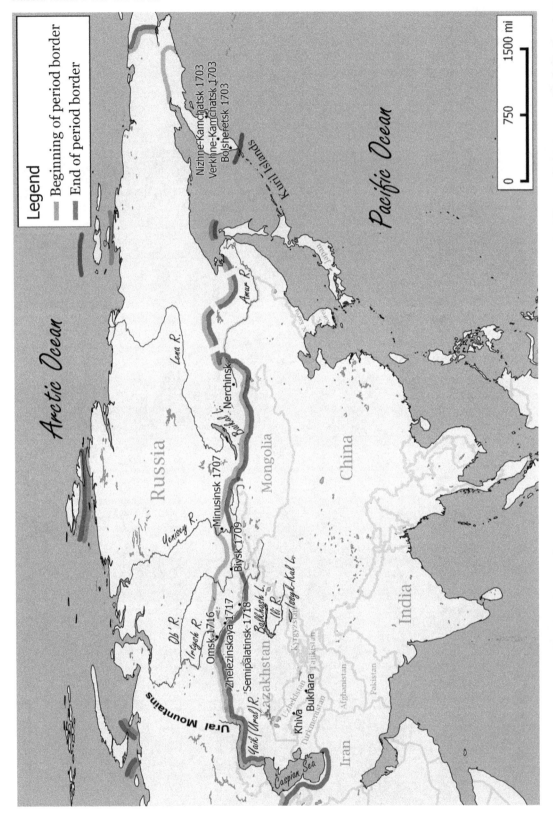

(July 18). Azov was abandoned by the Turks, and several thousand Russian families from nearby towns were resettled there.

After this first success, Peter undertook a tour of Europe as part of the 'Grand Embassy'. Its titular heads were F. Lefort, F. Golovin, and P. Voznitsyn. Travelling incognito gave Peter the most freedom of action as well as opportunities to visit places not on the embassy's itinerary, since in addition to diplomatic talks he intended to familiarize himself with every aspect of European life as best possible, to master for himself a number of crafts related to shipbuilding and military affairs, and also recruit foreign talent into Russian service. He visited Riga, Mitava, Libava, Königsberg, Amsterdam, London, and Vienna. The main diplomatic objective of the embassy was to press Austria and Venice into continuing military operations against Turkey. However, that objective was never met because Europe was then on the verge of a large European war (which entered history books as 'The War of Spanish Succession'), and Austrian emperor was not willing to expend energy on the fight against already weakened Turkey that no longer posed much threat to Austria. Peter managed to secure only diplomatic support. While he was away, in the summer of 1698, the government led by Naryshkin and Golitsyn crushed a new *streltzy* riot instigated by pro-Sophia party.

The change in overall European situation predetermined the pivot in Peter's foreign policy calculations. On the one hand, it was clear that Russia was unable to continue a major war with Turkey alone. On the other hand, new political alignments in Europe made for more favorable conditions for redirecting efforts to the north, since Sweden's European allies (now involved in a major war), were no longer able to support it to the same extent as before. There followed efforts to forge an anti-Swedish alliance. Secret negotiations between potential allies began in late 1698. Russia's potential allies included Brandenburg-Prussia, Saxony, Poland (at the time it was ruled by Prince-Elector Augustus II of Saxony), and Denmark. The leader of Livonian knights, Johann von Patkul, played a significant role in the negotiations (the plan was to attract Polish ruling circles by promised incorporation of Livonia into Poland). The plans called for Russia to receive Karelia and Ingermanland (the area around present-day St. Petersburg) from Sweden. In the autumn of 1699, treaties of alliance with Denmark and Saxony against Sweden were finally concluded.

However, Russia could not enter the war before completion of peace negotiations with Turkey. This was compounded by the fact that Russia's allies in the 'Holy League' succeeded in making their peace with the Ottomans at the Karlowitz Congress of October 1698 (with mediation by England and Holland), and Russia had to negotiate with the Turks separately in a situation where Austria and Poland came out of the war. On January 14, 1699, P. Voznitsyn concluded a truce with the Turks. The compromise gave Kerch back to Turkey, but kept Azov and Taganrog for Russia. That outcome did not satisfy Peter though. He ostentatiously sent an embassy to Constantinople aboard a warship accompanied by a small naval squadron. After nine months of negotiations, new peace was concluded on terms more favorable for Russia. Russia retained Azov and lands near the Mius River, as well as lands in the direction of Kuban River to the distance of a 10-hour horseback ride from Azov. Towns along the lower Dnieper had to be left with the Turks (on condition of their demilitarization), and Russian maritime trade was confined to a single port, Kerch. Additionally, annual tribute payments to Crimean Khanate were canceled.

Once the Russian troops received word of peace treaty with Turkey, they marched off towards the Swedish border. Russia's allies had already started military operations by that time. In February 1700, the Saxons took Dinaburg (now Daugavpils in Latvia) and laid

17

siege to Riga, but the siege dragged on. After capturing several fortresses in Holstein (which was Sweden's ally), the Danes too became bogged down. Peter decided in favor of an all-out attack on Narva (contrary to the wishes of allies, who were quite unhappy with the prospect of Estland and Livonia being seized by Russia).

Russian troops raised for this operation numbered more than 40 thousand. Infantry was divided into three divisions (led by A. Golovin, A. Weide, and Prince A. Repnin), and B. Sheremetev was in command of 11 thousand nobility cavalrymen. The siege of Narva began in late September 1700, but proved futile. Shoddy Russian cannon-pieces could not breach fortress walls. By that time, the Saxons retreated from Riga, while Swedish King Charles XII suddenly landed troops at the defenseless Copenhagen and forced Denmark to make peace with him and dissolve its alliance with Russia and Saxony. Then Charles quickly moved his troops into the Baltic provinces. On November 19, Swedish troops broke into the Russian siege camp during a snowstorm. The next day, after the loss of about 6 thousand men, the Russian army capitulated on the condition of free departure.

In order to keep King Augustus II from getting out of the war, Peter (in a new treaty concluded in February 1701) had to promise payment of a substantial subsidy, provision of some Russian troops for relief, and also relinquishment of claims to the Baltic lands. But in the summer of 1701, Charles XII defeated the Saxons near Riga and advanced on Poland. After recovering from earlier defeat, Russian troops numbering about 40 thousand were amassed near Pskov and Novgorod, while another 20 thousand (led by Prince A. Repnin) were sent to the aid of King Augustus. In the autumn of 1701, Russian troops (led by B. Sheremetev) started active operations in Livonia, and dealt the Swedes a series of defeats. In the summer of 1702, some more victories were won in the Baltic provinces; on October 11, Peter captured the fortress of Noteburg (*Oreshek* in Russian) at the source of the Neva. In April 1703, Nyenschantz fortress (located where Okhta River joins the Neva, now part of St. Petersburg) was captured. On May 16, St. Petersburg was founded on this newly-conquered territory, and the island fortress of Kronstadt was built. In May and June of the same year, the Swedes were completely driven out of the region of Ingria (Yam, Koporye, and Marienburg were captured). In the summer of 1704, Russian troops stormed and took Dorpat (now Tartu in Estonia) and Narva. That gave Russia the entire territory of Livonia and Estland. The Swedes held on only to Riga, Pernau and Reval (now Tallinn, the capital of Estonia). The Swedes' attempts to attack Archangel and St. Petersburg were repulsed.

Meanwhile in Poland, King Augustus II suffered a severe defeat from Charles XII and lost Warsaw. In 1704, pro-Swedish party elected Stanislaw Leszczynski to be King of Poland. Nonetheless, a considerable part of Polish army remained loyal to King Augustus, and Narva Treaty with Russia (concluded in the summer of 1704) kept him from entering a separate peace. That state of affairs did not last. In 1705, Russian troops took Mitava and Grodno, but in February of 1706 the Swedes defeated the Saxons who were marching to reinforce King Augustus, and in September they defeated Augustus himself in Saxony. From that time on, King Augustus (without formally breaking with Peter) had in fact abandoned the alliance by abdicating the crown of Poland and by offering Saxony as an operations base to Charles XII. On July 30, 1705, another *streltzy* riot broke out in Astrakhan, where several hundred military commanders and foreign merchants were killed. To put down the riot, Peter had to dispatch his best commander, B. Sheremetev, who took Astrakhan at the beginning of next year and executed key figures of the riot.

By May of 1706, Peter amassed troops near Kiev, and after Charles departed for Saxony, Russian troops gave support to pro-Russian elements in Poland by entering it and occupying lands up to the Vistula River. Consequently, Russia and Sweden now faced off toe-to-toe without any allies. Military action that followed spanned the vast expanse from Pskov to Ukraine, where Peter stockpiled forage and food, arranged defensive lines of felled trees, etc. Early in 1708, Charles XII moved on the offensive by taking Grodno and pushing Russian troops back near Golovchin. After taking Mogilev, he intended to march on Moscow, but a series of battles forced him to drop the idea, and he headed for Ukraine, where he was counting on support from Hetman Mazepa (who betrayed allegiance to Russia). General Lewenhaupt's corps of 16 thousand men was marching from Riga to join forces with Charles, but on September 28 it was completely destroyed by the Russians near Lesnaya village (that was the biggest victory since the beginning of the war).

During these difficult times, the situation was further complicated by a rebellion that broke out on Don River and was led by Kondratyi Bulavin. By the end of the 17th century, mostly Cossack[8] lands along the Don had attracted much volatile human flotsam and jetsam consisting of runaways and outlaws. Once Russia planted itself more firmly around the Sea of Azov and towns were built, government investigators looking for runaways could operate more efficiently there, which bred resentment. Besides, peace with Turkey deprived freemen and outlaws along the Don of their main source of income – war booty. Bulavin took advantage of that discontent and called for 'thieves and robbers' to gather under his command in so-called 'charm letters'. On October 9, 1707, Bulavin's men wiped out Russian detachment commanded by Prince Yu. Dolgoruky, but soon afterwards they suffered defeat from Cossack Host chieftain, L. Maksimov. However, in the spring of 1708, the rebellion spread to several southern districts (Voronezh, Tambov, and others) and to Sloboda Ukraine[9]. In April, rebels crushed the Cossack army, took Don Cossack Host's capital of Cherkassk, executed chieftain Maksimov and proclaimed Bulavin to be the new chieftain. Large warbands of Bulavin's men advanced on Izyum and Saratov, while his main forces advanced on Azov, but were defeated there. In summer, Bulavin was killed, but the rebellion (mostly along the Volga) lasted until March 1709, drawing off a part of Russian troops.

In Ukraine, Mazepa failed to attract any significant support. His only support came from Zaporozhye Cossacks[10] (Peter stopped their stipends as punishment for robbing

---

[8] Don Cossack settlements emerged in the 14th–15th centuries and consisted mostly of runaway serfs and other free men at loose ends. By the 16th century, they evolved into a Don Cossack Host, a quasi-state of men who lived largely by plundering raids on their southern neighbors and were arms-bearing farmers in peacetime. Early on, Don Cossacks allied themselves with Moscow and became in effect military settlers in the buffer zone between Russia and its troublesome and largely lawless neighbors to the South. Don Cossacks played a prominent role in the conquest and colonization of lands along the lower Volga and Ural Rivers (where a related Ural Host emerged) and along Kuban and Terek Rivers in the Northern Caucasus (Kuban and Terek Hosts), as well as led the conquest of Siberia. While they served as the tool of Russian expansion and the shield from depredations by southern neighbors, their traditions of proud independence, personal freedom, and democratic self-rule also made them prickly and rebellious as Moscow tried to establish tighter control.

[9] On today's map, that is a swath of Eastern Ukraine running roughly from Kharkov to Mariupol.

[10] The informal republic of this group of Cossacks (known as *Zaporozhye Sich*) centered on Khortitza island on the lower Dnieper. While they were similar to Don Cossacks in origins and way of life, their location in a power vacuum zone between Polish-controlled Ukraine, Russian-controlled Ukraine, and Crimean Khanate gave them greater freedom of action and made them into an opportunistic quasi-state, which allied itself in turns with all three of its neighbors or went to war with them.

foreign merchants, which helped provoke war with Turkey). His headquarters city of Baturin was stormed and burned down, and on November 6, 1708 I. Skoropadsky was elected a new Hetman of Ukraine. Charles XII with his main force headed for Poltava, where he hoped to join forces with Polish troops led by Leszczynski and with a Swedish corps dispatched from Poland. However, those two forces were tied down in Poland thanks to dexterous moves of Russian troops commanded by general Goltz. In early April, Poltava was besieged by the Swedes, but successfully repulsed assaults until the approach of Russian army.

Russian army engineers prepared the battle site with skill and built earthworks. The site chosen put the Swedes at every disadvantage. The battle royal that unfolded on June 27, ended in a complete rout and destruction of the Swedish army. In pre-dawn hours, the Swedes attacked Russian redoubts, but after breaking past them with huge losses they were defeated in a head-on encounter with the main Russian force. After the cavalry attacked the Swedes' right flank, they took to flight. Russian infantry was led by B. Sheremetev, cavalry by A. Menshikov, and artillery by Jacob Bruce. This brilliant Russian victory came at a cost of only 1.3 thousand Russian dead, while the Swedes lost 9.3 thousand dead with another 19 thousand captured (mainly on the Dnieper during pursuit). Charles XII and Mazepa managed to escape to Turkey.

Poltava victory not only marked a turning point of the war, but was also hugely important diplomatically. Stanislaw Leszczynski was forced to flee, and King Augustus II, with whom a new treaty was concluded in October 1709 (it recognized Russian sovereignty over Estland in addition to Ingria), returned to Poland and regained the Polish crown. Denmark renewed its alliance with Russia as well. In addition, in October a defensive treaty with Prussia was made, and in June of 1710 a similar treaty was made with Hanover. Thus, the Northern Alliance was revived and expanded. Even France, the only European power to consistently support Turkey, offered to mediate Russian-Turkish talks. Only Britain and Holland remained clearly unfriendly to Russia, since they did not like its newly acquired strength on the Baltic Sea.

The campaign of 1710 was marked by a number of victories of Russian arms. In the Baltic provinces, the cities of Riga, Reval and Pernau (till then in Swedish hands) were taken, as were important fortresses of Vyborg and Kexholm in Finland.

As a result, the Swedes were completely driven out of Estland, Livonia and Karelia. All three became Russian. The marriage of Duke of Courland, Friedrich Wilhelm to Peter's niece Anna Ioannovna established Russia's strong domination in Courland. The Baltic nobility of German extraction ('Ostsee' nobility), which at the end of 17th century suffered from partial confiscation of estates by the Swedish treasury, willingly entered Russian military service since Peter returned their property and restored traditional privileges and institutions. In Poland, Russian troops operated successfully under A. Menshikov. In 1712, Russian troops started taking action against the Swedes (the corps of General Krassow) in Pomerania, where their allies had been fighting Sweden since 1711. Stettin and Stralsund were sealed off, then Russian troops defeated the Swedes at Friedrichstadt, and some of the Swedes capitulated in Tönning. However, due to British intrigues, the campaign did not bring anticipated success.

After conclusion of Peace of Utrecht (1713) which ended the War of Spanish Succession, Britain even made an attempt to ally Holland, Austria and Prussia against Russia, but failed. In fact, Prussia concluded a treaty of alliance with Russia (June 1714) containing mutual guarantees of the ownership of lands captured from Sweden. Following that, Peter primarily focused on war efforts in Finland, where a special fleet of 200 shallow-draft galley ships was built in order to harass the Swedes in the waters around numberless inshore islands. Russian troops took Helsingfors (now Helsinki) and then Wasa, which gave them control of all the eastern coast of the Gulf of Bothnia. On July 27, 1714, the Swedish navy was defeated at Cape Gangut, then Abo and Umea fell, and the whole of Finland was occupied by Russian troops. By moving all the maritime trade of Archangel to St. Petersburg in 1713, Peter had not only reaped the economic advantage he sought, but also cleverly drove a wedge between Britain and Sweden, since Charles XII started capturing British and Dutch merchant ships on their way towards St. Petersburg. To protect its merchant shipping Britain had to send its navy to the Baltic. Moreover, in October 1715, Peter signed a treaty of alliance with the new British King George I (who was Prince-Elector of Hanover, a member of the Northern Alliance).

By 1716, Russian troops were stationed along most of the Baltic coastline: in Finland, in the Baltic provinces, in Pomerania, and in Denmark, while position of Sweden, against which all its neighbors had united (Peter even commanded the combined British-Russian-Dutch-Danish squadron for a while), was unenviable. But then, the situation changed dramatically again due to a change in British policy. After ascending the British throne and consolidating his position, George I came to see himself as King of Britain first, and only secondly as Prince-Elector of Hanover. Duty-bound to pursue a policy promoting British national interest, he started pitting Denmark against Russia. It all resulted in a completely new alignment of European powers. On August 15, 1717, in Amsterdam, Russia, France and Prussia entered into the treaty containing mutual guarantees of each other's possessions. In view of that, Sweden had to make concessions, and peace negotiations finally began at Aland Congress that opened in May 1718, but late in the same year Charles XII was killed (during the siege of a fortress in Norway). By that time, there evolved an anti-Russian alliance of Britain and Austria, Augustus II joined it, and after winning concessions from Sweden, Britain formed an alliance with Sweden.

For Peter, the situation was aggravated by the fact that his son and sole heir Alexey, who did not display his father's ability or evince any interest in his father's pursuits, and whose entourage was deeply hostile to Peter's plans, fled to Austria in the autumn of 1716. Allied Britain and Austria suddenly got a brilliant opportunity to turn Peter's heir against him, and they inspired Alexey's written addresses to Russian church hierarchy and the Senate. Austrian court refused to extradite Alexey to Peter. It took P. Tolstoy (who was sent to Vienna to secure Alexey's return) great effort and many months of negotiations with Alexey through the intermediary of his mistress to convince him to return to Russia. On his return in early 1718, a special investigation brought to light the plot in which over 50 persons were implicated. All of them were arrested and executed. Alexey was forced to abdicate in favor of Peter's infant son and was put on trial. Sentenced to death, Alexey died in prison before the execution.

Russian troops began the campaign of 1720 against the backdrop of strained relations with Austria and Britain and benevolent neutrality of France and Prussia. They landed on the west coast of the Gulf of Bothnia, defeated several Swedish garrisons, and on July 27, 1720, the Swedish navy suffered a serious defeat at Grengam, while the British fleet did not dare to step in to save the day. In April 1721, negotiations in Nystad (today's Uusikaupunki in Finland) were opened (even as military action continued). Meanwhile, a force led by P. Lassy landed on Swedish territory and marched for about 300 kilometers across Sweden, which certainly applied psychological pressure on the Swedes. Finally, on August 30, 1721, the Treaty of Nystad that ended the Great Northern War was signed.

Thus ended the uphill struggle with Sweden in the Baltic. It became the prime achievement of Peter's lifetime. Under peace terms, Sweden ceded all the lands between the Courland border and Karelia to Russia in perpetuity (part of Karelia including Vyborg became Russian too). That swath of land includes all of Livonia, Estland with the adjacent islands of Dago, Ezel and Mohn (today's Hiimaa, Saaremaa and Muhu in Estonia), as well as Ingermanland. Russia received its long-sought access to the Baltic Sea and had become one of Europe's great powers. In the north, the goals set by Peter at the opening of the 18th century were achieved. To top it off, in 1724 Russia signed a treaty of alliance with a weakened Sweden.

By war's end, the circle of closest associates of Peter the Great assumed its final shape. Those were the people playing key roles in running the country. In addition to A. Menshikov, who was made Field Marshal General and granted the title of the Most Illustrious Prince, 13 other senior officials received the rank of 'privy councilor' (the Table of Ranks had not yet been adopted nor old *Duma* ranks yet abolished, but that new rank was above any other). They were F. Apraksin, B. Sheremetev, Prince D. Golitsyn, G. Golovkin, Princes Yakov, Grigory and Vasily Dolgoruky, Prince B. Kurakin, A. Matveev, I. Musin-Pushkin, T. Streshnev, P. Tolstoy, and P. Shafirov. Another group of the most influential grandees bore traditional highest ranks. They were boyars P. Apraksin and P. Buturlin, Princes Pyotr, Boris and Alexey Prozorovsky, Alexey and Pyotr Saltykov, Yu. Urusov, F. Sheremetev, royal carvers V. Saltykov and K. Naryshkin, and Moscow's Governor Prince M. Gagarin. 17 others had lower *Duma* ranks.

Although Russia met all of its objectives in the northwest, it fared much worse in the south. In the midst of the Great Northern War, tensions in relations with the Ottoman Empire escalated. That was engineered in part by Charles XII (who stayed in Turkey after the Poltava debacle), and in part by some leading European powers, especially Britain and Austria. Having seen Russia's new military capabilities, they were fearful lest Russia would grow too strong not only in the Baltic but also in the Black Sea. In the autumn of 1710, as Russia's main forces were engaged against Sweden in the north, Turkey seized the opportunity and declared war on Russia. Russian ambassador P. Tolstoy was imprisoned. Early in 1711, Crimean Tatars attempted an attack on Kharkov, but were repulsed. In the Right Bank Ukraine, the Tatars, the Cossacks and the Polish troops did not succeed against the Russian troops either.

Turkey fielded an army of about 120 thousand against Russia. With help from its allies (Crimean Khanate and Zaporozhye Cossacks) that army could be beefed up to 200 thousand. Russia could dedicate a much smaller force against the Turks, but Peter intended to execute the war on the offensive and reach the Danube, where he counted on aid from King Augustus II troops, and on support from the Serbs in Austria and two Orthodox Christian vassals of the Ottoman Empire, Brancovan, ruler of Wallachia and Cantemir, ruler of Moldavia.

The Prut River campaign began with Russian troops led by B. Sheremetev (the bulk of committed forces) marching all the way from Riga. They reached the Dniester River behind time. By then, the Turks had already built bridges across the Danube to let their immense army cross. The ruler of Wallachia betrayed Peter and didn't allow Serb detachments to pass through his territory, whereas the ruler of Moldavia joined the Russian army with only a small force and failed to provide promised food supplies. Help from King

Augustus never came. By the end of June 1711, (after a hard crossing of burnt-out steppes) Russian troops amassed near Iasi, but were left without allies. Nonetheless, they set out south along the Prut River. On July 8, in the area of Stanilesti, that force of 38 thousand found itself surrounded by the Turkish army of 130–135 thousand. The next day the battle began, and the Turks were beaten back with heavy loss of life. On July 10, negotiations began and on July 12, P. Shafirov managed to sign a peace agreement (in 1713, the Peace of Adrianople reconfirmed its terms).

The terms of this peace made under such dire circumstances for Russian troops and Peter personally (he was with the troops and could not rule out death or captivity) were, of course, extremely unfavorable to Russia. Russia pledged to return Azov, raze down the fortifications in Taganrog and Kamenny Zaton, and refrain from interfering in Polish affairs. Thus, in the south Russia not only failed to reach the Black Sea, but also lost its key gains from Azov campaigns.

After the conclusion of the Treaty of Nystad, Peter, who was granted the title of Emperor by the Senate, turned his attention south and east again. Now that Russia became one of the great European powers, its interests broadened dramatically. Peter sought to create a trade route to India and establish links with Central Asia and Iran. In 1716, he sent an expedition led by Prince A. Bekovich-Cherkassky to Central Asia. That detachment of 5 thousand men tried to build two fortresses on the east coast of the Caspian Sea, but due to pestilent climate and heavy toll of the sick that effort had to be abandoned. In the spring of 1717, the prince went to Khiva with a detachment of 600 men, but it was completely wiped out by the Khivans. However, attempts to gather information about Central Asia continued. In 1718, the expedition of F. Benevenni was sent to Bukhara by way of the Caucasus and Persia, and in 1722–1724 I. Unkovsky explored the shores of Lake Issyk-Kul' and lands along the Ili River.

In Siberia, large areas in the upper reaches of the Irtysh, Ob' and Yenisey rivers were annexed to Russia during Peter's reign. In 1707, the city of Minusinsk was founded on those new lands, as was Biysk in 1709. After I. Buchholz's expedition that sailed along the Irtysh River in 1715–1716, Omsk was founded in 1716, Zhelezinskaya fortress (today's Zhelezinka in Kazakhstan) in 1717, and Semipalatinsk (now Semey in Kazakhstan) in 1718. Those were the beginnings of the so-called Siberian Line, a chain of outposts and fortifications stretching from Omsk to Semipalatinsk and beyond, with Irtysh River becoming the new Russian border. Many expeditions were sent to Eastern Siberia and the Far East. In the 1690s, valuable information on Kamchatka was received from V. Atlasov and L. Morozko-Staritsyn, and in 1703 Bolsheretsk, Verkhne-Kamchatsk and Nizhne-Kamchatsk were founded there. In 1716, the first maritime expedition set out for Kamchatka. After information about the proximity of land (America) across the strait was received in 1711, expedition led by I. Evreinov and F. Luzhin was sent out to verify it (1719). In 1711, the Kuril Islands were first explored and mapped. In 1720–1724, D. Messerschmidt's expedition explored the upper reaches of River Lena and lands beyond Lake Baikal.

In the Caucasus, by the early 18th century there still remained Cossack villages along the Terek River engaged in perpetual bitter struggle to survive. In 1707, they were devastated by Kuban Khan Kaib-Sultan, but surviving Cossacks held fast on the Terek. In 1711, the Governor of Kazan and Astrakhan P. Apraksin led a military expedition to Kuban River area, where (helped by allied Kalmyks) he defeated the Kuban Tatars in two battles. In 1712, Greben Cossack Host was relocated from Sunzha River to the left bank of Terek

River. That laid the foundations of Terek defensive line (later to evolve into the famous Caucasus Line).

In 1717, Artemy Volynsky who was sent to Iran as ambassador concluded a trade agreement that allowed Russian merchants to freely buy raw silk. Soon after, Iran was convulsed by civic unrest and riots. The Shah's throne was seized by Afghani warlord Mir-Mahmoud, while Turkey exploited the turmoil to draw plans for the capture of Iranian lands, the Trans-Caucasia in particular. Such a scenario would have been quite contrary to Russia's interests, and Peter demanded from Turkey to give up its claims to lands in the Trans-Caucasia populated by the Russians' co-religionists, Georgians and Armenians. In addition, Peter was planning to establish himself on the southern coast of the Caspian Sea. The Caspian campaign unfolded in the summer of 1722. In mid-August, Russian troops crushed the army of 16 thousand hill-men and entered Derbent. In November, Colonel Shipov led a landing party of two battalions by sea and occupied Rasht. In July 1723, the main force led by General Major M. Matyushkin took Baku, and then quickly occupied the entire western and southern coast of the Caspian. At the same time, the Turks launched an offensive from the west and occupied Georgia. In those circumstances, Tahmasp, the son of the deposed Shah, whom Russia considered the legitimate heir to the throne, made a choice in favor of Russia. On September 12, 1723, his ambassador in St. Petersburg concluded a treaty of alliance under which Russian troops were to assist Tahmasp in the fight against the Afghans. Under the treaty, Russia acquired Iranian provinces Dagestan, Shirvan, Gilan, Mazandaran and Astrabad, including such major cities as Baku and Derbent.

But in those times Russia was not capable of conducting large-scale military operations so far from its heartland. Besides, Russian troops suffered heavy losses due to disease in an unfamiliar climate, and the distances involved made it hard to replenish those losses. And it certainly could not afford to launch a new major war with Turkey. Therefore, under the terms of Russian-Turkish agreement concluded in 1724 in Constantinople, Russia was forced to accept the annexation of Georgia and Armenia by Ottoman Turkey.

However, these events highlight just how far this new Russia extended its vision of gaining the best possible geopolitical position in all directions. During the reign of Peter the Great, Russia acquired a completely new international standing by becoming Europe's second empire. Previously, only the Emperor of Austria bore that title (but only as the emperor of Holy Roman Empire, which still existed, largely as a fiction). European countries had to reconcile themselves to new international realities created by Peter's policy. In Northern Europe, Russia reigned supreme. The French ambassador Kampredon noted that Peter was "the only northern prince in a position to make others respect his flag" since "at the slightest display of his fleet or a movement by his troops neither the Swedish nor Danish nor Prussian nor Polish crown dares to take a hostile step or move its troops". Military and political success had been supplemented by establishing marital ties with smaller states in northern Germany, which were to become the anchors for Russian influence in Europe. Guided by these considerations, Peter arranged the marriage of one of his nieces, Anna, to the Duke of Courland, of her sister Catherine to the Duke of Mecklenburg, and of his own eldest daughter Anna to the Duke of Holstein.

Peter's territorial acquisitions were not all that extensive in land area, but enormously important strategically and politically. At no time in the past, had Russian troops penetrated deeper than Byelorussia in the west, whereas now they saw action not only all over Poland but also in Germany, Denmark, and Sweden. In the south, they reached the Danube River, and in the south-east they reached Iran. It is noteworthy that during those wars Russian troops nearly always (whether successfully or not) fought on enemy soil. For the first time, Russia went into a large-scale offensive in the west as it prepared to fulfill what it saw as its main historic mission – reunification of Russian lands of ancient times. That mission appeared self-evident to people of late 17th century, including those who were not part of Moscow establishment. As Hetman of Ukraine I. Samoilovich wrote in 1685, "Since the whole of that side of the Dnieper, Podolia, Volhynia, Podgorye, Podlyashie and the entire Red Rus' have belonged to a Russian monarchy from the beginnings of local history, there is no sin in quietly seeking back what is your patrimony whenever opportunity beckons". The first quarter of 18th century became just such an opportune time when the mission finally began to get realized.

System of government

One of the first reforms was that of municipal government. Peter's idea was to improve efficiency of taxation by removing cities (that is to say, tradesmen classes) from the jurisdiction of provincial governments, and place them directly under the tsar's control, while also introducing municipal self-government. The decree of October 30, 1699, demanded election of city stewards (*burmister* in Russian, which is derived from German *burgermeister*), who had to serve in city halls (*Burmister* Chambers, or *Rathauses*). Those bodies were to have the authority to govern cities and collect taxes. The Main Burmister Chamber (*Rathaus*) established in Moscow was put in charge of all city stewards across Russia. Its members had the right to report directly to the tsar. By 1708, that chamber was collecting up to a half of all treasury revenue. But the system did not last long.

As to the central government, for nearly two decades after Peter's reforms began it remained essentially the same old system of *prikaze*. Interestingly enough and contrary to accepted wisdom, for all the broad sweep of Peter's reform efforts, he avoided abrupt dismantling of existing institutions. His approach was primarily that of creating new government bodies that took over the functions of their predecessors, which were left to wither away. This applies even to the supreme body, the Boyar Duma, which was not formally abolished (Duma ranks registry was maintained until 1712). But it stopped holding sessions (presumably around the year 1704), and its ranks were effectively not replenished (in 1702–1712, only 3 persons were granted the rank of boyar, 4 were created junior boyars, and 2 more Duma nobility), which led to its gradual natural death. In 1699, the so-called Close (Privy) Chancellery was established as part of the Duma to deal with fiscal oversight. From 1704, it became the venue for meetings of *prikaze* heads. From 1708, these meetings became known as Council of Ministers. Until the Senate was established, that Council ran government business in the tsar's absence. From 1704, there also existed the so-called Cabinet under the Tsar, which served as Peter's private chancellery (it was headed by cabinet-secretary A. Makarov and was abolished in 1727).

The *prikaze* system kept changing shape adopting itself to needs created by the reforms. Some *prikaze* were merged, while new *prikaze* and chancelleries had been established (such as the Main Close Chancellery, the Chancellery for Supply of Uniforms, and even the Chancellery for the Baths). Most of those changes were driven by the creation of a new army. Cavalry Prikaz and *Inozemsky* Prikaz (in charge of foreigners in Russian service) were merged into Prikaz of Military Affairs, and new specialized *prikaze* were set up, such as Maritime, Artillery, and Victualling ones. County Affairs Prikaz (*Zemskih Del*) replaced the abolished *Streletzkyi* Prikaz. Great Russia Prikaz, Little Russia Prikaz, and

Smolensk Prikaz were merged into *Posolskyi* Prikaz (which handled foreign affairs). Prikaz of Stables (*Konyushennyi*), Palace Court Chamber, and Prikaz for Masonry Construction were incorporated into Prikaz of Grand Palace.

In the end, the reforms dramatically changed administrative machinery. The Ruling Senate took place of the Duma as the highest authority. That body was established on February 22, 1711. Before setting out for his Prut campaign, Peter entrusted the running of the country during his absence to this collegial body of nine. The Senate's first members were V. Apukhtin, Prince G. Volkonsky, Prince P. Golitsyn, Prince M. Dolgoruky, N. Mel'nitskyi, Count I. Musin-Pushkin, G. Plemyannikov, M. Samarin, and T. Streshnev. The Senate had jurisdiction over governance at large, issues of justice, financial matters, commerce, and industry. Senators had equal voting rights. Positions of governorate commissioners were created for communication with the provinces (known as governorates). Attached to the Senate was the office of chief investigator (*ober-fiscal*), who was the head of the whole new institution of investigators (*fiscals*) charged with conducting secret investigations of abuses of office. Those were not salaried officials. Instead, their incentive lay in the right to keep part of property seized from the perpetrators. Every city had one or two investigators, and every province had four. Four more investigators (two from the nobility and two from the merchants) worked under the chief investigator. Investigative reports were sent to the Chamber of Judgement (*Raspravnaya Palata*) and then to the Senate. With the creation of the system of collegial boards, all board presidents also became Senate members.

In 1722, the position of Prosecutor-General was established. He was directly answerable to the tsar and was made the head of Senate. The first Prosecutor-General of Russia was P. Yaguzhinsky. The system of prosecutorial oversight was extended to all agencies, both central and provincial. Its primary function was the general oversight of justice and public order. The corps of investigators was placed under Prosecutor-General as well. Thus, the Prosecutor-General came to occupy the key position in government. He had the right to appeal against decisions of the Senate as well as suspend their execution. Other new positions under the Senate included that of King-of-Arms (with oversight of service obligations of the nobility, its registry, and responsibility for its education) and that of the Ombudsman (who received complaints from the public and reported them to the Senate).

The Synod occupied a special position. That was a new body set up to run church affairs. After the death of the last Patriarch Adrian, no election was held for a new patriarch, who was replaced with the Synod established in 1721. Stefan Yavorsky, who held the position of Guardian of Patriarchal See, became its president, and Pskov Archbishop F. Prokopovich became its vice-president. It was he who penned the Church Regulations – the set of rules to direct all aspects of church life from then onward. These measures were intended to do away for good with any aspirations by the church to have a political role in the state (as it happened under Patriarch Nikon). Collective church leadership and prohibition to meddle in temporal affairs fully addressed that goal. Moreover, the Synod members swore allegiance to the tsar just as any other official, and when it came to crimes against the state, priests were ordered to violate the seal of confession.

Prikaze system was replaced with new agencies known as collegial boards. The first boards were set up as early as 1715, but the system was instituted in full in 1718. A special building in St. Petersburg was built to house collegial boards. They were 11 in number: Foreign Board, Military Board, Admiralty Board, Board of Mines, Board of Manufactories, Commerce Board, Palace Board, Board of State Offices, Audit Board,

Justice Board, and Patrimonial Estates Board. The creation of this system of boards signaled the arrival of Russia's first well-structured state apparatus with detailed statutes and procedural rules. The General Statute regulated operation of the entire system. Regulations for each of the boards were adopted as well. Those documents described in detail the structure, functions, procedures, and document management rules of every board. Board decisions had to be taken collegially (hence their name in Russian – 'colleges'). The principles of their operation were meant to rule out abuse of office for personal gain (in striking contrast to erstwhile *prikaze*). Some matters remained in the remit of bodies smaller than boards (Armory Chamber, Prikaz of Posts (*Yamskoy*) and Palace Prikaz, Salt Chamber, Medical Chancellery). The functions of secret political police in Peter's time were vested in Preobrazhensky Prikaz (originally a palace chamber in charge of 'amusement' regiments). In addition, the Secret Chancellery was established in 1718.

In 1708–1710, the governorate reform was implemented. It laid the foundations of a new system of administrative divisions of the country. The country was divided into eight governorates, those of St. Petersburg, Archangel, Smolensk, Moscow, Kazan, Kiev, Azov and Siberia. In 1713–1714, Nizhny Novgorod, Astrakhan and Riga (to replace Smolensk) were added. Heads of governorates (with titles of Governor or Governor-General) exercised both military and civilian governance functions on their territories. Their staff included positions of Vice-Governor (chief deputy), Chief Commandant (responsible for military affairs), *Ober-Commissar* (responsible for collection of revenue), Chief of Army Victualling (responsible for collection of the governorate's quota of grain supplies), and *Landrihter* (with oversight of justice).

Smaller territorial units, *uezds,* were historically headed by *voevodas*, who were rebranded commandants in 1710. From 1715, they were headed by councilmen (known as *landrats*), who were elected by local nobility from their own ranks, but otherwise were the same officials as all the others serving in the provinces.

The governorates were excessively large in land area, and their chancelleries were overwhelmed with governing numerous smaller territorial units. Therefore, in May of 1719, governorates were further divided into provinces, totaling 50 in number. Those were headed by commandants and had on their staff a *kamerir* (responsible for tax collection) and a *rentmeister* (responsible for local treasury). Every province had a regiment stationed in it, which was supported by tax take from one of the *uezds*. The governorates were preserved, but governors exercised real power only in a single province – the one eponymous with capital city of a governorate and surrounding it. Provinces had more specialized agencies as well, bureaus and offices responsible for such matters as military recruiting, law enforcement, procuring timber for shipbuilding, and the like. The size and strategic importance of a province determined the rank of the official presiding over it. The most important provinces were governed by governors or governor-generals, and less important ones by *voevodas*. In the second half of 18th century, provinces became the basis for redrawn division into new, smaller governorates. Provinces were subdivided into districts, headed by a district commissioner (known as *Zemsky Komissar*) who combined administrative, policing, and tax collection functions. Below them were so-called lower commissioners, who dealt directly with traditional elected headmen of rural communities (the latter mostly performed rural policing functions).

Prior to 1721, provincial *voevodas* had jurisdiction over the cities on their territory, but with the creation of the Main Magistrate cities passed under its control, and city tradesmen classes were no longer under the jurisdiction of *voevodas*. In 1723–1724, city magistrates were established (analogous to *Burmister* Chambers). Those were collegiate bodies elected from amongst "townsmen of high standing" and consisting of a president, 2 to 4 city stewards and 2 to 8 junior councilors. They were in charge of all city business (administration, policing, city funds, court of justice, and city property and services). Tradesmen were united into craftsmen guilds and merchant classes (ranked on declared worth).

It was Peter who first attempted to create a judiciary system independent from the executive. But it was too early for its time and never took root (just as his city home rule system). The highest level of the judiciary consisted of the Senate and Justice Board. In some, but not all provinces (in large cities), there were established courts of appeal and provincial lower courts with judge panels. The latter were hearing all civil and criminal cases involving peasants (except for monastery-owned peasants) and those townsmen who did not belong to tradesmen classes. In areas with no judge panel courts, there were lower courts with a single judge. However, provincial *voevodas* were soon given the right to control provincial courts, and in 1722 lower courts were abolished, while in the provinces with no courts of appeal provincial courts headed by the *voevodas* were established.

The most important innovation was the development (by Peter himself) of the 'Table of Ranks'. That document describes the full hierarchy of civilian, military, and court ranks and codifies the rights of their holders. Its adoption in 1722 ushered in an entirely new foundation of public service in the Empire. For two subsequent centuries, the principles laid down in the 'Table' remained the cornerstone of Russian state's institutions. They profoundly changed not only the civil service, but also the social structure of the country by establishing the first regular channels for upward social mobility.

The armed forces

Reformist efforts of Peter the Great were directly related to the need for addressing foreign policy challenges. They also were a direct extension of Peter's youthful passions, and therefore started with the creation of a new army and navy. Immediately after the Azov campaigns, as Peter prepared for new campaigns against Turkey, he ordered fleet construction to begin in the area of Voronezh. The project was expected to be completed in 2 years. As early as 1697, 150 young noblemen were sent abroad for training, so that the country could have a native officer class. One-third of them were to be trained for naval service. Foreign engineers were invited for the construction project itself. Naturally, so unprecedented an undertaking required new approaches. The construction was carried out by partnership companies (*kumpanstva*) formed by Peter's special decree. Those companies included members of the nobility, the clergy, and city tradesmen. Over 30 such companies were set up. Funding had to be obtained through extraordinary exactions, and labor service was exacted as a non-monetary obligation (masses of people were mobilized for the construction). By the spring of 1699, more than 20 ships were built, and in the summer of that same year, they sailed from Azov to the port of Kerch, making a great impression upon unsuspecting Tatars and Turks.

Immediately after that, steps were taken to create a regular army. In November 1699, there followed orders to assign 'people given for service' (*datochnye liudy* in Russian) for permanent service in the army. In effect that was a mandatory levy to provide a set percentage of young men from every local community as army recruits, and it was to be borne by all classes of the population except those already in service to the state. That laid the foundations of the recruit system of supplying the army with soldiers, which remained in place for nearly two centuries. But recruits were not the only source of enlisted men. Volunteer regiments began to be raised at the same time, and stipends paid to those who freely enlisted were twice what the *streltzy* got. The former 'amusement' regiments, Preobrazhensky, Semyonovsky and Lefortov, made up the core of this new army. Newly created regiments had uniform tables of personnel (1152 men, including a lieutenant-colonel, a major, 9 captains, a lieutenant-captain, 11 lieutenants, 12 ensigns, a regimental train clerk, 36 sergeants, 12 quartermasters, 12 warrant officers, 48 corporals and 12 company clerks), and they were armed with fusils and bayonets. Fusils had the range of 300 steps and effective stopping power at 60 steps. The decision was made to raise from nobility ranks dragoon-type cavalry. Yet the majority of noblemen still served in traditional mounted militias.

On the eve of the Great Northern War, the troops were trained in accordance with Russia's first ever drill regulations of 1699. As the war progressed, a whole number of army regulations were issued ("Order of March", "Rules for Military Battle", "Guidance for Combat", and others). Three volumes of "Articles of War" were published in 1716. Naval service regulations were developed as well: "Navy Articles" of 1716 and "Instructions and Articles of War for the Russian Navy" (published in 1710). In 1722, lessons learned in the war were summarized in "Naval Manual" and "Rules of Admiralty", and alongside with the "Articles of War", they laid the foundation of subsequent Russian military thought.

The officers of regular army regiments were drawn from the old contingent of military commanders controlled by *Inozemskyi* and *Reitarskyi prikaze*, from old-timer reiters, hussars and lancers (these categories of cavalry were drawn from the lower strata of nobility, and in 1701–1702, regiments of lancers, reiters and hussars were disbanded), from the nobility assigned to such service by *Razryadnyi prikaz*, and from seasoned soldiers of Preobrazhensky and Semyonovsky regiments. During the Grand Embassy of 1698, up to 700 foreigners were recruited for Russian service. Some foreign officers, intending to throw in their lot with Russia for good, converted to Orthodox Christianity. The proportion of foreign officers was especially high in the infantry. In 1701, three 'generalships' (divisions) that made up a field army had 1137 officers, about a third of whom were foreigners or recent converts, while senior officers were all foreign. By contrast, all cavalry officers (there were 9 dragoon regiments in 1702) were Russian (unsurprisingly, since Russian nobility traditionally preferred service in the cavalry). Naturally, such a large percentage of foreign officers appeared highly undesirable, especially after the year 1700, when foreign officers accounted for themselves poorly at Narva (where almost all of them surrendered themselves prisoner, their commander, Duke von Croy included). But they were a necessary evil, since at that time overwhelming majority of native Russian officers simply did not have the requisite military skills. Even in later years, the government twice advertised the campaigns to recruit foreigners for Russian military service (in 1702 and 1704).

In terms of the role of foreign officers, the Great Northern War has been a unique chapter in the history of Russian Army. Never again would it be so high. Many of those officers stayed in Russia for good and started prominent family lines of officers. It should be noted though, that while Peter recruited a large number of foreigners out of necessity, other things being equal he preferred to rely on Russian-born officers. In 1700, the recruitment of officers from the ranks of Russian nobility began on a wide scale. It extended to Moscow nobility with 40 or more peasant households. They were screened and trained, and 940 were commissioned officers prior to taking to the field. Moscow nobility were considered priority candidates for promotion to officers. When it came to forming dragoon regiments, all colonels and captains were recruited from Moscow nobility, while junior officers were recruited from old-timer reiters and lancers. In the early years of the Northern War, junior officer positions in the infantry were increasingly filled with Russian officers, and native Russian regimental commanders appeared as well.

During the Great Northern War, Russia's army had grown both in numbers and in battle worthiness. By 1700, in addition to the three original 'amusement' regiments, there were formed 2 dragoon and 29 infantry regiments. By 1708, the number of dragoon regiments grew to 33, and of infantry ones to 52. Cannonry lost at the walls of Narva was replaced with new artillery pieces of remarkably high quality (which wiped away Swedish infantry, then the best in Europe, in the Battle of Poltava). In 1702–1704, construction of naval ships for the Baltic Fleet unfolded on rivers close to the Baltic war theater, with over a hundred different ships built. Ten years later, shipbuilding capacity extended to large men-of-war with 50 to 60 guns. By the end of the war, Russian Army had more than 100 thousand men on active duty and 71 thousand in 55 garrison regiments (including 4 dragoon regiments). Besides, there existed irregular cavalry forces of 125 thousand raised from among Don and Ukrainian Cossacks, the Bashkirs, and Kalmyks. Russian fortresses were defended by 8100 cannon. Russian Navy then numbered 29 ships of the line and 6 frigates (with a total of 2128 guns and 16 thousand crewmen). In addition, there existed a galley fleet of 171 galleys and 23 thousand marines. By 1722, there were about 300 various (mostly small) ships in the Caspian Sea.

By the time of Peter's death, Russian field army had 73 regiments of infantry and cavalry (131 thousand men along with 2620 artillerymen) and 55 garrison regiments (72 thousand men along with 2295 artillerymen). Irregular troops numbered 113 thousand (30 thousand of them Kalmyks). Russian artillery was armed with three-pounder cannon, mortars and howitzers – over 15 thousand pieces in total (including 9891 cannon and 788 mortars in garrisons and fortresses). It was one of the top European armies. For the first time in Russian history, it was uniformly armed and outfitted (the infantry wore green, and the cavalry had blue coats and black hats).

Most enlisted men were drafted through recruit drives. From 1699 to 1725, there were 53 recruit drives which delivered a total of 284 thousand men. Recruits were selected by local communes in their traditional assembly gatherings. Just like the nobility, recruits had to serve all their lives (or until they were invalided out). The nobility made up a significant proportion of the army. At the beginning of 18th century, after Narva debacle, noblemen's cavalry accounted for only 1% of the whole army, but if all branches are added together the nobility accounted for about 25% (several thousand officers, dragoon regiments fully manned by the nobility, plus many of gentle birth who served alongside peasant recruits as common infantry soldiers).

The army's needs for supplies were fully met by domestic armaments industry. Its cornerstones were two weapons factories (in Tula and Sestroretsk) and two gunpowder factories (in St. Petersburg and Okhta (now part of St. Petersburg)). Those factories continued to be the flagship ones in their sectors in the future. Raw materials for military factories were supplied by ironworks in the Urals, in the North, and in Central Russia. Uniforms were also produced in Russian manufactories.

The state of education was another factor affecting political and military capabilities of Russia. Just as was the case with reforms in other areas, the great reformer's top priority was specialized education, which under the conditions of permanent war meant military and naval education. In 1697, when first travelling to Europe, Peter took along a few bombardiers from Preobrazhensky regiment, who then became the instructors at the first military school established under the bombardier company at the opening of 18th century. There they taught mathematics, art of fortification, and artillery. In 1701, the School of Mathematical and Navigational Sciences was established in Moscow. The school accepted sons of "the nobility, clerks and junior clerks, from the houses of boyars and other ranks" of ages 12 to 17 (later extended to 20-year-olds). Those who had owned over 5 peasant households had to pay their own expenses, while the rest received a stipend for living expenses. Those graduates who were noblemen went on to serve in the Navy as engineers and artillerymen, while the graduates hailing from lower classes (who studied only literacy and numeracy) went on to become clerks, architect's assistants, and other employees in the Admiralty. With the founding in 1715 of Naval Guards Academy in St. Petersburg, which became the main source of officers for the Navy, the school lost its standing and became the prep school for the Academy. By 1712, Moscow had an Engineering School, which was later merged with St. Petersburg Engineering School (established in 1719). In 1712, another artillery school was added to the original one at the bombardier company. One more artillery school (for continued education of 30 already serving artillerymen) was set up in 1721 in the so-called St. Petersburg Laboratory House. However, shortly after Peter's death those artillery schools went out of existence.

Economic reforms

Of great importance was the monetary reform. By the late 17th century, the monetary system was extremely primitive. In fact, the only coin in circulation was a silver kopeck (penny) crudely minted from silver rods. For petty payments, it had to be cut into halves, thirds, and quarters. In order to provide small coin for circulation, in March 1700, copper coins were introduced: denezhka (1/2 kopeck), polushka (1/4 kopeck), and polupolushka (1/8 kopeck). At the same time, large denomination silver and gold coins were introduced. What evolved was a very orderly decimal coinage system. One kopeck, 3 kopeck, 5 kopeck, 10 kopeck, 25 kopeck, 50 kopeck, and ruble coins were minted in silver (the three lower denominations were later minted in copper). Gold ruble coins were introduced as well. In 1718, they were replaced by 2-ruble gold pieces. As early as 1702, circulating money supply increased almost tenfold.

This system met all the needs of the economy and brought huge royalty profits to the Treasury in the most difficult period of the Great Northern War (with a pound of copper priced at 6 to 8 rubles, face value of coins minted from it was 20 rubles in 1711 and 40 rubles in 1718). With the start of this monetary reform, royalty profit from mintage came to account for about 27% of all budget revenues (while in pre-Petrine times it was 2.6%). That largely replaced the revenue from direct taxation (in 1701, tax revenues accounted for 20% of the total instead of previous 34%). It is noteworthy that during the Great Northern War Peter not only managed without foreign loans, but himself provided financial aid to allies. Peter's financial advisor, A. Kurbatov came up with the idea to introduce stamped paper for important documents. Its price depended on the sum of money involved in the transaction recorded (while contracts and other business deeds drawn on plain paper were considered void). In 1704, all the inns were placed directly under the treasury, and collection of commercial duties was centralized even earlier.

31

By the end of Peter's reign, the country switched from traditional household-based taxation to capitation-based taxation. The decree of November 28, 1718, ordered a census of all males who were subject to taxation, but review of its results in 1722 has identified about 2 million uncounted people. When repeated or 'revision' census was taken, it found 5.4 million males, who were duly taxed (and from then onward censuses came to be officially called 'revisions'). By 1724, capitation tax yielded 54% of total revenues, while indirect taxes supplied 25% of the revenue, salt tax accounted for about 8%, and coin mintage for 2.5%. All told, budget revenues at constant prices have tripled compared to 1680 (from 24.9 to 76.7 million rubles).

Under Peter, the vast majority of budget spending went to military needs, since most of his reign was dominated by bitter struggles with Turkey and Sweden. In the first decade of 18th century, the army and navy expenditures accounted for 70% to 80% of budget outlays. By the end of Peter's reign, that proportion went down somewhat to about two thirds (62.8%). Another major line item of expenditures was public administration. Under Peter, education and healthcare expenditures emerge in the budget for the first time (1%).

Peter's measures in the field of industrial development were largely driven by the needs of the military. While industry for wartime needs had to be created fast, the country offered little opportunity for wide-spread private enterprise and had no labor market. Therefore, the state (as represented by Peter) took the task upon itself. Some potential labor was available as there were all sorts of 'people at loose ends,' but that source was quickly exhausted. The government began assigning state peasants (i.e. those not bonded to individual landowners) to various mills as workforce in exchange for exemption from taxes and non-monetary obligations. At the same time, the authorities encouraged private enterprise, and many private mills were built with government support and assistance.

Following the creation of the system of collegial boards, industrial development became the responsibility of Board of Manufactories and the Mining Board (the latter was also tasked with geological surveys). The state controlled every aspect of manufacturing: output, production process, and quality. It also assisted private entrepreneurs by helping with labor supply, with hiring foreign experts, and with training domestic ones. In addition, the state extended preferential loans to entrepreneurs (through the boards). The boards could also transfer some state-owned enterprises to private owners, and vice versa. Since private entrepreneurs were interested in having regular labor (assigned state peasants were not the answer as they worked in factories only a few months a year), in 1721 Peter took the bold step of allowing people from outside the noble estate (who were the majority among entrepreneurs) to buy and own serfs for work in the factories. Previously that right belonged to the nobility alone.

As early as 1701, Kamensky and Nevyansky ironworks appeared in the Urals, joined by Uktussky (now part of Yekaterinburg) ironworks in 1702 and Alapaevsky in 1704. Ironworks were also being built in the North: at Ustyuzhna, Olonets, and in *Belozerye* (around lake Beloye). In 1703, Petrovsky and Povenets works were built in Karelia, as well as Konchezero and Beloozero *uezd* works in 1704–1705. In 1704, industrial-scale mining of silver began in Nerchinsk, which crucially supported successful monetary reform. Ironworks continued to be built after the Northern War. Yekaterinburg (named after Peter's wife, future Empress Catherine I) ironworks appeared in the Urals in 1723. As a result, by the time of Peter's death, Russia was the third-largest European producer of iron and base metals.

In the 1720s, the government built Yagushihinsky, Lyalinsky, Polevsky, Vyshne-Pyskorsky and Nizhne-Pyskorsky works (*zavod* in Russian) to exploit large copper deposits in the Urals. Private copper smelters were started in the Urals as well. In total, during Peter's reign about 30 ironworks and copper smelters (both private and state-owned) appeared in the Urals, while Central Russia had about 40 ironworks. Large shipyards were built in St. Petersburg, Voronezh, Moscow, Archangel, and Olonets. Various textile and canvas and sail-making manufactories mostly supplied the needs of the army and navy. Textile manufactories numbered about 40 (over half of them in Moscow). Some were quite large, with dozens, or even over 200 looms. Large woolen manufactories existed in Moscow, Kazan, Putivl and Lipetsk. Numerous small chemical works (making paint, sulfur, turpentine, vitriol, etc.) emerged as well.

All told, during Peter's reign about 180 large industrial enterprises appeared in Russia, half of which were state-owned. As a result, in 1726, finished products made up 52% of Russian exports, while raw and semi-finished materials accounted for less than a half (finished products accounted for 51% of imports).

Chapter 3

Russia under the successors of Peter the Great

For all his grandiose achievement as a reformer, Peter the Great was not happy in his private life, and died without a legally capable male successor to carry on his work. While suffering from a grave illness since 1723, Peter did not consider his own mortality, and was not ready for death till the very end. He died in the morning on January 28, 1725, without any instructions on who was to be his heir. That turned personal tragedy of that reformist ruler into a tragedy for the empire he built. For years afterwards, the country faced the danger of losing its hard-won standing in the world.

As it invariably happens when a new power emerges on the international scene, great European powers of the time viewed Russia's successes with cautious jealousy, yet sought to turn it into an ally. None of them had reasons to favor Russia's ascendancy. France's traditional policy in opposing hostile European powers was to rely on countries at a distance from France with whom there would be no overlapping interests. That meant Turkey in the south and Sweden in the north. With both being Russia's principal enemies, France could hardly welcome their weakening. Britain was the first to assume a hostile stance towards Russia. It feared Russia's growing naval power as a possible threat to British maritime trade. In case of Austria, Russia was a natural ally against Turkey in the south, but then again Austria was most exercised about the strengthening of Russia's positions in Poland. Under those conditions, domestic political instability in Russia hampered the conduct of robust foreign policy.

The empire's highest dignitaries were divided on the issue of succession. Peter was survived by his second wife Catherine (officially crowned in May 1724), and his preteen grandson, the son of Prince Alexey. In his Order of Succession decree of 1722, Peter enshrined in law the emperor's full discretion in the appointment of heirs to the throne, but due to illness and death he never expressed his will in that matter. Therefore, decision on the issue fell to the late emperor's immediate circle where opinions were split.

The idea of enthronement of underage Peter was supported mainly by the aristocratic circles led by Princes Dolgoruky and Golitsyn and Prince A. Repnin. The majority of Peter's less high-born or commoner associates led by A. Menshikov, I. Buturlin, Count P. Tolstoy, Count P. Yaguzhinsky, and A. Makarov preferred the elevation of Catherine. This later group had the backing of household troops – Preobrazhensky and Semyonovsky guards' regiments (where not only officers but also the vast majority of men were the cream of Russian nobility). At the conference held in the palace, Count P. Tolstoy's speech in favor of Catherine was rather bluntly supported by the arrival of guards' officers, while their two regiments were lined up beneath palace windows.

While Catherine I fully shared Peter's plans and vision, she lacked the capacity to carry on his policies independently. Alexander Menshikov assumed dominant position at

34

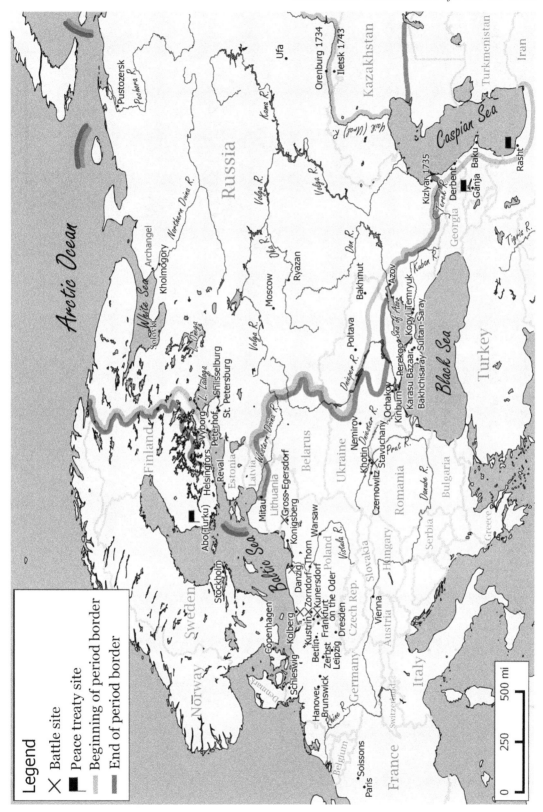

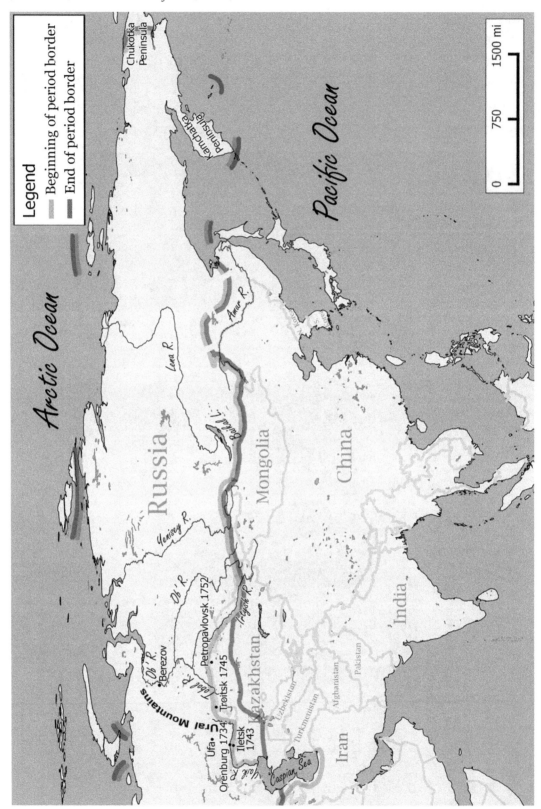

the helm of the state, and his boundless ambition was strongly resented by all the other dignitaries. At the suggestion of Count P. Tolstoy, on February 8, 1726, there was established a collegial body under the empress, the Supreme Privy Council, and Catherine became its chairperson. The Council included Count F. Apraksin, Prince D. Golitsyn, Count G. Golovkin, Prince A. Menshikov, A. Osterman, Count P. Tolstoy, and Duke Karl Friedrich of Holstein who was married to Anna, the eldest daughter of Peter and Catherine. That body became the ultimate authority for all major decisions, and the Senate could not issue any decrees without its endorsement. However, Menshikov's thirst for power did not abate, and he conceived the plan to marry his daughter Maria to Peter Alexeyevich. He also managed to sideline P. Tolstoy, I. Buturlin, and their supporters and to bring official disgrace on them.

Catherine's foreign policy continued international alignments established under Peter the Great. The alliance with Sweden remained in place, and in April 1726 Russia sought to bring Austria into it by signing an agreement to that effect. Counting on Swedish backing, Catherine decided to support Holstein (which was in personal union with Russia through ties of marriage) against Denmark in order to secure the return of Schleswig captured by the Danes. However, as the Russian troops prepared to march on Copenhagen in the spring of 1726, the Anglo-Danish naval squadron suddenly appeared near Reval, and it emerged that it was Russia's ally Sweden who granted the English navy access into the Baltic (the British and French promised Sweden the return of areas lost during the Northern War).

Russia managed to gain predominant influence in Courland, where its interests overlapped those of Poland, Prussia, and Sweden. After the death of Anna Ioannovna's spouse, Poland in 1726 insisted on the election as Duke of Courland of Moritz of Saxony, illegitimate son of Polish King Augustus II, while the pro-Russian party nominated the self-promoted candidacy of Alexander Menshikov. The Polish Diet elected Moritz of Saxony, and thus snubbed Menshikov had to desist and withdraw his candidacy because of the threat of war with Turkey. Yet, in 1727, Russian troops entered Courland (while Moritz of Saxony was denied entry) and Russian predominance was established.

By that time, realignments in European politics produced two large alliances. The Hanover Union included Britain, France, Sweden, Denmark, and Holland. Its counterbalance – the Vienna Union included Austria, Spain, Prussia, and Russia.

Early in May 1727, Catherine succumbed to a grave illness and decided to establish the order of succession. It was as follows (succession to the next heir to be occasioned by childlessness of the previous one): 1) Peter Alexeyevich upon his maturity (age 16) and his descendants, 2) Anna Petrovna and her descendants, 3) Elizabeth Petrovna and her descendants, 4) Natalia Alexeyevna (the elder sister of Peter) and her descendants.

The empress soon died, and 11-year-old Peter, now Peter II, who was engaged to Menshikov's daughter Maria, ascended the throne. As Menshikov looked for allies among the old aristocracy, he elevated the standing in court of the two Princes Dolgoruky: Alexey Dolgoruky became head of household court of Natalia Alexeyevna, while his son Ivan became close friends with Peter. However, this helped wean Peter from Menshikov's control, something that Peter's tutor, Count Osterman conspired in. In September of 1727, Menshikov was arrested and exiled with his family first to Ryazan Governorate, and then to the town of Berezov (today's Beryozovo in Russia) beyond the Arctic Circle, where he died on November 12, 1729. All his vast property was confiscated.

Following the coronation of Peter II, Princes A. G. and V. L. Dolgoruky were brought into the Supreme Privy Council, while Princes V. V. Dolgoruky and I. Trubetskoy were elevated to field marshals. Just like Menshikov before them, princes Dolgoruky schemed to become Tsar Peter's relatives by marrying him to Prince A. Dolgoruky's daughter, Catherine. The engagement was announced on November 30, 1729, but on the very day appointed for wedding (January 18, 1730) Peter II (who was weakened by a severe cold contracted earlier) died of smallpox.

During the reign of Peter II, Russia had to conduct a cautious foreign policy and seek to prevent a war between large European coalitions. Any such war would have been extremely disadvantageous to Russia, since all its northern neighbors in the Baltic were allied against it. At Soissons Congress of 1728–1729, Russian diplomacy strove to appease Britain and Denmark by stressing the benefits of sea-borne trade with Russia and withdrawing the demand to return Schleswig to Holstein.

The death of Peter II raised the question of succession again. By that time, five out of eight members of the Supreme Privy Council were Dolgorukys and Golitsyns. The predominance of old aristocracy caused the order of succession established by Catherine I to be rejected. The candidacy of Elizabeth Petrovna found no support (and Anna Petrovna died abroad in 1728 leaving an infant son). The Dolgorukys and Golitsyns preferred the rule by descendants of Ivan, Peter the Great's brother and onetime co-ruler. At the suggestion of Prince D. Golitsyn, final choice was made in favor of the widow of Duke of Courland, Anna Ioannovna (Ivan's daughter). By then, Anna was 37 years old, she was widowed early, and had lived for the previous 20 years in Mitau, Courland's capital.

That choice was mainly driven by the fact that Supreme Privy Council did not expect Anna to be a self-willed ruler, and intended to rule in her name while preventing the emergence of some powerful favorite behind the throne. The idea of limiting royal powers was vested in the so-called 'Conditions' drawn by Supreme Privy Council. Those limits on royal powers were fairly drastic and left the empress essentially a nominal head of state: she could not command the armed forces, or decide issues of war and peace, or make appointments to senior positions, or even award the nobility with estates (as well as deprive them of estates). The 'Conditions' were carried to Mitau by Prince V. L. Dolgoruky.

But the designs of Supreme Privy Council leaked out to wider circles, and caused widespread resentment in Moscow, which was then packed by the noblemen come to witness the planned wedding of Peter II. Although Anna had warning of that, she signed the 'Conditions', which were promulgated on February 2 at the joint meeting of Supreme Privy Council, the Senate, the Synod, and the generals. The attendees' reception of 'Conditions' was quite chilly though, and the protocol was never signed. Moreover, there emerged alternative projects coming from various groups of the nobility. On February 10, when Anna reached Vsesvyatskoye village near Moscow, she was visited by representatives of guards' regiments and declared herself a colonel of Preobrazhensky Regiment. By that time, the feelings of the guardsmen and of the majority of nobility regarding the 'Supremos' project were quite obvious to her. On February 25, 1730, Anna was petitioned to consider all the proposals submitted by the nobility compiled into a single package. Anna agreed to that, but allowed just a few hours to do the job. In the afternoon, Prince A. Cherkassky acting on behalf of a group of about 150 noblemen submitted the proposal stipulating autocratic form of government, disbandment of Supreme Privy Council and restoration of the Senate of 21 members. Prince Cherkassky also declared that the 'Conditions' were drawn up without consent of the nobility. Anna Ioannovna play-acted being deceived by

Prince V. L. Dolgoruky. She ordered that the 'Conditions' be brought out and publicly tore them up. Having abolished the Supreme Privy Council, the empress took her time about persecuting its members. The first to fall into disgrace were the Dolgorukys. Initially, they were banished to their estates, then exiled to far-off places (Berezov, Pustozersk, Solovki), and only in 1739 the four Princes Dolgoruky were executed.

Anna Ioannovna's long-time favorite, Courland nobleman Ernst Johann Biron, emerged as the top figure in the state due to his unlimited influence on the empress. The pressure applied by Anna and reinforced by the presence of Russian troops got Biron elected Duke of Courland. However, Biron (who freely used his position for personal gain and to render patronage to his fellow countrymen from Courland) had little patience for the work of governance. During Anna's reign, affairs of state were in fact devolved on two prominent figures: Vice Chancellor Count A. Osterman (de facto prime minister) was left in charge of foreign policy and civilian affairs, while matters military were entrusted to Field Marshal B. Minich. In those years, many foreigners entered Russian service, and many of them were quickly catapulted to top positions. Sometimes such meteoric career climbs were due to a person's closeness to Ernst Biron and his immediate entourage. This fanned discontent among native Russian nobility. Cabinet Minister A. Volynsky (who enjoyed Anna's strong confidence) emerged as the center of opposition to "Biron's misrule". To him gravitated the like-minded figures (President of the Commerce Board P. Musin-Pushkin, Attorney General of the Senate F. Soimonov, P. Eropkin, A. Khrushchev, and others). Following their personal clash on the issue of monetary compensation to Poles for the passage of Russian troops, Biron categorically demanded that Volynsky be removed. Volynsky was soon arrested, accused of conspiracy, and executed along with his supporters.

By the time of Anna Ioannovna's accession to the throne, there occurred new dramatic changes in the alignment of powers in Europe. In 1729, Britain and France, having made every concession to Spain, entered into the Treaty of Seville with it, thus snatching Spain from the Vienna Union. However, only two years later, in 1731, Austria concluded a second Treaty of Vienna with Spain, which was also joined by Great Britain and Holland, while Hanover Union ceased to exist. France found itself in isolation, and since Austria (its main continental rival) and Russia remained allied, French policy was now focused on the creation of an anti-Russian belt of states that were hostile to Russia, while traditionally friendly to France – Turkey, Poland, and Sweden. However, since continuing realignments (the alliance of Russia with Great Britain and the warming-up of Russia's relations with Denmark) left Sweden isolated in the Baltic it chose to renew its alliance with Russia (in 1735).

While the French schemes with regards to Sweden failed, France stepped up its efforts in Poland. Although huge in land area, from the 17th century Poland was a very loose political conglomerate. In place of a strong royal power it had what amounted to a republic of the nobility with an elective king and eternally warring factions aligned with one or another European power. Poland's neighbors – Austria, Russia and Prussia – were naturally much in favor of maintaining that status quo. After the death of King Augustus II in 1733, Russia supported the candidacy of his son Friedrich Augustus, Elector of Saxony, while the pro-Austrian and pro-Prussian parties advocated for Portuguese Prince Emmanuel. France insisted on the candidacy of father-in-law to Louis XV, Stanislaw Leszczynski (who was the Swedish protege on the Polish throne during Northern War), and encouraged Sweden to back him as well. Russia and Austria finally agreed on the candidacy of the Elector of Saxony, entered into an alliance with 18-year term with him, and exacted the promise that Polish form of government would remain unchanged.

In September 1733, the majority of the gathering of about 60 thousand mounted noblemen near Warsaw declared for Stanislaw Leszczynski (French money helped). However, the minority did not recognize that decision and invoked the Diet's principle of unanimity ('liberum veto'). The dissenters included the most influential Polish magnates, such as princely clans of Radziwills, Sapiehas, and Lubomirskys. They called on Russia to act in defense of the Polish form of government, and convoked their own confederacy, which duly elected King Friedrich Augustus III. This opened the War of Polish Succession, in which Russia got deeply involved.

Russian troops under the command of P. Lassy entered Poland and occupied Praha (a suburb of Warsaw). Unable to resist the Russian corps of 20 thousand, Leszczynski fled to Danzig. After taking Thorn in January 1734, Russian troops laid siege to Danzig. A French squadron arrived to help Leszczynski and landed troops, but the squadron was chased away by the Russian fleet and the landing force defeated and largely captured. Danzig capitulated and recognized Augustus as king. Stanislaw Leszczynski fled to France. The battle for Danzig became history's first direct fight between Russian and French armies. Russia's ally, Austria was at that time at war with France too. Russian troops marching west from Poland reached the banks of the Rhine, and their appearance brought closer the end of that war in 1735.

After losing in Poland, France turned its attention to the south and the third potential opponent to Russia – Turkey. Despite the fact that there had been no hostilities between those two powers for over two decades, antagonism between Russia and Turkey was ancient and deep-seated. Whether they were at war or not at any given moment depended on specific circumstances. Many millions of Orthodox Christians lived under the Turkish rule, including the Slavs, who viewed their coreligionists in Russia with hope. Christian holy places in Palestine were also under Turkish rule. Control over the Black Sea and Sea of Azov coasts as well as the Crimea, enjoyed by the Ottoman Empire and its vassal Crimean Tatars constituted a deadly threat to southern and central regions of Russia whenever it was distracted by conflicts in other regions. Even in peacetime, during 1711–1735, the Tatars constantly raided Left Bank Ukraine (areas around Poltava and Bakhmut), Right Bank Ukraine, and areas north of the Caucasus mountains, taking away thousands of captives and preventing the settlement of southern territories. Finally, Turkish advances in the Trans-Caucasia and Iran threatened Russia's trade links in the East.

Unable to fight Turkey in the mid-1720s, Russia was forced to recognize Turkish conquests in Trans-Caucasia and could not respond to repeated appeals by the Armenians for help against the Turks. In turn, Turkey was tied down by its war with Iran. In 1725, the Turks began to suffer defeats. In the north, they had to abandon Armenia, while in the south they retreated to the bank of the Tigris. But even after making peace with Iran in 1727 (facilitated by France, Great Britain, and Sweden in order to give Turkey a free hand to fight), the Turks were in no hurry to launch war against Russia for fear of losing Georgia, which they still controlled.

Russia's strategic position in the south was difficult. In fact, it was little better than at the end of the 17th century. The Crimea, that principal threat to the southern reaches of Russia was virtually impregnable. Even after a successful march across parched grasslands, Russian troops would have had to storm a narrow isthmus protected by a rampart and a moat. Inside Crimea, the troops would be welcomed by more sun-scorched grasslands, while the Tatars could easily avoid battle by hiding in the mountains. At the same time, the Tatars could make sallies from the Crimea with impunity. In the Sea of Azov region and in Northern Caucasus, Russian troops relied on a thin defensive line of small forts incapable of resisting the Turkish army. It was also not feasible to maintain substantial forces in the south without such key outposts as Azov (ceded under the Peace of Prut in 1711).

However, war became inescapable after 1735, when the Crimean Tatars fought their way through Russian possessions as they marched to attack Persian lands near the Caspian Sea (according to Ganja Treaty of 1735, lands south of Terek River were ceded to Iran). In the autumn of 1735, Russian troops took advantage of the fact that the Tatars' main forces were away (on the campaign to seize Derbent) and marched to the Crimea under the command of M. Leontiev. After suffering heavy losses from hunger and disease in the grasslands, they were forced to return before reaching the Crimea. Next year's campaign was led by B. Minich himself, who had the foresight to build food supply depots along the road to the Crimea. With about 50 thousand men under him, he reached the Isthmus of Perekop while repelling Tatar counter-attacks and fought his way into the Crimea. In June of 1736, Russian troops took the Khanate's capital of Bakhchisaray and Sultan-Saray, but the Tatars avoided battle royal, and after losing half his army to disease, Minich hastened to retreat from the Crimea ahead of the return of Tatar's main forces from the Caucasus. Even as the Crimean campaign unfolded, the Russian force of 20 thousand laid siege to Azov, which surrendered in mid-June.

The following year's campaign took place at two war theaters. P. Lassy with the army of 40 thousand re-entered Crimea and took Karasu Bazaar after a series of battles, yet just as Minich before him was forced to retreat due to the heat and lack of water. Minich himself led the Russian army of 90 thousand to Bessarabia, and after a hard crossing of the grasslands stormed and took Ochakov fortress in July, but heavy losses from hunger and disease stalled his advance. The Turks sued for peace, but peace negotiations in Nemirov (started in August 1737) proved futile. Meanwhile in the Caucasus, in April 1736, a horde of 40 thousand Kalmyks allied itself to Russia and defeated the Nogais (some part of the Nogais then swore allegiance to Russia), and acting together with Don Cossacks and Terek Cossacks took the Turkish fortress of Kopyl (where Kuban River empties into the sea) and ravaged the Tatars' possessions along the Kuban River. In the spring of 1737, the Kalmyks took Temryuk, massacred its Turkish garrison, and joined Lassy's army.

In 1738, the third annual campaign of Russian troops to the Crimea ended in failure for the same reasons as the prior ones, while the main Russian force of 100 thousand led by Minich failed to move beyond the Dniester River. On top of it all, a severe plague epidemic broke out among the Russian ranks, and in September of that year Russian troops abandoned previously seized seaside fortresses of Ochakov and Kinburn. The campaign of 1739 fared better. Minich headed to Khotin by way of Czernowitz, and in August defeated the Turks in the pitched battle near Stavuchany and captured Khotin. The entry of Russian troops culminated in the conclusion of the treaty by which Principality of Moldavia accepted Russian sovereignty with the preservation of its traditional autonomy.

Russia waged that war in alliance with Austria. Austrian troops took to the field in the summer of 1737 and advanced on two fronts, in Bosnia and Wallachia, where they had some success. But later, the Austrians suffered a series of defeats, and Austria violated its agreements with Russia by signing a separate peace with Turkey, which freed up large Turkish forces. In those circumstances (besides, a new war with Sweden in the north was brewing), Russia also had to make peace with Turkey and lose almost all the fruit of its victories. However, Azov (with its fortifications razed), the adjacent grasslands to the west of it, and Zaporozhye region remained Russian. Essentially, this restored the situation that existed after Peter's Azov campaigns.

Russia's standing vis-à-vis Iran weakened in this post-Petrine period due to domestic developments in Iran itself and to its relative strengthening after military successes in the war against Turkey. In dealing with Iran Russia preferred to make concessions, both because Iran did not pose such an immediate threat as the Ottoman empire and because maintaining Peter's conquests there was simply too difficult. The troops were constantly harassed by highlanders of Dagestan and by the Persians, and unfamiliar climate took its toll as well. Russia restored previously conquered provinces of Mazandaran and Astrabad to Iran when Peter II was on the throne. The treaty signed in 1729 with Shah Ashraf granted the right of free transit across Iran for Russian commerce with India and Bukhara. However, when Shah Tahmasp won back his throne, he demanded a new treaty. Under the terms of treaty of Rasht (1732), Russia was to return Gilyan province and promise eventual return of Derbent and Baku. When Iran strengthened even further under Shah Nadir and defeated the Turks in the war of 1730–1736, Russia and Iran concluded the Ganja Treaty (March 10, 1735) under which Russia had to cede not only Baku and Derbent, but even the strip of land to the north all the way to Terek River, where the only remaining Russian fortress was Kizlyar (laid down in 1735). Although the treaties of 1732 and 1735 upheld Russia's right of transit trade through Iran, and bound Iran to fight as Russia's ally in case of a new Russian-Turkish war, such significant territorial losses made Russian border retreat far to the north and significantly worsened its defensive position in the Caucasus should Iran itself attack. Such a war with Iran seemed imminent in the early 1740s when newly installed Shah Nadir marched with his troops into Dagestan and kept on moving north. Although a rebellion in Iran forced him to interrupt the campaign, the defensive line along Terek River was kept in the state of high alert until his death in 1747.

Russia's advance to the southeast into the grasslands along the Yaik (Ural) River required construction of defensive border lines and fortresses. In 1734, there was launched the so-called Orenburg expedition led by I. Kirilov. Among other things, it was tasked with establishing two schools for teaching Russian to the Bashkirs and other non-Russian native people of the area. Another such school opened in Ufa in 1739. Construction of the fortresses provoked a major rebellion of the Bashkirs in 1735–1736. The rebels devastated Russian, Mordovian and Chuvash villages. By 1740, the rebellion was fully suppressed and steps taken to convert the natives into Christians. Those attempts provoked a new rebellion in 1755, incited by the Muslim clergy and inspired by the slogan of *jihad* (holy war). Its leaders were counting on support from Turkey. It took an army of 50 thousand to put down that rebellion, which was achieved fairly quickly, yet afterwards the policy of conversion of the Bashkirs was suspended.

Several fortresses were built along the Yaik (Ural) River, with Orenburg (founded in 1734) becoming the principal center of the region. In 1743, Iletsk fortress was built south of Orenburg to guard the strip of annexed lands to the south of Yaik River. In 1748, there was formed the Orenburg Cossack Host, and work started on Orenburg defensive line. Later, in 1754, that line was pushed further south to Iletsk. Lands beyond the Yaik (Ural) River and Tobol River were the domain of nomadic Kazakhs, who were divided into three loose tribal confederations (known as the Junior, Senior, and Middle *Zhuz*). Those lands saw constant fighting between the confederations, as well as clashes between the Kazakhs and Dzungarian Khanate. The Junior *Zhuz* bordered directly with Russia, and as its leader, Sultan Abulkhair sought protection against his enemies he asked for Russian suzerainty, which was duly granted by Anna Ioannovna in 1731. In 1740–1743, Russian protectorate was extended to the Middle *Zhuz* as well.

Development and exploration of new lands continued in the Far East. The first Kamchatka expedition of Vitus Bering and Alexey Chirikov was sent by Peter the Great. It explored the eastern coast of Kamchatka and the eastern and southern coasts of Chukotka. In 1733–1743, it was followed by the second Kamchatka expedition, which was led by the same two explorers but arranged on a far grander scale (with about a thousand men on 13 ships). It explored the northern and eastern coasts of Siberia and confirmed the sea passage between Asia and America.

By the early 1740s, domestic political situation in Russia worsened again. Empress Anna Ioannovna chose as her heir the son of her niece – Anna Leopoldovna, Princess of Mecklenburg. She was the daughter of Anna Ioannovna's elder sister Catherine (who died in 1733), and was married to Prince Anton Ulrich of Braunschweig (Brunswick), who had been in the Russian service for several years by then and saw action in the war against Turkey. On August 12, 1740, the couple had a son named Ivan Antonovich, who became the heir. In the autumn of 1740, as the empress lay dying (she died on October 17), she signed a manifesto appointing Ernst Biron the regent for the infant heir until his maturity. That appointment was supported by Cabinet Ministers A. Bestuzhev and Prince A. Cherkassky, and favored by B. Minich and A. Osterman. The discontents started to coalesce around Prince Anton Ulrich of Brunswick, but were captured and executed, with the Prince dismissed from all his positions. However, Biron did not enjoy strong enough support either at court or from the guards' regiments. That became patently obvious when only three weeks into his regency Biron was arrested by 80 guardsmen led by Field Marshal Minich (who had explicit permission from Anna Leopoldovna).

But even after that, relations between Minich (appointed the new First Minister), A. Osterman, and Anton Ulrich remained tense. Personal enmity was compounded by genuine disagreements over foreign policy. Following the death of Austrian Emperor Charles VI in October of 1740 (he bequeathed the throne to his daughter Maria Theresa), Austria and Prussia were on the brink of war over Silesia, which was coveted by Friedrich II of Prussia. Anna Leopoldovna and Anton Ulrich leaned to the Austrian side, while Minich preferred neutrality, and in December of 1740 even signed a treaty of alliance with Prussia. Since by that time Prussian troops had already invaded Silesia, that act looked like a direct challenge to a friendly Austria. As chastisement, Anna Leopoldovna's decree reduced Minich's powers. Offended, he handed in his resignation, which was accepted (quite contrary to his expectations). A. Osterman took over from him. In April 1741, the treaty of alliance with Great Britain was signed. Its terms (good for 20 years) were very favorable to Russia. That treaty was in the works even 6 years previously, but due to self-serving scheming by Biron it was replaced at that time with a trade agreement so favorable to Britain that it lost any incentive to add political clauses (those terms on trade were grandfathered into the new treaty). A French attempt to induce Russia to oppose Austria failed. Moreover, it was understood that Prussia incited Sweden to go to war with Russia.

Meanwhile, a court intrigue involving Peter' daughter Elizabeth began to unfold. She was still unmarried, even though several attempts to marry her off were made in the preceding decade (so as to rule out for good the possibility of her laying claim to the throne). After a decade-long predominance of foreigners at the court, many saw her first and foremost as her father's daughter and someone to continue the course Peter set for the country. She was especially popular with the guards' regiments, as was revealed on several occasions when plots hatched by the guards were uncovered in the reign of Anna Ioannovna.

With a new big European war brewing, the French diplomacy (through the Ambassador in St. Petersburg Marquis Chétardie) sought to prevent Russia taking part in it as an ally of Austria, France's principal enemy (that course was favored by the Brunswicks). France attempted to neutralize Russia by drawing it into war with Sweden and Turkey, which would make Prussia (then a French ally) secure from being attacked from the rear. Acting through Elizabeth's personal doctor Johann Lestocq, Chétardie as well as Swedish ambassador tried to convince Elizabeth that Sweden is prepared to declare war on Russia for the purpose of elevating Elizabeth to the throne and delivering Russian court from its domination by foreigners (when the war began in July 1741, a manifesto to such effect was in fact issued by the Swedish commander-in-chief). In return, the Swedes demanded from Elizabeth a written promise of concessions favoring Sweden, especially territorial ones. Elizabeth gave no promises, and negotiations led nowhere, but A. Osterman and Anna Leopoldovna knew of them and of Elizabeth's popularity with the guardsmen, and grew alarmed.

The crunch came on November 24, 1741, when the guardsmen were ordered to prepare for a march from St. Petersburg to Vyborg. Influenced by her entourage (M. Vorontsov, P. and A. Shuvalov, A. Razumovsky), Elizabeth decided to act. In the night of November 25, she showed up at the barracks of Preobrazhensky regiment, and spoke to the soldiers. Several hundred guardsmen immediately swore the oath of allegiance to her, and the regiments were rallied within an hour. Escorted by one company of Preobrazhensky regiment, Elizabeth headed for the Winter Palace, and sent out teams to arrest her main opponents. The Brunswick family was arrested and deposed.

A council convened to write the new oath of allegiance included Chancellor Prince A. Cherkassky, Senate Prosecutor-General Prince N. Trubetskoy, Field Marshal Prince I. Trubetskoy, Admiral N. Golovin, A. Bestuzhev, and others. The next day, all the guards' regiments swore that oath. Minich, Count Osterman, and Count Golovkin were imprisoned in Schlisselburg fortress (and were later exiled), while the Brunswick family was sent into exile in Kholmogory.

Elizabeth immediately asked Chétardie about stopping hostilities since the formal cause of that war was pre-empted, but the French ambassador now openly spelled out the war's true objective – revenge for the defeat in the Northern War. Going through Elizabeth's doctor again, he started pressuring her to make concessions to Sweden. However, Elizabeth, who could well resist pressure even from people closest to her, took the side of the new Vice-Chancellor A. Bestuzhev, who insisted on continuation of the war, which Russia had every reason to do by that time. Even though formally allied Prussia refused Russian request for assistance, in August of 1741 Swedish troops invading Finland were routed by the Russian army of 20 thousand led by P. Lassy. Their retreat continued during 1742. In March of 1742, Elizabeth issued a manifesto with a promise of independence for Finland, which won over the local population to the Russian side. In August, the core of the Swedish army capitulated at Helsingfors (although combat continued elsewhere). After long negotiations held in Abo (Turku), Russia signed (on August 7, 1743) an advantageous peace treaty, that gave it several fortresses in Finland. In the autumn of the same year, Sweden, fearful of attack by Denmark, even persuaded Russia to send to its aid a corps of 10 thousand, which landed at Stockholm. The Franco-Prussian intrigue completely backfired.

Almost immediately after her accession to the throne, Elizabeth summoned to Russia her nephew (Anna Petrovna's son) Karl Peter Ulrich, the Duke of Holstein. He accepted Russian Orthodox baptism under the name of Peter Feodorovich, and was declared heir to the throne as early as November 7, 1742. That was all the more important to Elizabeth because those factions who were hostile to her (as well as Austria) pinned their hopes on infant Ivan Antonovich. Elizabeth also took time to search for a bride for her heir, and her choice fell on Princess Sophie Auguste Friederike of Anhalt-Zerbst, who arrived in Moscow early in 1744, and was received into the Orthodox Church under the name of Catherine Alexeyevna. In the summer of 1745, she was wed to Peter. While Elizabeth showered her heir with attentions, she was soon gravely disappointed in him. Being congenitally mediocre, and afflicted with some mental health issues, Peter, who was orphaned early in life, also received a very poor upbringing, which made him quite unfit to become a statesman. Even worse, he felt an overwhelming disgust for the country he was called upon to rule, the disgust he neither could nor cared to hide. He made a point of wearing the uniform of Holstein, surrounded himself almost exclusively with fellow natives of Holstein, behaved inappropriately during worship services, and was generally quirky. He idolized the Prussian King Friedrich II. Pious Elizabeth was driven to distraction, but was powerless to do anything about it: after all, this Peter was the only grandson of Peter the Great.

Dramatic strengthening of Prussia during the reign of Friedrich II (who created Europe's best army of the time and enriched the art of war with new tactics) prompted a new political realignment. Unlike short-lived alliances of the first third of the century, this new European architecture had a longer life. After the seizure of Silesia by Prussia, confrontation between Austria and Prussia became one of the cornerstones of European international politics (while Franco-Prussian alliance persisted). This led to the rapprochement between Austria, Britain, and Russia. In 1745, Russia and Austria entered into a new treaty of alliance with a term of 25 years. Russia also signed an agreement with Britain stipulating military aid to Britain should its continental possessions be threatened by France and Prussia. It was against this backdrop, that Europe's War of Austrian Succession (1743–1748) ended. In 1750, Russia completely severed diplomatic relations with Prussia.

In the mid-1750s, Prussia, intending to secure itself from Russian threat, reoriented its policy from alliance with France to that with Britain by promising protection of British possessions from a French attack. In January 1756, Britain was negotiating the same with Russia, but since Russia primarily sought to strengthen the anti-Prussian coalition, it agreed to protect British possessions only against threats from Prussia. However, Britain turned around and concluded a non-aggression pact with Prussia. This triggered yet another realignment of powers in Europe, as in May of the same year France (betrayed by Friedrich II) responded by a treaty of alliance with Austria. Thus emerged the coalition of Austria, France, Russia, and Saxony opposed by that of Great Britain and Prussia. The two coalitions launched a new European war known as the Seven Years' War (1756–1762).

In August 1756, the Prussian troops suddenly attacked Saxony and took Dresden and Leipzig, while troops of allied Austria were defeated as well, and Saxony surrendered. That loss was offset in May 1757, when Sweden joined the anti-Prussian coalition. Russia declared war on Prussia right after Prussia's aggression became known. Russian troops led by Field Marshal S. Apraksin entered East Prussia in summer of 1757, took a number of cities, and set off for Königsberg. In a major battle at Gross-Egersdorf Russian troops defeated 40 thousand-strong army of Prussian Field Marshal Levald. Apraksin (who was a Friedrich sympathizer) did not acquit himself well in that battle, but the day was saved by the successes of another army led by P. Rumyantsev. W. Fermor was appointed commander in Apraksin's place and took Königsberg and later the whole of East Prussia.

The following year Russian troops besieged the fortress of Küstrin. Unexpectedly for Fermor, Friedrich II arrived with the army of 33 thousand to relieve the siege. Fermor had to abandon the siege, and redeployed his army of 42 thousand to poorly chosen positions near the village of Zorndorf. Prussian attack came on August 25, but the bloody battle did not give victory to either side. In the summer of 1759, a new commander, P. Saltykov, entered the territory of Brandenburg. After defeating a Prussian corps, he seized Frankfurt on the Oder, and now posed a direct threat to Berlin. Russian troops (about 41 thousand) were joined by 18.5 thousand strong Austrian corps of General Laudon. Friedrich led against them the army of 48 thousand men, and battle royal took place on August 1 at Kunersdorf. Friedrich stubbornly attacked Russian troops entrenched on the heights, but made no progress. Then Saltykov switched to the counterattack. Bayonet charge by the Russians rolled Prussians back and forced them to flee (their losses exceeded 18.5 thousand, while the Russians and Austrians lost 15 thousand). The bulk of the Prussian army scattered, and Friedrich left with only 3 thousand men barely escaped capture. The road to Berlin lay open, yet the Austrians insisted that the main thrust be redirected to Silesia. Feeling resentful, Saltykov resigned, and Field Marshal A. Buturlin took his place.

Next year, in the autumn of 1760, while the main Prussian forces were tied down in Silesia, Russian troops approached Berlin, which capitulated on September 28. The campaign of 1761 mostly unfolded in Silesia, but P. Rumyantsev's corps took parallel action in Pomerania. In December 1761, helped by naval support, he took the fortress of Kolberg, which was under siege since 1760. By early 1762, the position of Prussia was absolutely untenable, and Friedrich II planned to abdicate in favor of his nephew. However, the death of Empress Elizabeth changed everything and saved Prussia from a complete debacle. On December 25, 1761, Elizabeth died, and the first action of Peter III who ascended the throne, was to cease hostilities against Prussia. Moreover, on April 24, 1762, he signed a "perpetual peace" with Prussia, and General Chernyshov was ordered to march against yesterday's allies to Prussia's aid.

Upon assumption of the Russian throne, Peter III continued to see himself as the Duke of Holstein rather than the Emperor of Russia. After conclusion of peace with Prussia, which deprived Russia of all the fruit of its victory, he declared war on Denmark, Holstein's traditional enemy. He openly admired Friedrich II, adopted Prussian military uniform for the troops, ordered to remove most icons from Orthodox churches, and embarked upon secularization of church properties. Unsurprisingly, all of that was bitterly and widely resented by Russian nobility. Such sentiment was particularly strong in guards' regiments whose proximity to court gave them a ringside view of the new emperor's behavior.

All the discontents gravitated towards Peter's wife Catherine, who was his polar opposite on every point that caused aggravation. Fated to become a ruler's wife by the circumstances of her birth, she was preparing herself for that role since childhood. She was intelligent, well-read, and strong-willed. While perfectly fluent in French, upon moving to Russia, she quickly learned Russian. At court, she always comported herself with good grace and was diligent in observing all the religious rites (which won her love from Elizabeth). But most importantly, unlike her husband, Catherine came to be fully dedicated to the interests of the country whose empress she was destined to become. The contrast between the spouses (whose relations were cold, as Peter publicly humiliated and insulted his wife) was plain to see. She enjoyed the sympathy of both the guardsmen rank-and-file (while a few dozen officers were her determined supporters) and of a number of prominent dignitaries, including attorney-general A. Glebov, police director N. Korf, commander of army artillery A. Vilboa, Prince M. Volkonsky, Count N. Panin, and the Hetman of Little Russia Count Razumovsky.

Just as in 1741, the coup was precipitated by the order for the guardsmen to march out to fight Denmark. On June 27, 1762, unrest erupted in Preobrazhensky regiment. One of its officers and Catherine's supporter was arrested. Accompanied by A. Orlov (sent by the regiment), Catherine hastened from her suburban residence in Peterhof to St. Petersburg, where she called to arms Izmailovsky regiment (which swore the oath of allegiance to her), and Semyonovsky regiment followed suit. The guardsmen took positions in the Winter Palace where Catherine received the members of Senate and Synod, all of whom swore the oath to her. Upon learning of what has happened, Peter attempted to hole in at the island fortress of Kronstadt, but was denied entry there. He abdicated, was whisked away to a country residence, and assassinated there a week later. On July 6, a manifesto proclaiming accession of Catherine II was issued, and on September 22, she was crowned in Moscow.

Catherine II broke the alliance with Prussia, but did not resume the war. In November 1762, Austria and France signed a truce with Prussia (final peace treaty was approved in February 1763). Resounding victories of Russian army in the Seven Years' War (won against Europe's best army, that of Friedrich II) boosted Russia's prestige enormously, but ill-fated reign of Peter III robbed it of any tangible gains. Even Courland which had been within Russia's sphere of influence for a long time was not annexed.

In summary, the period from 1725 to 1762, saw Russia score some successes in the west and in the south, but territorial gains were quite modest (a small part of Finland and recaptured Azov). In the east, the Caspian coastlands south of Terek River were lost, but the broad swath of land from the upper reaches of Tobol River and to Irtysh River was gained (towns of Troitsk and Petropavlovsk were established there in 1745 in 1752 respectively), while the nomads across much of the huge expense of dry Kazakh grasslands further south became Russia's vassals. Russian successes in European wars (war over the Polish Succession and the Seven Years' War) once and for all made Russia one of the top four European powers, and an integral part of European politics.

System of government and military-economic potential

Following the abolition of Supreme Privy Council at the start of Anna's reign, the role of supreme government body running all daily affairs of state belonged to the Cabinet of Ministers. Established on October 12, 1731, it consisted of three ministers (the first ones were Count A. Osterman, Prince A. Cherkassky and Count G. Golovkin). In 1735, the Cabinet was granted a legislative role as well (its unanimous decision carried the same weight as a decree from the empress). Under Elizabeth, the Cabinet was abolished, and she restored her father's practice of running affairs through a personal chancellery, known as Her Majesty's Cabinet. In 1756, the Imperial Court Conference was established; it was mainly engaged in issues of foreign policy. During the short reign of Peter III, the supreme body was the Imperial Council of 8 members. During Anna's reign, the Senate functioned as an executive body under the Cabinet of Ministers, but Elizabeth restored its former role of supreme government body. It was in charge of all the machinery of state (down to appointment of officials), of finance, and management of the economy, while also serving as the court of last resort.

The system of collegial boards had not changed significantly in the period from 1730s to 1750s although some boards were merged or abolished. But their staff was halved: from 1726, a board was allowed to have only a president, vice president, 2 councilors and 2 assessors. In the 1720s and 1730s, two special boards were set up to manage affairs of state in Livonia and Estland, where the nobility continued to enjoy its historic special privileges (as stipulated at the absorption of those provinces into the empire). The Secret Chancellery was abolished in 1726, and Preobrazhensky prikaz in 1729. For a while, crimes against the state were investigated by the Senate and Supreme Privy Council, but in 1731, the functions of erstwhile Preobrazhensky prikaz and Secret Chancellery were inherited by newly created Secret Investigative Office headed by A. Ushakov. It mostly investigated cases falling under the first two articles of Decree on State Crimes issued in 1715 (malicious designs against the emperor, rebellion, or treason). Some central institutions of lesser importance were created as well – the Printing Bureau, Siberian prikaz, *Doimochnyi* prikaz (responsible for default tax collection). All court offices now reported to the Main Palace Chancellery. In 1754, the Nobility Bank and the Merchant Bank were instituted.

Local government system underwent significant changes. In 1726–1727, *uezds* were restored in place of districts, while numerous local offices (dealing with forest management, recruiting, tax collection, etc.), as well as the positions of local (*zemstvo*) commissioners were abolished. In 1729–1730, the corps of local secret investigators (*fiscals*) was also abolished. Local government reform was summed up in the circular of 1728, which made governors in governorates and voevodas in provinces and *uezds* the sole centers of both executive and judicial powers. Specialized local chancelleries were placed directly under them. In 1730, the requirement for rotation of *voevodas* every 2 years was introduced, but in 1760, their term of service was extended to 5 years. By that time, there were 14 governorates, 47 provinces, and over 250 *uezds*.

The Main Magistrate was temporarily abolished (between 1727 and 1743), while city Magistrates had their powers limited and were placed under *Voevodas* and Governors. The Magistrates were in charge of collecting taxes, customs duties, and oversight of drinking establishments, and also had some judicial functions. But in any of those areas Magistrates were reporting to *Voevodas* and Governors, who could also rule on appeals against Magistrates' judgments.

By the middle of 18th century, Russia had Europe's biggest army. By 1754, it numbered 331 thousand men, of whom 172 thousand served in the field army (133 thousand infantrymen and 40 thousand cavalry), 75 thousand served in garrison troops, 28 thousand in local militias, 13 thousand in artillery and engineering troops, and 44 thousand were irregulars. If necessary, the field army could be augmented to 220 thousand men.

The infantry consisted of 3 guards' regiments and 46 army regiments, each made of three battalions. The cavalry consisted of 1 guards' regiment, 3 cuirassier regiments and 29 dragoon regiments, which broke down into squadrons and companies. Garrison troops consisted of 49 infantry regiments, 7 dragoon regiments, 4 separate battalions, and 2 separate squadrons. The local militias (serving to protect boundaries exposed to raids by Crimean Tatars or the Kazakhs and other nomads) had 20 cavalry regiments of dragoons in Ukraine, and 1 infantry regiment and 3 cavalry regiments in the borderlands south-east of the Kama River. Irregular units were made of 6 hussar regiments (raised from the Serbs, Moldovans, Hungarians, and Georgians), Don Cossacks (9 thousand men), 5 Cossack-type regiments in Sloboda Ukraine (5 thousand men), as well as smaller detachments raised from such non-Russian groups as the Kalmyks, the Tatars, and the Bashkirs. An infantryman was armed with a bayonet rifle and a smallsword. A cavalryman was armed with a smallsword, a pair of pistols, and either a bayonet rifle (dragoons) or a short rifle (cuirassiers).

Russian artillery of that time was the best in Europe. It consisted of field artillery (including regimental pieces), siege artillery and fortress artillery. The usual assortment of cannon and mortars aside, it was armed with the so-called '*shuvalov*' howitzers (so named after their inventor Count Shuvalov). Those had somewhat elliptical cross-section of the barrel which ensured wide scatter of grapeshot. Another type of cannon, known as 'unicorns', had a shortened barrel providing for overhead and grazing fire and capable of shooting bombs, cannonballs, and grapeshot. An infantry regiment's table of equipment included 2 three-pounder cannons and 4 six-pounder mortars, while a cavalry regiment had 1 cannon and 2 mortars.

Prior to the Seven Years' War, the Russian Navy was hardly involved in military operations at all. In the 1730s and 1740s, the number of ships shrank and combat readiness deteriorated. In 1733, the navy was a significant force with 37 ships of the line and 15 frigates in the Baltic Sea (more than at the time the Northern War ended). However, by 1757, only 27 ships of the line and 8 frigates remained.

Calls for recruits were announced as necessary, with recruits chosen and supplied by landowners and peasant communities without any oversight by the authorities. Governors were responsible for meeting their quotas of recruits, while delegated military officers at assembly stations ensured compliance with recruit health requirements. Length of service remained unlimited. Soldiers becoming unfit for service were placed in the care of monasteries or given plots of land (as per the Decree of 1736, they got about 10–15 hectares of land and a cash payment of 5–10 rubles). All the males of noble birth were enlisted as common soldiers at age 16 and served in perpetuity too. In 1736, the length of service for the nobility was limited to 25 years, while it was mandated that between the ages of 7 and 20 they must get an education.

During that period, the system of military education was further enhanced. In 1735, an Artillery Drawing School for 30 children of the nobility and officers was established in St. Petersburg. Its graduates became non-commissioned artillery officers. Soon, it was merged with Artillery Arithmetic School for the sons of artillerymen, which was training military clerks. The combined school became known as St. Petersburg School of Artillery. In the early 1730s, a similar school appeared in Moscow. The graduates were enlisted as non-commissioned officers, and could be commissioned as officers based on the recommendation of their superiors. Low achievers graduated as common soldiers. In 1758, the Corps of Engineers commander, Count P. Shuvalov merged the School of Engineering and the School of Artillery into the new Nobility School of Artillery and Engineering.

On July 29, 1731, upon an initiative of Count P. Yaguzhinsky, a cadet school built on the Prussian model was established in St. Petersburg. The school accepted literate children of noble families aged 13 to 18. The program of study consisted of 4 grades, three senior grades amounted to 5–6 years of study. In 1732, there were 360 cadets at the school, and in 1760 their number reached 490. In 1743, the school was named Ground Forces School. Graduates received the ranks of non-commissioned officer or ensign, while the best graduates could be directly commissioned as junior lieutenants, or even lieutenants. In

1752, the Naval Guards Academy was expanded to become the Nobility Naval School, which subsequently became the main supplier of officers for the Navy.

Russian industry of the time continued to provide for all the needs of the military. By 1750, there were about 100 iron mills with an annual output of up to 33 thousand tons of iron, which made Russia the world's top producer. Copper production tripled between 1725 and 1750. Most iron mills were owned by Demidov family (up to 60% of total output). A number of mills and factories belonged to Stroganov, Osokin, Batashev, Maslov, and Goncharov families. Tverdyshev and Myasnikov families owned large copper mills. Many copper smelters were state-owned. Between Peter the Great's death and mid-18th century, there appeared 62 new linen, silk and woolen cloth manufactures. Woolen manufacture fully met the state demand (for military uniforms). Among other industries there were 15 papermaking mills, 10 glass-making, and 9 chemical manufactories.

Chapter 4

Russian society in the first half of the 18th century

From the late 1600s till the 1760s, Russia's population had been growing exceptionally fast, at a rate higher than in any other European country. That growth was almost exclusively driven by natural increase (this period predated later expansion into vast and densely populated areas). By the early 1680s, Russia's population stood at 11.2 million, by 1719 it grew to 15.6 million, and by 1762 it reached 23.2 million. Accordingly, by the end of this period Russia became the most populated country in Europe. The vast majority of Russia's population at the time (78%) lived in areas that belonged to Russia as far back as mid-17th century. Population density across Russia's vast territory (14.5 million sq. km) was very low - only 1.1 person per square kilometer. Even in European part of Russia (west of the Urals) it amounted to only 3.5 persons per square kilometer.

Ethnic composition of that population changed very little over the first half of 18th century. In 1719, the population considered to be Russian (in the empire, no distinction was drawn between Great Russians, Little Russians (or Ukrainians), and White Russians (Byelorussians)) accounted to 86% of the total, and by 1762 that proportion stood at 83.6%. The largest indigenous non-Russian groups were Estonians and Latvians (3% of the total at both dates), the Tatars and Bashkirs (3% and 3.9%), the Chuvash (1.4% and 1.2%), and the Finns (1% and 2.7%), while no other ethnic group exceeded 1%.

At that period, the structure of Russian society was the same as in all European countries in that it broke down into well-defined social categories or estates. The main estates were the nobility, the clergy, townsmen (of whom merchants made the highest stratum), and the peasantry. All those social strata existed in pre-Petrine Russia as well, but from the early 18th century their status, rights and obligations were more clearly defined in law. In that sense, the structure of Russian society underwent significant transformation during this period.

First and foremost, it affected the interests of the highest estate (the serving class), i.e. the nobility. Its internal structure and the way it was replenished were dramatically altered. Generally speaking, the reforms did not replace old serving class families with new ones. With rare exceptions, Peter's trusted circle of reformers belonged to the same families which formed the core of serving nobility in the 17th century (the only thing different was that exclusive hold of a few dozen clans of the highest nobility over top government positions was broken). The Senate, collegial boards, top and senior military ranks consisted almost entirely of pre-reform noble families (apart from foreigners, whose tenure in the Russian service was in most cases temporary). In other words, the pre-reform nobility (numbering about 30 thousand at the start of the 18th century) formed the base of post-reform officer corps and officialdom. Yet, even if the reforms initially left the actual cast of nobility characters intact, they fundamentally changed the principle of subsequent replenishment of that serving class by making possible the entry of newcomers based only on their service record, and thus providing for constant renewal and rejuvenation of that class with fresh blood.

Transformation of the noble estate underway in the years 1700–1710 took the route of transforming servicemen 'by patrimony' into the officers of the new army and the bureaucracy and officialdom of the new government machinery (given that those vacancies were significantly fewer than the numbers of nobility, at that time, most members of the noble estate served as common soldiers). A series of measures made that class more homogeneous. In 1714, an estate given for service was put on the same legal footing as patrimonial lands, i.e. became the unconditional property of its owner. Soon afterwards, as part of taxation reform, a significant number of erstwhile petty nobility whose de facto circumstances and way of life were now viewed as incompatible with membership of the upper class, were expelled from nobility ranks. The census of male tax-paying population was carried out in 1717, and a 'revised' census taken almost immediately afterwards (hence it became known as the first revision of five revisions, or simply censuses of the 18th century). During the revision, most petty servicemen 'by patrimony' in the south (where they concentrated in large numbers) were reclassified as a special social group – smallholders. Smallholders were levied the same poll tax as their peasants, and no longer had to show up at annual servicemen musters. Nevertheless, the number of nobility (including family members) almost doubled compared to pre-Petrine period. By 1719, their numbers increased by 146 thousand to the total of 304 thousand (2% of the population).

Upper class membership was strictly conditional on service, and that service now became far more rigorous than before. While in old Muscovy most servicemen spent almost all their lives on their estates, were summoned only for military campaigns, and served an average of two months a year, the creation of regular army and full-fledged government apparatus turned service into a permanent and daily duty. Furthermore, Peter decreed that the term of service be open-ended, meaning that noblemen could return to live on their estates only in advanced age or when disabled. A non-serving member of the nobility (except for cripples and minors) was not allowed to hold an estate or to be considered a member of the noble estate (one could refuse to seek promotion into officer or civil servants ranks, but in that case one remained a private soldier all his life).

At the same time, the noble estate, being previously closed to people of non-noble ancestry, now became wide open to entry 'from below'. Peter attached great importance to elevating the social status of those serving the state (especially in the military). This noteworthy entry appeared in his notebook around 1711 or early 1712: "All officers to be the nobility and have precedence over others". This describes the tsar's intention quite unambiguously. Firstly, he wanted to ennoble all the officers by statute; secondly, he wanted to give officers preference over all other nobility. The decrees of 1714 and 1719 confirmed the availability of officer commissions to men of low origin (commoners), and the Decree of 1721 confirmed the granting of nobility status to all the officers and their children.

The decree addressed to the Senate in 1721 and the *Table of Ranks* of 1722 (paragraphs 5, 11 and 15), stipulate that persons of any origin, who obtained the first officer rank – of 14th grade in the Table (ensign), were to be elevated to hereditary nobility (with that status shared by their children and wives). As far as civil service is concerned, hereditary nobility was attained with promotion to a rank classified as grade 8 (collegiate assessor), while ranks belonging to grades from 14 to 9 conferred only the non-hereditary nobility status (unless one came from the family of hereditary nobility), which extended to one's wife, but not to children. Further fine points in the system stipulated that only children born after a commoner obtained his noble status by becoming an officer would be considered hereditary nobility, while those born earlier would be classified as part of a special estate of 'junior officer children'. However, if an officer had no male issue born after he obtained his officer rank and membership of the noble estate, any one of his sons born earlier could inherit his hereditary nobility status.

The *Table of Ranks* promulgated in January 1722 summed up the process of nobility transformation into an open service class. Army hierarchy of military ranks was used as the template to assign all then existing government service positions (over 90% of them predated the Table) to one of 14 grades. Military ranks themselves broke down into army, guards, artillery, and naval ones. All civil service and court ranks had a corresponding military rank. Initially, the *Table* was quite cumbersome, since it had to break into 14 grades 262 then recognized government service positions (which were then synonymous with ranks). Military positions dominated the list (126 or 48%), civil service accounted for 94 (36%), and 42 (16%) were the court positions. There was no real difference between ranks and positions at the time: there existed a certain number of positions, and people who held them bore a corresponding rank. In other words, a rank was not detached from one's position: a brigadier indeed commanded a brigade, a colonel was a regimental commander, a major was a battalion commander, and so on. The same applied to the civil service – the names of civil ranks are those of positions initially occupied by civil servants of that rank (e.g., a collegiate secretary indeed served as a secretary on one of the collegiate boards, and so on). Over time, the list of government positions significantly expanded, and it was impossible to reflect all of them in the *Table of Ranks*. Therefore, the separation between ranks and positions developed. Ranks in grades from 9 to 14 were considered to be junior officer ranks, ranks in grades 6 through 8 were considered staff officer ranks, and all ranks above were considered to be generals. The *Table* also codified forms of address to people belonging to a defined group of ranks, and the use of those forms survived until 1917. Ranks in grades 1 and 2 were to be addressed as 'High Excellency', 3 and 4 as 'Excellency', ranks in grade 5 as 'Noble Sir', those in grades 6 to 8 as 'Right Honorable', and all lower ranks were to be addressed as 'Your Honor'.

Relative permeability of the walls separating estates was essential for social and political stability. Russia was the only European country, where the 18th and 19th centuries did not bring about the ossification of class barriers (by contrast, in France the walls between estates hardened in the 18th century, and creation of new nobility practically stopped). Moreover, the trend in Russia was exactly the opposite: while previously such estate walls were nearly impenetrable, now the entry of outsiders into the nobility steadily grew. By the early 1720s, 30% to 40% of the officer corps and a much higher proportion of civil servants were not nobility by birth.

During Anna's reign, the onerous duties of the nobility were somewhat eased. The Manifesto of December 31, 1736 decreed that "all young noblemen must study from age 7 to 20, and do their military duty afterwards". The term of service was now limited to 25 years. In 1737, there was compiled the register of all male nobility older than age 7. At age 12 they had to pass knowledge assessment, and those who so wished could be enrolled in schools. At age 16 they were summoned to St. Petersburg, and another knowledge assessment determined what would happen to them next. Those with sufficient knowledge could start as civil servants right away. The rest were sent home with an obligation to continue studies and report back at age 20 to be enlisted in military service. Those deemed uneducated at 16, were enlisted as common sailors without the right of promotion to officer.

At the time, the vast majority of the noble estate were landlords. By 1727, there were 64.5 thousand landlords (including widows and minors), the vast majority of whom (38.3 thousand or 60%), were petty landlords with less than 20 peasants; another 20.5 thousand (32%) had estates with 20 to 100 peasant souls, and only 5.7 thousand (8%) had more than 100 peasants. Most members of the nobility at the time served as private soldiers or non-commissioned officers, or, less frequently, in clerical jobs in civil administration. That happened simply because the number of officer positions and ranking civil service positions was quite limited. In 1701, there were only 2078 officers, and by mid-18th century they numbered about 9 thousand. In the mid-18th century, there were only 5379 civil servants (including 2051 ranking ones), and 61.8% of those ranking officials did not own peasant serfs. In later years, the proportion of officials without landed estates only grew.

By the early 18th century, the clergy was for all practical reasons a closed estate, since its replenishment from the outside was negligible. Peter's reforms did not significantly alter its composition. Just as was the case with nobility, the first half of 18th century made this estate more consolidated and brought it new privileges. In 1711, monks were attached to their monasteries, and in 1719 the parish clergy were attached to their parish churches. In 1719, the clergy were exempted from direct taxation, and in 1724–1725, they were exempted from supplying recruits as well. All crimes committed by the clerics (except the most grievous ones) and disputes between members of the clergy were removed from the jurisdiction of general courts, and from 1722 onwards the sole jurisdiction belonged to the Synod. From 1735, grave crimes and litigation between clergymen and laity fell under the courts of general jurisdiction with the proviso for mandatory presence of special clergy representatives. Just like the nobility, clerical hierarchy was to enjoy stipulated forms of address: for metropolitans and archbishops it was 'Eminence', for bishops it was 'the Right Reverend', for abbots, priors, archpriests, father superiors, and rural deans it was 'the Very Reverend', and for all other priests – 'Reverence'. The number of clergy (including monks, priests, deacons and sextons) with their male family members grew significantly. In 1678, it stood at about 40 thousand, while by 1719 it climbed to 140 thousand. By the end of the 1730s, so-called white (or marrying) clergy consisted of priests (37% of the total), deacons (10%), and the rest were minor parish officials. From 1722, one needed theological education to become a priest, therefore the first seminaries appeared in the 1720s, and in 1739 every diocese was required to have one (in the 1720s through 1740s, 71% of their students had family origins in the clergy). In general, by the 1730s, 96% of the clergy came from within that estate which was almost entirely self-reproducing.

At the start of 18th century, townsmen (formerly known as town tradesmen) were granted broad rights of self-government, both on citywide level (in the form of elected magistrates and special courts for members of different estates) and for various tradesmen guilds. In 1721, urban population was divided into so-called 'regular' and 'irregular' townsmen. 'Regular' townsmen consisted of merchants (divided into two ranks depending on their declared capital), craftsmen (with their guilds organized by trade), and people of independent professions (doctors, pharmacists, artists, shipmasters, and others), as well as the class formerly known as servicemen 'by selection'. All the other city residents, who were not members of guilds and mostly worked as hired hands made up 'irregular' townsmen (who had no right to participate in the election of magistrates). In 1724, the entire urban population was divided into three grades, the first two included large and medium-sized merchants, entrepreneurs, and factory owners, while the third one was everyone else. After the death of Peter the Great, the rights of city self-government were curtailed, and special estate courts for townsmen abolished. In 1724 townsmen numbered 185 thousand males, and by 1744 that number grew to 212 thousand. Merchants accounted for 27% of that number (9% of the first rank and 18% of the second).

As before, peasants constituted the largest estate, accounting for about 90% of the total population. They were further divided into state peasants (free peasants with obligations directly to the state), palace peasants (those owned by the tsar and members of his family), landlord estate peasants (i.e. the serfs, including all former bonded servants), church peasants (on lands owned by monasteries), and so-called factory peasants (attached as bonded labor to factories and manufactories). Peasant estate also included non-Russian populations in the Volga basin, northern areas of European Russia, the Urals and Siberia. Those people generally paid their tax in kind (mostly in furs, the tribute known as *yasak*), and were formally labeled *yasak natives*. Above all, serfdom meant that the state transferred most of its rights and authority as it applied to the peasants to landowning noblemen (or the church), who were to be held responsible for the peasantry. That was very important from the perspective of public administration (considering how limited the machinery of state then was). The serfs constituted the majority of national population, and by delegating its administrative and judicial functions with regards to the serfs to their landlords the state relieved itself of associated costs. From 1741, landlords' peasants did not have to swear the oath of allegiance to newly enthroned emperors. In 1761, they were also prohibited to issue promissory notes and to post bail or surety. Since 1760, they could be forcibly relocated for the resettlement in Siberia (which counted towards their owner's quota of recruits). According to the first revision (census) of 1719, state peasants constituted 25.9% of the peasantry, landlords' and factory peasants constituted 54%, palace peasants 7.7%, and church peasants 12.4%. Transitions from peasant estate to townsmen were then quite few, only 2 thousand individuals from 1719 to 1744.

For a long time (formally until 1835), the Law Code of 1649 remained the fundamental law of Russian legal system. Its individual articles were amended by new decrees, regulations, and other acts. Early in the 18th century, Peter's "Articles of War" of 1715 assumed great importance. Although they addressed the issues of crime and punishment for military ranks, in practical terms the same provisions largely applied to civilians. Age of marriage capacity at the time was mainly determined by church law, which set it at 15 for men and 12 for women. The government considered that to be too early (thus in 1714, Peter the Great forbade guardians to marry off orphans of noble parents in their charge before age of 17 for women and age 20 for men), but in general left those church canons alone. However, under Peter the Great, the age of legal competence (to conduct transactions, enter contracts, etc.) was raised to 20 years. For the first time, exceptions were introduced for those mentally ill or accused of depravity (the insane, those stripped of rights by court order, and those under guardianship due to extravagant living were recognized legally incompetent).

Since the beginning of 18th century, private contracts were usually made in writing, drawn up by officials, and recorded at special offices. In 1739, regulations were passed to grant merchants the right to pay by means of promissory notes. In 1754, it was first allowed to charge interest on a debt (not more than 6% annually). Inheritance law did not undergo significant change. Peter's 1714 attempt to introduce the principle of primogeniture for the nobility did not take hold, and in 1731 that law was abrogated. In case of intestate death, property had to be divided equally among the sons (daughters with living brothers received 1/14 of immovable and 1/8 of movable property). In the absence of sons, property passed to grandsons, and in the absence of grandsons – to daughters; a surviving spouse received 1/7 of immovable property and 1/14 of movable property, while parents inherited property only in the absence of both lineal and collateral descendants. Land (which only the nobility were allowed to own as private individuals) was classified into three categories: ancestral, granted for service, and purchased, while structures were classified either as residential property (compound) or commercial premises. Town tradesmen were allowed to sell their buildings sitting on city land to others. In 1714, movable property was legally separated from immovable, and acquired the character of fully private property.

Family law established the husband's primacy (the husband's and father's estate defined what estate the wives and children belonged to), but in terms of property rights spouses were recognized as equals: they owned property in common (including property held by each spouse before marriage) and were jointly liable for debts and sureties. Grounds for divorce included adultery, inability to consummate, a spouse's disappearance or retirement into a monastery, (but not loss of estate rights by court order). The fine imposed for refusal to marry after betrothal was scrapped in 1702. In 1716, fathers were charged with responsibility to support their illegitimate children and their mothers, even though under the law (in case of intestacy) such children could not inherit. Marriages with non-Christians remained banned, but in 1721 marriages between Christians of different confessions were allowed. In 1722, parents were forbidden to force their children to marry, and mentally retarded and mentally ill were forbidden to marry. In 1753, joint obligation of spouses for debts was revoked.

According to church law, the age of criminal responsibility started at 7, and the same applied to civil law. Children over 7 could not get capital punishment, and some other punishments were relaxed for them. The age of full criminal responsibility was first established in 1742 and set at 17 years old. For children from 7 to 16 the punishment by horsewhipping and banishment was lightened to giving the lash and heavy labor at a monastery for 15 years. Criminal code was at its harshest in the first quarter of 18th century when death penalty was prescribed for about 200 offences (although in most cases it was commuted to something else). To previously known punishments were added imprisonment with hard labor and deprivation of rights (i.e., loss of one's estate privileges). Just as before, grave offences carried punishment by maiming (robbery, rebellion and perjury were punished by cutting off the nose and ears) and horsewhipping, while for lesser crimes one was flogged or caned. Punishment for offenses against the faith and the church remained cruel: apostasy by joining a non-Christian cult was punishable by burning, changing one's Christian confession was punishable by exile to a monastery for life, becoming an Old Believer was punishable by hard labor (and death penalty in case of priests). During Empress Elizabeth's reign, all punishments were substantially mitigated, and death penalty no longer used. From 1753–1754, it was replaced by deprivation of all rights, flogging and exile to Siberia. In 1757, severe punishments for women were abolished.

Early 18th century marked the beginnings of secular education in Russia. Peter the Great took the first steps towards creating a network of public education, most of all elementary schools. By the end of his reign, there were 42 elementary schools, mostly enrolling children of parents with reading and writing skills, such as *prikaze* clerks. Those schools were mostly located in provincial cities. The network of diocesan schools was greatly expanded (such schools appeared in the 17th century, and took in children of the clergy); by the end of Peter's reign there were 46 of them, and church regulations made them mandatory for future priests. Finally, garrison schools were established for soldiers' children. A number of special schools existed as well, such as the Medical College in Moscow, the translator school (under *prikaz* of foreign affairs), the Mining School at Olonets iron factories, schools for children of artisans and clerks in the Urals, and the school for training of clerks (established in 1721). The two institutions of higher learning were both church ones: the Slavic-Greek-Latin Academy in Moscow (in 1727 it was put under the Synod) and the Kiev-Mohyla Academy in Kiev, each with over 500 students.

In 1724, the Academy of Sciences was founded in St. Petersburg (it had mathematical, physical and humanities departments). Its initial 12 members included major European scientists of the time. Initially, it was partly an educational institution including a preparatory school and a university, as well as the *Kunstkammer* (in effect, a natural history museum) and a library. In 1728, the Academy started publishing a scientific magazine 'Brief Annals of Academy of Sciences Notes'. In 1755, it started publishing Russia's first popular science magazine 'Monthly Works for Public Benefit and Amusement'. The first Russian newspaper, '*Vedomosti*' ('News') with the circulation of several hundred copies appeared in 1702 in Moscow (and from 1711 in St. Petersburg). 'St. Petersburg Vedomosti' first came out in 1728 (it survived till 1917), accompanied by the monthly edition of magazine of 'Notes on History, Genealogy, and Geography'. Russia's first university with three departments (philosophy, law and medicine) was founded in 1755 in Moscow at the initiative of Mikhail Lomonosov and Count Ivan Shuvalov. A preparatory college with two departments, one for the nobility and another for commoners, was affiliated with the University. In 1756, the University started publishing its newspaper 'Moscow Vedomosti' which survived until 1917 and eventually became one of the main newspapers of official record. Three privately published magazines appeared in 1759–1760 (the 'Idle Time' and 'Busy Bee' published by A. Sumarokov in St. Petersburg, and M. Heraskov's 'Useful Amusement' in Moscow).

Simplified Russian type for secular use was introduced in 1710 and gave an impetus to book printing (Moscow Printing House was its center). Works of writers of Antiquity were published in Russian, including historical writings of Julius Caesar and Josephus Flavius, as well as history books of European authors. Even though Russia lagged behind Europe in technology, Peter's times saw a number of important inventions, primarily of applied nature, A. Nartov designed a number of metal-working machines, and Ya. Batishchev designed a machine tool for machining rifle barrels. Applied geology was much advanced: more than 120 ore deposits were discovered over the first decade of the century. A variety of treatises on geography and history were written.

Chapter 5

Russian Empire from the beginning of the reign of Catherine II to the end of the 18th century

By the time Catherine II was enthroned, the overall architecture of relations between European nations was again in a state of flux, caused primarily by tangibly real prospect of resolving the Polish question. By then, Poland had lived with effectively no real central authority for about a century, and it was clear that lands it seized during its medieval heyday would eventually be lost. The issue of partition of Poland came to a head as early as in the 1730s during the 'War of the Polish Succession'. Yet for all the Russian claims and protests regarding the status of Orthodox Christians in Poland, Russia did not resort to partition at that time because it was not yet strong enough to assume a lead role in it. But now that the Seven Years' War was over and brought about much greater ability of Russia to influence Polish affairs, the key goal of Russian policy in the western theater – reunification of all lands of erstwhile Kievan Rus' – became a part of the immediate agenda.

It was clear and inevitable that such a move would alienate Austria which harbored designs on some Polish territories itself. By contrast, Prussia actively sought closer ties with Russia because even after the Seven Years' War it saw Austria as its principal rival. While Austria increasingly grew estranged from Russia, it rapidly grew closer to France (which busily cobbled together anti-Russian European alliances throughout the 18th century). This created the real impetus for the alliance of Russia and Prussia to counter the two powers hostile to them.

Following the death of Augustus III of Poland, Catherine II advanced as a candidate for the vacant throne her former favorite Stanislaw Poniatowski. He was duly elected king by the Polish Diet in September 1764 (as Prussia looked on approvingly). Even earlier, in late 1762, she decided to replace Charles (the son of Augustus III who sat on the throne of Duchy of Courland) by bringing out of obscurity the former Duke, Ernst Biron. That move made Biron Catherine's puppet, while Courland became a complete dependency of Russia. In March of 1765, Russia and Prussia entered into a military alliance. The thinking of Count Panin (who presided over Russia's foreign policy at the time) was that the alliance would evolve into the core of future 'Northern Accord' – a broad coalition of northern powers (Russia, Prussia, Britain, Denmark, Poland, and Sweden) serving as a counterweight to the 'southern' coalition of Austria, Spain, and France. Yet, neither Friedrich II, nor Catherine II felt the need for such a broad coalition, while Britain was disinclined to join it (in 1766 it concluded a purely commercial agreement with Russia). The other potential joiners were by then weakened and of little value for Russia as allies. Besides, French diplomacy vigorously intrigued against Russia in Sweden. Britain agreed to support pro-Russian faction in Sweden, but systematically failed to pay that faction promised subsidies. Relations between

Russian Empire from the beginning of the reign of Catherine II to the end of the 18th century

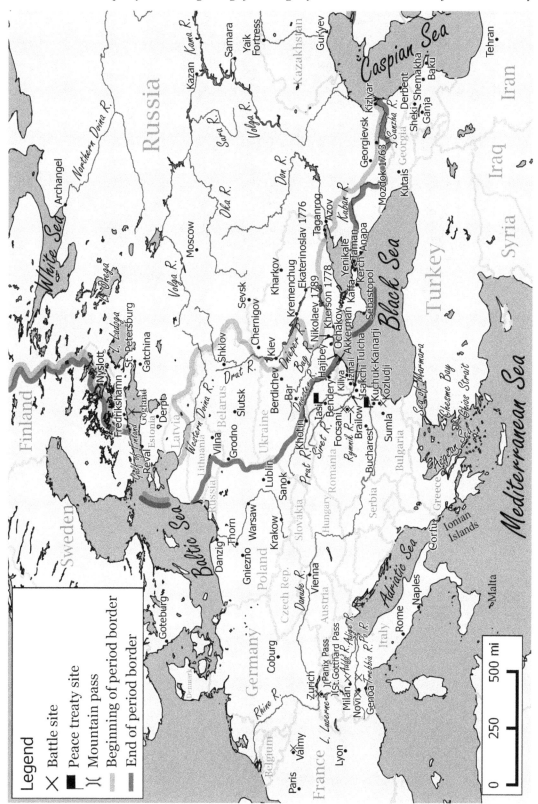

Legend
- ✕ Battle site
- ▪ Peace treaty site
-)(Mountain pass
- Beginning of period border
- End of period border

500 mi

0   250   500

59

Russian Empire from the beginning of the reign of Catherine II to the end of the 18th century

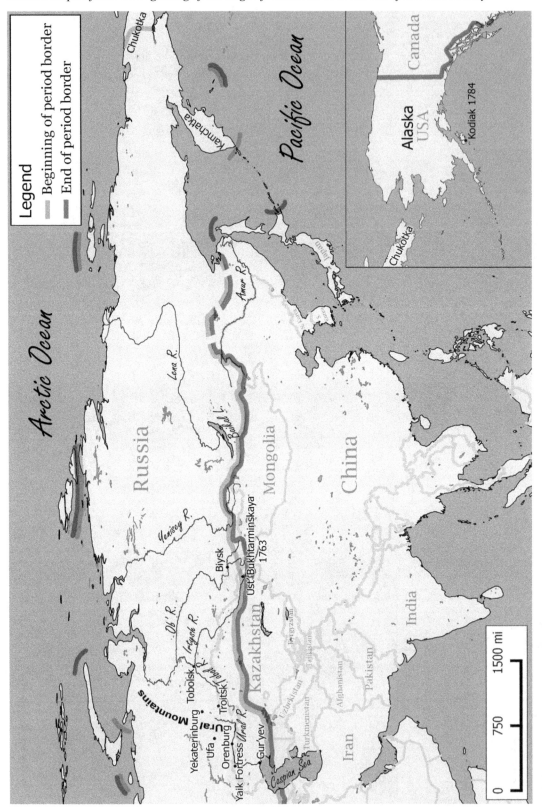

Russia and France deteriorated to the point that diplomatic relations were severed from 1767 to 1772.

In the early 1760s, Russia felt itself to be very much on firm ground in Europe. By contrast, its geopolitical position in the south was unsatisfactory. Along the broad salient from Moldavia to the Caucasus, Russia faced off with Turkey, and the antagonism between the two was existential. Orthodox Christians in the Ottoman Empire continued to see coreligionist Russia as a natural ally in seeking liberation from Turkish rule. Anti-Turkish movement was always simmering in Moldavia and occasionally erupted in rebellions (the latest big one happened in the area of Iasi in 1759). Predatory Crimean Khanate posed perennial threat to southern areas of Russia, the threat Russia could not counter as it could not maintain a fleet in the Black Sea or even fortify the port of Azov. The Khanate's influence extended to the western part of Northern Caucasus, where petty local rulers were Crimea's vassals. Turkey's ownership of the coastal strip of the Caucasus and its fortified bases there enabled vigorous policy of conversion of native peoples to Islam. Muslim clergy was active in proselytizing, and the ruling classes of the Kabardians and Circassians fell under its influence. In the Northern Caucasus, Terek defensive line maintained by three Cossack hosts (Greben, Kizlyar and Terek) was constantly harassed by raids from local tribes who felt Turkey's support behind them. In 1763 the new fort of Mozdok was established, and in 1769 the line was strengthened by the Cossacks resettled from the Volga River.

Christian peoples south of the Caucasus range – Armenians and Georgians – were completely cut off from Russia and suffered constant depredations by Turkey and Iran. The rulers of Eastern Georgia (the kingdoms of Kartli and Kakheti were merged under one ruler by the mid-17th century) sought help from Russia by sending an embassy as early as 1752. King Solomon I, the ruler of Western Georgia (Imereti) who fought the Turks in the 1750s (and allied himself with Eastern Georgia in 1758), also sent his envoys to Russia (in 1760 and 1768). Armenians, who had no country of their own and whose lands were split between Turkey and Iran, migrated to Russia in large numbers. Many then played a prominent role in commerce, while some enlisted for Russian service. Armenian spiritual leaders, *Catholikoi* (church Patriarchs), appealed for Russian protection several times to the extreme chagrin of Ottoman rulers.

Meanwhile, the so-called 'dissident question' flared up again in Poland. That was the issue of relations between majority Catholics on the one hand and Orthodox and Protestant communities on the other. While the king, Stanislaw Poniatowski fully depended on Russian subsidies, just like his predecessors he had no real power and therefore could not pressure the Diet for a decision favorable to dissidents. Catherine's demand to give the Orthodox full equality of civil rights with Catholics was adamantly rejected by the Diet's Catholic majority. Since the dissidents could count on implied support from Russia and Prussia, they took the route by then well-established in Poland, that of creating an opposition confederacy. In March 1767, dissident confederacies were formed in Thorn and Slutsk. In autumn of the same year, Russian troops advanced on Warsaw, and on February 1768, the pressured Diet acceded to the dissidents' demands. They were granted the right to open their churches, schools, cemeteries, and printing houses, to freely print religious books, and to occupy any position in the state (with the sole exception that king and queen had to belong to the Catholic church, which was recognized as the dominant one). Inter-confessional marriages (between Christians) were allowed as well.

Yet, the granting of equal rights to dissidents led to civil war. This time it was the Catholics who refused to accept equal rights for dissidents. They immediately launched their own confederation in the town of Bar, and opened hostilities against the king and government. Confederation of Bar found support in many parts of Poland, and in March 1768 the Polish Senate asked Catherine for help. After defeat in northern Poland (Lublin, Gniezno), the confederates retreated to Podolia. After Russian troops seized Bar and Berdichev, they regrouped around Sanok and Krakow. Yet, they lost Krakow in August of the same year, while Russian troops continued to advance in southern Poland.

Russia's traditional southern foe – the Ottoman Empire – was not remiss in exploiting all these developments. Podolia has long been coveted and claimed by the Ottomans, and the appearance of Russian troops there became a major aggravation to them. For its part, French diplomacy did what it could to propel Turkey to war with Russia, while the confederates directly appealed for Turkish help. In the end, the Sultan found himself in the bizarre role of advocate for the Catholics. On September 25, 1768, he demanded from the Russian ambassador assurances that the Diet's decision on dissident issue would be revoked. Upon the ambassador's refusal, he was duly arrested, which was tantamount to declaration of war. Catherine was not at all fearful of the prospect of war. Her complete confidence in the strength of the army was well-founded: no other European nation of the time had such an efficient tool of war. The army's strength lay not only in its numbers, but also in experience gained through victories over Europe's best armies, and in its cutting-edge artillery and other military gear. Besides, it appeared self-obvious that a war with Turkey in some immediate future is in any case unavoidable.

Catherine decided to make the most of potential help from the Christians in the Balkans and Trans-Caucasia. An embassy sent to Georgian rulers reached agreement on joint action against the Turks, after which the corps under General Totleben was dispatched to Georgia. Russian emissaries were sent to foment rebellion against the Turks in the Balkans, while two navy squadrons were sent to the Mediterranean to support such a rebellion (the total of 10 ships of the line, 3 frigates, and ancillary ships). Work began on strengthening the fortifications of Azov and Taganrog, and orders were given to start building a fleet for the Black Sea and Sea of Azov operations there. Moldavia and Wallachia were expected to become the major theater of action, especially since Russian troops chasing Polish confederates were already on the edges of that region.

Early in 1769, Crimean Tatars carried out two raids into Russian (and for good measure Polish too) territory and then returned to the Crimea. One of two Russian armies amassed in the general area of Kiev and commanded by Prince A. Golitsyn marched off toward Khotin in April of the same year, while another (commanded by P. Rumyantsev) was to give it cover by deploying to the Dnieper downstream of Kremenchug. Golitsyn campaigned somewhat languidly, but both Khotin and Iasi were taken in September of 1769. Meanwhile, in the Caucasus the corps under General Medem advanced on Kabarda, and after a number of clashes Kabarda swore allegiance to Russia. The Ossetians became Russian subjects at the same time (they petitioned for it even prior to these events). Totleben's corps entered Georgia, took Kutais, and then cleared of Turks all of Imereti kingdom.

During 1770 campaign season, the first army was commanded by P. Rumyantsev, and the second by P. Panin. In spring, the main Ottoman forces amassed on the Danube near Isakchi and began to cross the river. Rumyantsev with a force of 40 thousand set out to meet them. In mid-June, he defeated a mixed force of the Tatars and Turks at the left bank of River Prut and continued his advance with defeating on July 7 another army of 80 thousand Tatars and Turks at the confluence of Larga (left tributary of Prut) and Prut rivers. The Tatars fled to the south-east, and the Turks withdrew to the south. Next, Rumyantsev detached a force of 10 thousand against the Tatars (who rallied and tried to cut him off from the east), and marched against the main body of the Turks (150 thousand strong) with only 28 thousand men. The two forces met by the Kagul River (in the Prut basin) on July 20, and the Russians attacked at full pelt. The Turks were routed. They fled towards the Danube after losing about 20 thousand as casualties and abandoning their artillery and train (in two days, the Russians caught up with them at the river crossing and inflicted severe losses again). The Russian troops seized Izmail, Akkerman, and Kiliya, and in autumn also Brailow and Bendery. That same summer, the Russian navy launched its campaign in the Mediterranean. The rebellion of Greeks in Morea was suppressed, but in late June after a naval engagement at the Strait of Chios, the Turkish fleet fled into Chesme Bay, where it was completely destroyed two days later (on June 26). Meanwhile, in the Northern Caucasus there was constant engagement with the Tatars, Circassians, and Chechens. Nomadic Horde of Nogai withdrew from the war and swore allegiance to Russia.

Victories of that year were jealously watched by Austria. Much concerned, it offered mediation in peace talks which began in the spring of 1772. But prior to that, in 1771, the troops led by Prince V. Dolgoruky advanced to the Crimea, and on June 14 successfully stormed the Isthmus of Perekop. They forced the retreat of a 60 thousand-strong army led by Khan Selim-Giray himself, and seized Kaffa (now Feodosia), Kerch, and Yenikale. On July 27, the new Khan, Sahib-Giray signed the treaty of eternal friendship with Russia. In its peace talks with the Ottomans Russia demanded recognition of Crimea's independence, the granting of independence to Moldavia and Wallachia, freedom of Russian navigation on the Black Sea, and transfer of one of the islands in the Aegean Sea. Austria (extremely upset by those demands) and Prussia submitted to Russia their versions of peace terms for the Turks, which they tried to bundle with the resolution of Polish question. Austria insisted that Russia's territorial gains be limited only to Azov district and Kabarda. While Prussia leaned toward recognition of Crimea's independence, it suggested the return of Moldavia and Wallachia to Turkey, with Russia compensated by getting a bigger slice of Poland.

The partition of Poland de facto started in 1770 when Austria seized a number of districts (with Prussia's approval). Confronted with that fait accompli (which also led to a rapprochement between Prussia and Austria), Catherine finally agreed to the partition as well. Following the talks by three powers in 1772, it was decided that Austria will get Galicia, Prussia will have the Baltic coastal area and part of Greater Poland, while Russia will get back part of Kievan patrimony – eastern part of White Russia (Byelorussia), with the new boundary to run along Western Dvina, Drut, and Dnieper rivers.

Truce was concluded in May of 1772, and direct peace negotiations with Turkey started in July, but immediately deadlocked. On October 29, new peace talks were launched in Bucharest and truce extended till March 1773, but in March Turkey walked out of negotiations. By that time, Russia's hand in the talks was weakened due to a major plague epidemic (which began in 1771) that hit the army and finally reached Moscow. Battles with confederates who avoided a decisive engagement continued in Poland. But what complicated Russia's position most of all was the Pugachev rebellion which broke out in the Urals and along the Volga River.

Pugachev was a Don Cossack who rebelled and deserted in 1770. In the spring of 1773, he escaped his prison cell in Kazan, declared himself to be "sovereign Peter Feodorovich" (in other words, Catherine's husband Peter III, assassinated in 1762), and rallied to himself the most restless elements among the Cossacks. The band of his followers quickly grew to about two thousand. After a failed bid to capture Yaik fortress (now Oral in Kazakhstan), they moved upstream, took several fortresses and finally besieged Orenburg. Pugachev was joined by many non-Russians: the Bashkirs, Kalmyks, and Tatars with their own leaders. Thus fortified, he twice defeated government troops sent to relieve the siege of Orenburg. In December 1773 – January 1774, his followers attacked the city of Ufa. Another hotbed of rebellion developed in the central Urals. Pro-Pugachev bands ranged across a huge swath: from Samara to Tobol River along east–west axis, and from Gur'yev (today's Atyrau in Kazakhstan) to Yekaterinburg along the north–south one. That called for deployment against them of significant government forces. After a series of defeats in the spring of 1774, Pugachev with a small band retreated to the Urals, where he again built up a 10 thousand strong army of followers. In May, Pugachev was routed near Troitsk fortress, but recouped his strength in just a month. In July, Pugachev with a force of 20 thousand broke into the city of Kazan, but failed to seize the citadel and was defeated by arriving government troops. With only 400 Cossacks he fled to the right bank of the Volga. His manifestos issued in the name of Peter III attracted much peasantry there, and the rebellion flared up anew. Over 3 thousand noblemen and civil servants were murdered. Then, Pugachev turned south from Sura River with the purpose of gaining lower Don River. During that trek south he seized and abandoned several cities, but government troops were always at his heels. They finally caught up with him and routed his force on August 24, 1774. Pugachev with two hundred Cossacks managed to flee, but was soon betrayed by some of his last followers who handed him over to the authorities (he was executed in Moscow in January 1775).

Following the failure of peace talks with Turkey, the army under P. Rumyantsev was sent to the right bank of the Danube in order to advance on Sumla, but the danger of exposed lines of communication forced Rumyantsev to return. Campaigning in autumn of 1773 brought no victories either. In the Caucasus, the Khan of Kalmyks fell out with General Medem and led his people first to the Volga and then beyond it. By the end of 1773, a Turkish corps of 10 thousand materialized on the banks of Kuban River and seized Taman'. In March 1774, it advanced to the Russian border but was defeated. In summer, the remnants of that Turkish force were dispersed by General Medem. Meanwhile, Russia's position was further complicated by a coup in Sweden, which strengthened royal power there and raised the prospect of a new war against Russia. In June of 1774, Russian troops crossed the Danube again and inflicted several defeats on the Turks. In the largest of those battles, at Kozludji (now Suvorovo in Bulgaria) the division of 8 thousand commanded by Suvorov defeated a Turkish army of 40 thousand while suffering only 75 casualties.

The defeat forced Turkey to the negotiation table, and the peace treaty of Kuchuk-Kainarji ending that difficult war was finally signed on July 10, 1774. Peace terms recognized Crimean Khanate's independence from Turkey. Russia won the right of free commercial navigation on the Black Sea and the Sea of Marmara, and was to receive war reparation of 4.5 million rubles. Russia had to abandon its designs regarding Moldavia and Wallachia, yet Turkey recognized Russia's right to be the protector of Christian Ottoman subjects, which somewhat improved their plight (thus Georgia was freed of delivering as tribute teenage girls and boys). The principal outcome of the war was that Russia for the first time established a firm foothold on the Black Sea. It received the fortresses of Kerch, Yenikale and Kinburn, as well as the wedge of land between the rivers Bug and Dnieper. In the Caucasus, Kabarda was transferred to Russia. Following the war, Russian influence in European politics grew even more. From now on, no single issue of European politics could be resolved without involvement of Catherine II. She could now afford the luxury of disregarding anyone else's interests and no longer needed to seek allies. In fact, now the other powers sought her friendship and help. When Prussia and Austria went to war over Bavaria in 1778, a stern word from the Russian Empress proved enough to end it in 1779. In 1780, Catherine and Austrian Emperor Joseph II reached an agreement on mutual assistance against Turkey and on maintaining the status quo in Poland (just as Friedrich II insisted on its soonest final partition).

Rather than continue to seek agreements with Britain, Catherine now took an openly hostile stance. In 1775, when Britain asked for 20 thousand Russian soldiers to help suppress rebellious colonies in North America she refused. Five years later she helped the colonists' cause by promulgating the famous 'Declaration of Armed Neutrality' postulating armed resistance to British navy's efforts to inspect ships sailing under neutral flags. The declaration made a blockade of new North American states impossible. It was immediately joined by Austria, Prussia, Holland, Sweden, and Denmark and recognized by France and Spain (then at war with Britain).

Gains made in the war with Turkey opened up to Russian colonization and development the region of *Novorossiya* (literally meaning New Russia, as the swath of land to the north of Black Sea came to be known). The city of Ekaterinoslav (now Dnipro in Ukraine) was founded in 1776, and Kherson in 1778. The Crimea remained an open issue though. Since its independence from Turkey was a transparent fiction, the Crimean Tatars posed a persistent threat to newly settled territories. In 1778, Russia facilitated the resettlement of about 30 thousand Greeks and Armenians (on whom Crimean commerce critically depended) from the Crimea to Novorossiya. Next year, Ottoman Empire recognized as khan Shakhin-Giray who was a Russian puppet. Yet Ottoman machinations in the Crimea continued. Assisted by the Nogais, Turkey seized mainland possessions of Crimean Khanate in Kuban River basin. When Turkey fomented an uprising in the Crimea in 1782, Shakhin-Giray had to flee to Russian-held fortress of Yenikale (within city limits of today's Kerch).

That brought the denouement closer. Shakhin-Giray abdicated, and Catherine published a manifesto on the annexation of Crimea by Russia (signed on April 8, 1783). Nogai nobility who acted as Turkish stooges in Kuban River basin were soundly defeated. That gave Russia lands to the north of Kuban River which previously constituted the mainland part of Crimean Khanate. So ended the centuries of Russia's struggle with Crimean menace. Extremely fertile lands of the south that remained unplowed for centuries for fear of Tatar raids from the Crimea now saw vigorous settlement and development. That latter fact was tremendously important. Since infertile lands of Russia's historic heartland could support only marginal and high-risk farming barely capable of feeding the country, Russia faced the danger of eventual stagnation as a primitive agrarian society with too much population tied down in farming and unavailable for more sophisticated pursuits. Also, Russia could now build a full-fledged Black Sea navy with the main naval base in Sebastopol. In the Northern Caucasus, areas along the defensive line saw the beginnings of Russian settlement too. In 1783, the governor of the Caucasus, Count Paul Potyomkin dealt a serious defeat to the Chechens beyond river Sunzha, and in 1785, large forces of hill-men led by Sheikh Mansur were defeated in Mozdok area.

Ottoman interests suffered a serious setback in Trans-Caucasia as well. In the treaty signed in Georgievsk on July 27, 1783, the ruler of eastern Georgia (Kartli and Kakheti kingdoms) declared himself a Russian subject. That created a Russian bridgehead beyond the main range of the Caucasus. The chain of Turkish possessions along the Black Sea coast could be threatened from there (although a similar agreement with western Georgia, or Imereti Kingdom, had to be postponed). In 1784, Russia pushed through an agreement under which the Sultan gave up his right to remove at will rulers of his vassal dependencies of Moldavia and Wallachia.

Throughout these years, Turkey contemplated revenge, which made a new war with it inescapable, especially as Turkey was encouraged by three foreign powers. Britain could not forgive Russia for its stance in the war with North American colonies. Prussia hoped that distraction of Russian energies to the south will give it exclusive options on new land grabs in Poland. France simply continued its traditional pro-Turkish and anti-Russian policy. While believing the war to be inescapable, Catherine would have preferred to delay its outbreak, but Turkey forced her hand. In the summer of 1787, Turkey demanded that Russia recognize Ottoman sovereignty over Georgia and also admit Turkish consuls in the Crimea. On August 15, Russian ambassador was given an ultimatum to return the Crimea immediately. Having refused, he was arrested on the spot, and the second (of Catherine's reign) war with Turkey began.

Less than a week later (August 21, 1787), the Turkish fleet attacked Russian ships anchored off Kinburn fortress. Two Turkish landing parties (in September and October) were completely wiped out by the fortress garrison commanded by Suvorov. Overall command of all forces engaged against Turkey was given to Count Grigory Potyomkin. The bulk of his army (132 thousand men), as well as the Black Sea fleet, were deployed against well-fortified Turkish fortress of Ochakov. The main forces of the Turkish navy (about a hundred ships) were also at Ochakov. In 1788, admiral Ushakov defeated that Turkish fleet by the *Zmeinyi* (Serpent) Island in the Black Sea near the Danube delta. Turkish flotilla of rowing galleys operating in Dnieper-Bug estuary was soon destroyed (with much loss of life) as well, and finally, in December, Ochakov fortress was taken by assault. A secondary theater of war was in Moldavia, where the army led by P. Rumyantsev seized Khotin that same year. In Kuban River basin, Russia won several engagements with hill-men and in autumn of 1788 attempted to seize the seaport and fortress of Anapa. That attempt and the one next spring both failed with much loss of life.

In the meanwhile, British diplomacy took pains to put together an anti-Russian alliance in northern Europe. In the spring of 1788, it imposed a ban on Russian hiring of British vessels and seamen and on the purchases of provisions, and in summer Britain entered into an anti-Russian alliance with Prussia and Holland. Besides, it prodded Sweden (where revanchist mood strengthened after the coup reinforced royal powers) to launch war against Russia by demanding the return of all the territorial gains won by Peter the Great, as well as the return of Crimea to Turkey. In June of 1788, the Swedes laid siege to Nyslott (today's Savonlinna in Finland) and Fredrikshamn (now Hamina in Finland), while their navy entered the Gulf of Finland. Denmark joined the war on the Russian side, but dropped out of it following a failed siege of Göteborg. In July of 1788, Swedish fleet suffered defeat in the naval battle of Gogland, and in 1789 Russian troops started their land offensive in Finland. Three out of four more naval engagements were won by Russia.

From January 1788, Russia was in alliance with Austria in its continuing war against Turkey. Austrian troops were stationed as a border cordon all the way from the Adriatic to Siret River (a tributary of the Danube). A corps led by Prince of Coburg (about 17 thousand strong) was deployed at the contact point with Russian troops, a 10 thousand-strong division led by Suvorov. In the summer of 1789, the Turks tried to break through between the two allies, but were defeated by Suvorov at Focsani. Undeterred, the Turks launched two new offensives: a strike north from Izmail and from Brailow to Focsani. On September 8, the corps led by Prince Repnin repelled the force advancing from Izmail, but the principal Turkish force (about 90 thousand men with 83 guns) went after the corps commanded by Prince of Coburg. Suvorov marched to aid the Prince with only 7 thousand under his command. On September 11 by Rymnik River, Suvorov won one of his most brilliant victories. The Turkish army was soundly defeated having lost 10 thousand dead on the first day and 7 thousand more as it was chased on the next day. Suvorov's losses were only 45 dead and 133 wounded. The campaign of 1789 ended with Russian troops taking Bendery, Akkerman, and Hajibey (now Odessa in Ukraine) and advancing to positions between the Dniester and Siret rivers and to the lower reaches of the Danube.

On the other hand, those victories inspired renewed hostile diplomatic maneuvers by Britain and Prussia. Combined pressure of those two powers (including war threats) forced Austria to abandon its military effort against Turkey. Exploiting the involvement of most Russian military forces in the war against Turkey, Prussia orchestrated dramatic strengthening of anti-Russian factions in Poland. In 1789, Prussia forced Russia to evacuate the remainder of Russian troops in Poland and in 1790 concluded a Prussian-Polish treaty of alliance. Yet, tensions in the north were somewhat relieved in August 1790, when the patent superiority of Russian forces convinced Sweden to seek peace restoring prewar status quo.

In the campaign of 1790, Russian fleet commanded by Ushakov won more engagements with the Turks. In autumn, Russian troops acting in concert with galley fleet on the Danube seized the fortresses of Kiliya, Tulcha, and Isakchi. The siege of Izmail – the Turks' key stronghold on the lower Danube – began on November 21. On December 11, Suvorov led the force of 31 thousand men on an all-out assault of Izmail (defended by the garrison of 35 thousand). The assault cost Russian forces 2 thousand dead, but the fortress was reduced. The victors executed 26 thousand Turks and imprisoned the rest. On September 30, 1790, the corps operating in Kuban River basin squashed the Turkish army of 50 thousand led by Batal Pasha.

Such an outcome of 1790 campaign did not shake Britain's determination to deny Russia a successful overall outcome of the war with Turkey. British premier William Pitt made an effort to knock together a broad anti-Russian coalition of Britain, Turkey, Prussia, Denmark, Sweden, and Poland. Russia was being pressured to return Ochakov and accept British mediation in peace talks with Turkey. In view of expected war with Britain, Catherine brought up the strength of the Baltic fleet to 32 ships of the line and began redeployment of some troops to the west. Yet, Pitt's anti-Russian efforts crossed the line even in the eyes of British establishment itself. The prime minister was chastened to discover that the notion of a direct clash with Europe's most victorious army and the prospect of losing benefits from trade with Russia were far from popular in the country. Britain was not prepared to go to war, and the Anglo-Prussian-Dutch alliance fell apart. In the meanwhile, the campaign of 1791 gave Russia new victories at the Danube, while in the Caucasus the principal Turkish stronghold of Anapa fell to frontal assault in June. In July of

1791, commander-in-chief, Prince Repnin signed truce with the Turks, followed by peace negotiations in Iasi which were successfully concluded on December 23.

The Peace of Iasi gave Russia the fortress of Ochakov and all the seacoast up to the Dniester River. Wallachia and Moldavia with Bessarabia remained under the Ottomans. Turkey was to compensate Russia for damage caused by raiding of Russian territory by tribal bands from Turkish-held lands in the Northern Caucasus and was obligated to prevent attacks on eastern Georgia, but still refused to accept Russian sovereignty over Georgia.

To sum up the events of the late 1780s, unprecedented victories of Russian arms allowed the country to emerge creditably from the dire situation: simultaneous fight against its traditional foes in the north and the south against the backdrop of British-orchestrated anti-Russian alliance of half the European powers. Subsequent events engendered by the revolution in France brought about another abrupt shift in Europe's web of international relations and thrust Russia to the forefront.

The French revolution of 1789 dramatically altered France's position in Europe. Shaken by that upheaval at home, France discontinued its traditional policy of building anti-Russian alliances among Russia's neighbors. Now the French monarchy itself was hanging by a thread and needed support of the great powers. Moreover, royalist circles pinned their hopes on Russia above others. Catherine II even played the mediator in reconciling and bringing together various French royalist factions and provided them with substantial financial support. She also led the joint protest of European powers demanding that the revolutionaries set free the king Louis XVI. A corps of several thousand French émigrés led by Prince of Condé was accepted into Russian service. Besides, Russia became the spearhead of a pan-European coalition opposing revolutionary France. With Austria, Sweden, Prussia, Spain, Kingdom of Sardinia, and Kingdom of Naples as members, the only large power outside that coalition was Britain (which declared its neutrality). Only the nearly simultaneous deaths early in 1792 of Emperor Leopold II and King of Sweden Gustav III prevented the coalition from going to war. Soon thereafter, France itself declared war on Austria and Prussia. On September 20, 1792, the French defeated Austrian and Prussian troops at Valmy.

Following the execution of Louis XVI in January of 1793, Russia severed diplomatic relations with France and deported all pro-republican Frenchmen. Perceived need to oppose revolutionary France brought about rapprochement between Russia and Britain, with agreement to that effect signed in March of 1793. Russian ships joined the British navy in its naval blockade of France. Late in 1795, Russia, Britain, and Austria entered into the anti-French military alliance, and a Russian corps of 60 thousand was ready to march out when Catherine's death intervened.

Having shored up its positions on the Black Sea, Russia could now focus on its primary objective in the western direction – reunification of historic Russian lands that came to be ruled by Lithuania and Poland after the Mongol invasion. By that time, Prussian efforts made sure that Russian influence inside Poland dramatically declined. During the war with Turkey, Russian troops were withdrawn from Poland, and victualling depots closed. With Prussian backing, Poland even disallowed the transit of Russian troops to the theater of war against Turkey. When anti-Russian alliance of Poland with Prussia was concluded in 1790, Russian guarantees of traditional Polish form of government were rejected. In fact, the new constitution adopted by Polish Diet in 1791 did away with the principle of 'liberum veto'.

New European realities created by the French revolution brought Russia and Prussia closer again. In the summer of 1792, they signed a treaty of alliance and in January 1793 they agreed on a new partition of Poland. The agreement once more gave Prussia lands from Polish-speaking heartland (part of Greater Poland, Danzig, and Thorn), while Russia was receiving additional lands in White Russia and the Right Bank Ukraine. Poland responded to this partition with a rebellion led by Kosciusko which flared up in the spring of 1794. Russian troops led by Suvorov crushed the rebels and took Warsaw by assault. What followed was the decision to do away with Polish statehood altogether. For Russia, the third and last partition of Poland in 1795 meant that the goal it pursued for centuries in the western direction was almost completely gained. It now received back into the fold the western part of White Russia and Volhynia in Ukraine. Additionally, Russia now annexed Lithuania and Courland (the latter lay within the sphere of Russian influence for almost a century by then). Polish-speaking heartland of Poland was divided between Prussia (the north, including Warsaw) and Austria (the south with Krakow). Galicia (annexed by Austria) was now the sole part of Kievan patrimony remaining outside Russia. Thus, shortly before her death Catherine II completed the great task of gathering back western lands of historic Russia.

In 1795, Persian Shah Agha-Mohammed invaded and devastated Georgia. That was a direct insult and challenge to Russia in its capacity of Georgia's protector, and Catherine II launched war with Iran. A corps commanded by General Lieutenant P. Zubov was amassed in Kizlyar and marched off down the Caspian coast in April 1796. In May, Derbent was taken by assault, while another force under General Major Rakhmanov took Baku, and the force led by General Major Bulgakov subdued the Khanate of Kuba. Native rulers of Dagestan scrambled to the Russian camp with assurances of their submission. Following that, Russian troops seized Shemakha, Khanate of Sheki and Khanate of Karabakh in rapid succession. In December, a force of 3 thousand (under General Major Rimsky-Korsakov) sent west to assist Georgia's King Erekle subjugated Ganja Khanate along the way. The main force led by Zubov reached the grasslands of Mougan. With all these native khanates in present-day Azerbaijan subjugated, the road to Tehran itself lay open, and Russian advance parties reached Gilan. Catherine's death put an abrupt end to this victorious march. In early December, the troops vacated all the conquered areas and withdrew behind the Terek River.

When Catherine II died on November 6, 1796 she was succeeded by her son Paul I. Just like his father (Peter III) Paul was a passionate admirer of all things Prussian and of Friedrich II in particular. Paul's tutor, Count Panin, encouraged both his pro-Prussian sentiment and his dislike of the reigning mother (who did not involve Paul in affairs of state). Prior to his ascension to the throne at age 42, Paul had to content himself by drilling his own miniature army arranged along the Prussian lines while nursing hatred of all Catherine's deeds and innovations. Once enthroned, he sought to destroy her heritage, and most military leaders and statesmen who built Russia's greatness under Catherine now fell from official grace. Foreign policy took a pro-Prussian turn as well, yet European realities determined the continuation of previously set policy versus France.

Peace concluded in 1797 between France and the first coalition of its opponents did not satisfy either side or alter the overall situation in Europe. The French grab of Ionian Islands in 1797 was of immediate concern to Russia insofar as it could strengthen French influence (always anti-Russian) on Turkey. Napoleon's Egyptian expedition of 1798 carried the threat of complete domination of Turkey by France and of French predominance in the

Mediterranean. Accordingly, the year 1798 saw the creation of the second anti-French coalition consisting of Russia, Britain, and Austria and joined by Turkey and Kingdom of Naples. By that time, the French controlled all of Italy west and south of river Adige and everything west of the Rhine.

For this war Russia committed 75 thousand soldiers and 7 thousand strong corps of French émigrés under Prince of Condé. Those forces were shipped piecemeal to the theater of action through the years 1798–1799. The Russian Black Sea fleet under Ushakov entered the Mediterranean in autumn of 1798 and then proceeded to the Adriatic sweeping the French from Ionian Islands. The biggest military feat was the assault on the French main and well-fortified base on Corfu. In 1799, Ushakov's landing parties drove the French from Naples and Rome. In July and August of 1799, another Russian force of 17 thousand was dispatched to Holland.

Allied Austrian and Russian troops in Italy were placed under the overall command of Suvorov. On April 16, 1799 (less than two weeks after his arrival in Italy), he defeated the French at Adda River and entered Milan the next day. In a three-day battle at Trebbia River in June, he again inflicted a painful defeat on the French (who lost 3 thousand dead with 12 thousand captured). Following that, Suvorov planned to drive the remaining French from Italy and march on to Paris by way of Lyon. Yet at this point there emerged the difference between Russian and Austrian vision of war aims. Following his brief from Emperor Paul, Suvorov intended to restore the royal house of Piedmont, while Austria regarded Italy as a conquered country and felt that driving away the French was quite sufficient. On August 4 at Novi, Suvorov again defeated the French army which retreated with heavy losses, but Austrian Emperor Francis I did not allow Suvorov to continue the offensive into Genoese Riviera.

According to the new plan of war, Russian troops had to take the place of Austrian ones in Switzerland, while the Austrians would be redeployed to the Rhine in order to advance into Belgium. The withdrawal of Austria's main force from Switzerland left there a Russian corps of 24 thousand under Rimsky-Korsakov and 22 thousand Austrian troops under General Hotze faced with 84.5 thousand French troops under General Massena. On August 31, Suvorov set out on his legendary crossing of snow-covered Alps to join them in Switzerland. By mid-September, he wiped away French defenses at Saint Gotthard pass and reached Lake Lucerne. But in those same days the Russian and Austrian troops he was rushing to relieve were defeated by the French near Zürich and had to retreat beyond the Rhine. Suvorov with his worn-out troops and critically low supplies found himself in dire straits. Nonetheless, on September 19–20, Suvorov pushed back the French, escaped encirclement, and crossed another mountain pass, Panix, into the valley of Upper Rhine. In October, he withdrew his force to Bavaria. By that time, the differences between Paul I and Francis I escalated to the point where Russia quit the anti-French coalition.

Moreover, following the British seizure of Malta, Paul who previously took the title of Grand Master of Maltese Knights, performed a policy U-turn. He entered an alliance with France and declared war on Britain. The full strength of Don Cossack Host was ordered to march on India by way of Central Asia (that insane expedition was called off following Paul's death). Paul's reforms in the army along the lines of the Prussian model, his cruel personal rule, petty regimentation of every aspect of life in the country, endless fault-finding with others and violent mood swings caused broad discontent which culminated in the plot amongst the guardsmen, which was led by two leading statesmen,

Count Palen and Count Panin. On March 11, 1801, Paul was assassinated and his oldest son ascended the throne as Alexander I.

In geopolitical terms, the period from 1762 to 1800 was one of crowning achievement for the Russian Empire. Along western and southern frontiers, it achieved its principal objectives: the fulfillment of what it saw as historic mission and securing the status of great power. In the south, it secured broad access to the Black Sea and no less importantly made possible the agricultural development of enormous acreage of very fertile lands (both the newly acquired ones and those that could not be properly settled and developed earlier due to constant predatory raids from the south). In the Northern Caucasus, there now existed a coast-to-coast fortified line (primarily along the rivers Kuban and Terek), and Russia also established a bridgehead into Trans-Caucasia. A dramatic turnaround finally took place in the relative strength of Russia versus its historic foe in the south – the Ottoman Empire. Only Catherine's death prevented Russia from recapturing lands along the Caspian once won by Peter the Great. In Siberia, the frontier was pushed to the upper reaches of Ob' River south of Biysk (where Ust'-Bukhtarminskaya was founded in 1763). In 1768–1769, an expedition led by P. Krenitsyn and M. Levashov was sent to explore Russian America (Alaska), where the first permanent Russian settlement was founded on Kodiak Island in 1784, while the first settlements on Alaskan mainland appeared in 1786. In the west, almost all the lands of old Kievan Rus' were now recovered into the Russian fold. Those were densely populated and strategically important territories that gave Russia the ability to influence European affairs directly, since almost all European countries now lay within reach of Russian arms. By the late 18th century, Russia enjoyed preeminence in European affairs. The essential work was done. What remained was to safeguard this achievement against revanchist attempts from Russian Empire's rivals and to secure defensible borders in the south and the east.

System of government and military-economic potential

Starting with the enthronement of Empress Anna, attempts to limit a new emperor's powers after succession became practically an established routine. This time around, the effort was led by N. Panin, the tutor to royal heir, who wanted to transfer the power to approve all new legislation to Imperial Council. Yet, Catherine turned down the plan. The so-called Council at the High Court created in 1768 was merely a conference of top military and civilian leaders on matters of conduct of war with Turkey. In other words, it had no more weight than the 'Conference' during the reign of Elizabeth. Once the first Turkish war was concluded, the Council at the High Court was not abolished and continued as supreme advisory body to the monarch. In the 1770s and 1780s, its importance even grew, and at times it convened quite often (over 50 times from late 1773 to early 1775). The Council survived into Paul's reign, but its importance declined.

Her Majesty's Cabinet continued to operate as her personal chancellery, which was also in charge of Catherine's personal property and of the Hermitage (which was created to house imperial collections). One innovation that appeared in 1763 was the institution of positions of state secretaries. State secretaries handled petitions submitted to the monarch and all other affairs that required her personal involvement (the first two secretaries were G. Teplov and I. Yelagin, and the most prominent among later ones were A. Olsufiev and A. Khrapovitsky). The composition and responsibilities of personal chancellery finally crystallized under Paul.

The Senate retained its role of the highest executive body. Its head, the Prosecutor-General, enjoyed the right of daily report to the empress and was in a unique position as the key administrator dealing with heads of collegial boards and with regional governors (Prince A. Vyazemsky had a long tenure in this position). In December 1763, the Senate was split into 6 departments, two of which were located in Moscow. The first department ('affairs of state and matters political') was headed by Prosecutor-General himself and dealt with promulgation of laws, with finances, economic matters, and the management of government property. It also included the Secret Chancellery and the Chancellery of Confiscations. The second department dealt with matters of justice, with land surveying, and review of petitions submitted to the empress. The third department was in charge of roads and communications, education, public health, and also of territories with special privileges (Ukraine and the Baltic provinces). The fourth department was in charge of the armed forces. The two Moscow-based departments provided redundancy to departments one and two.

Development of new laws was entrusted to the specially convened Code of Laws Commission made up of deputies elected nationwide by each social estate. Election procedure stipulated that deputies would receive written instructions from their constituencies. A total of 1.5 thousand such instructions were submitted. Elected deputies were exempt from capital and corporal punishment for any crime, and sentences for assault on them were doubled. 228 deputies (40%) represented nobility, 208 represented townsmen (1 deputy per city), 43 – smallholders, 23 – state peasants, 45 – the Cossacks, and 50 – the non-Russian peoples of Volga Basin, the Urals, and Siberia. The Commission first met on July 30, 1767. By 1769, the Commission held 203 sessions and discussed multiple legislative initiatives including laws defining the condition of various estates: the nobility (including special status of German *('Ostsee')* noblemen in the Baltic provinces), merchants, townsmen, and state peasants, as well as matters pertaining to cities, arts and crafts, farming, judicial system, etc. As part of the Commission's work, there were set up 15 smaller commissions covering specific topics, and those deliberated until 1771.

The system of central and local government did not undergo significant change until the reforms of 1775. Prior to that, the only changes involved Ukraine. In 1764–65, the positions of Hetman and separate army chancellery and military court were abolished. The Collegiate Board for Little Russia (the name then commonly applied to Ukraine) was restored (it survived till 1786). Little Russia was split into two governorates (those of Sloboda Ukraine and Novorossiya). With the Tatars and Turks driven from the northern coast of Black Sea, *Zaporozhye Sich*, that informal republic of Dnieper Cossacks, outlived its military usefulness but not its restlessness, and was duly abolished in 1775. Zaporozhye Cossacks were resettled into the fertile basin of Kuban River and given extensive land grants there.

The reform of 1775 sought to broaden the purview of local governments. One side effect was the abolition of most collegiate boards, only three of which still existed by the late 1780s (those of foreign affairs, military affairs, and the admiralty). The responsibilities (much reduced) of other collegiate boards and some other central bodies were devolved onto smaller bodies known as expeditions. Thus, the remaining functions of Board of Revenues and Board of Mines were given to Expedition for State Revenues, those of the Board of Confiscations to the Expedition on Tax Arrears, and so on. The Senate had oversight of all the expeditions and of a number of other agencies: Postal Service Department, Land Survey Department, and St. Petersburg and Moscow treasuries. As a practical matter, Prosecutor-General was all ministers rolled into one (with the exception of army, navy, and foreign affairs portfolios).

Under Paul, collegial boards were restored, and their heads enjoyed the right of personal report to the emperor. Some agencies were removed from the Senate's jurisdiction or created for the first time (Department of Waterways, the Treasury).

Catherine's 1775 reform of local government was well thought-out. A special commission of the most senior civil servants toiled for 9 months to prepare the document called "Institutions for Administration of the Russian Empire's Governorates". The system it inaugurated proved so efficient that it survived in its essentials till the 1860s, while many features lingered till 1917.

A three-tier administrative division (governorate-province-*uezd*) was simplified to a two-tier one (governorate-*uezd*). Before the reform, there were 23 governorates, 66 provinces, and 276 *uezds*. By the mid-1790s, there were 50 governorates and 483 *uezds*. Those administrative divisions were of comparable population size and land area (other than in cases where it would have prevented maintaining efficient government control). Governorate population size was to range from 300 to 400 thousand, and that of an *uezd* from 20 to 30 thousand. Governorates were named after their principal cities (and occasionally after historically established place names). Every governorate and city (down to an *uezd* seat and sometimes lower) received a coat of arms.

The two governorates that were home to Russia's two capital cities and some strategically important regions (consisting of 2 or 3 governorates) were headed by viceroys who had extraordinary powers, and had the right to a seat in the Senate, as well as the privilege of direct report to the empress over the Senate's head. The viceroys also had 2 or 3 councilors and controlled army units stationed within their jurisdictions. During Paul's reign, those positions were abolished.

Governors ran the affairs of their governorates with the help of advisory councils. Directly under the governors were *prikaze* for public assistance staffed by lay judges of provincial courts of peers. Those *prikaze* were in charge of schools, hospitals, almshouses, and orphanages, as well as workhouses for the destitute and vagabonds and workhouses for petty offenders. They had their own money purses (a mix of government funds and donations), which they could manage as they saw fit (including investment and lending) for the public benefit. Under Paul, those *prikaze* were abolished.

All financial, commercial, and economic matters were placed under so-called treasury chambers. Those were chaired by vice-governors and included a director for economic matters, a councilor, two assessors, and a treasurer. Treasury chambers were in charge of censuses, management of state property (which included state-owned industries, buildings, lands, forests, and waters), taxation, financial oversight, leases for the sale of alcohol, salt sales, and general oversight of commerce and industry.

Courts of justice in governorates were a mixed system of courts of general jurisdiction and courts for individual estates. Courts of general jurisdiction were known as the chamber of criminal justice and the chamber of civil justice. Both chambers had a chairman, two councilors, and two assessors, all of whom were appointed by the Senate. In effect, the two chambers served as courts of appeal. Additionally, the system included so-called Courts of Conscience, which looked into cases involving persons legally incompetent due to age or insanity, into cases of damage caused by accidents, and also into civil litigation (primarily between relatives) where amicable settlement was possible. The two capital cities also had specialized courts dealing with cases involving the officials and so-called 'people of miscellaneous ranks' (the name applied to non-noble people who did not belong to major legally recognized estates). At governorate level, there existed three estate courts which operated as courts of appeal: one for nobility (known as upper *zemstvo* court), one for merchants and townsmen, and one for smallholders, state peasants, and post coach drivers. Chairmen of those courts were appointed by the Senate, while their lay judges (or assessors) were elected by members of corresponding estates. Every governorate also had a prosecutor with two aides known as solicitors, one for criminal and one for civil cases. All told, the governorate-level staff numbered 75 officials, about half of whom were elected judges of various estate courts. Under Paul, all the governorate estate courts and courts for officials in Moscow and St. Petersburg were abolished, and criminal and civil courts of general jurisdiction were rolled into one.

Top *uezd* official was the district police captain (who reported to the governor), while in towns serving as *uezd* seats the equivalent position was that of town governor (*gorodnichyi*). Police captains were elected by *uezd* nobility. The district police captain and two or three assessors formed an *uezd*-level (known as lower) *zemstvo* court, which was in charge of investigating criminal cases, of enforcing court rulings, and of implementation of decisions taken by governorate authorities. *Uezds* had their own treasuries reporting directly to governorate-level ones. *Uezd*-level court system also included three estate courts of first instance (or trial courts): one for nobility, one for townsmen, and one for state peasants and small landholders. Attached to the courts were two specialized agencies: board of trustees for members of the nobility (it consisted of *uezd* marshal of the nobility, court chairman, and the assessors) and so-called orphans' court (town governor, and elected magistrates). Board of trustees and orphans' court dealt with trusteeship of property of widows, underage children, and wastrels endangering family estate (appointed trustees managed property in return for 5% of income it earned). *Uezd* solicitors reporting to governorate prosecutors provided prosecutorial oversight. In 1796, Paul abolished *uezd* estate courts by giving *zemstvo* courts trial jurisdiction over all estates except townsmen. As per the reform of 1775, cities became independent administrative units (governed by their town governors and not *uezd* police captains). Town governors were appointed by the Senate from the ranks of local nobility, but town magistrates, courts of conscience and town hall councilmen were elected by town residents.

In 1782, town police (separated from *uezd* police) was overhauled. Police departments of the two capital cities were commanded by police commissioners, assisted by two investigators (one for criminal and another for civil cases), while elected prominent local citizens provided civilian oversight. In addition to the maintenance of public order, the departments conducted preliminary investigation of criminal cases involving damages of less than 20 rubles. In governorate capitals, police departments were commanded by police chiefs. Cities with over 4000 households were divided into precincts (200 to 700 households), commanded by precinct chiefs, who had their own administrative offices. Every precinct also had an elected judge for accelerated review of petty disputes. A precinct was further divided into blocks of 50–100 households controlled by block police inspectors. In 1798, Paul replaced town police departments with so-called *rathauses* (or town halls), German-style city governments combining administrative, economic, and partly judicial functions. A *rathaus* consisted of a president, director for commerce and elected members – *burgermeisters* and *ratsherrs*, who had to be confirmed by the emperor.

The biggest factor behind Russia's geopolitical successes in the second half of 18th century was the excellent state of its military. The system of recruit drives provided the army with homogenous (recruitment drives were almost exclusively conducted in central part of Greater Russia) and highly professional (because for them military service became the sole occupation) body of men. That gave the Russian military a distinct advantage over most contemporary European armies which were replenished by hiring mercenaries. For one thing, many mercenaries came from fringe or lumpen social groups (vagabonds, deserters from foreign armies, criminals, and the like). For another, mercenary systems were less stable and more dependent on the state of public finances. Through almost all of Catherine's reign recruits had to serve for life; only in 1795 the term of service was limited to 25 years. All told, 1241 thousand recruits were drafted from 1767 to 1799.

Through all of this period, Russian army remained Europe's largest. In 1767, the field army (that is to say excluding the guards' regiments, special troops, and irregulars) numbered 186 thousand men, by 1786 that number stood at 275 thousand, by 1795 at 318 thousand, and in 1798 at 221 thousand. Garrison duty troops numbered 91 thousand in 1767, 95 thousand in 1795, and 95 thousand in 1798. By 1795, all armed forces (including the guardsmen, artillery, and garrison troops) numbered 463 thousand men (an increase by 1.7 times over Catherine's reign), or 502 thousand men if the Cossacks and irregulars are included. Under Paul, the strength of regular troops was reduced to 358 thousand. Territorial militias were disbanded as early as 1769.

Military reform was among the first major undertakings upon Catherine's accession. A special commission to prepare it was set up as early as 1762. By 1763, that commission presided by field marshal Saltykov developed the new table of organization. Infantry regiment (2093 men) consisted of two battalions, each made up of five musketeer and one grenadier companies. Like before, an infantryman was armed with a bayonet rifle and a smallsword. Grenadiers (who were formerly armed with hand grenades) differed only in uniform and were considered to be the elite infantry. New soldier uniforms introduced in 1783–1786 on the initiative of G. Potyomkin were a real breakthrough and well ahead of their time. That remarkably comfortable uniform included a leather hat with woolen flaps (which could be tied under the chin in severe cold), a loose jacket with short flaps, wide trousers with leather leggings, and low-top boots.

At the start of Catherine's reign, infantry had 3 guards' regiments, 4 grenadier regiments, and 46 musketeer regiments (by 1767 the latter numbered 59). The year 1765 saw the establishment of a special ranger corps. Rangers were a kind of light infantry armed with rifled weapons and taught to fight in loose line formation. European armies adopted that innovation only twenty years later. Every regiment was required to have a ranger team, and by 1768 there were over 3.5 thousand rangers.

In the early 1760s, the cavalry consisted of one guards' regiment, 6 cuirassier, 20 carabineer, and 8 hussar regiments. A regiment broke into 5 squadrons, each of two companies. Carabineer regiments were formed out of former dragoons and mounted grenadiers. In effect, they were heavy cavalry who did not wear a cuirass, but were armed with carbines in addition to the backsword and handgun. In the 1770s and 1780s, the weight of carabineer and cuirassier equipment was reduced, and new regiments of mounted rangers and dragoons were introduced. Under Paul, all light cavalry regiments with the exception of hussars were disbanded.

In the early 1760s, field artillery mostly relied on 'Shuvalov-type' howitzers and so-called 'unicorn' howitzers (while the fortress and siege artillery counted an enormous

75

number of pieces of many designs and calibers). Every infantry regiment had four three-pounder guns, and each cavalry regiment had two. Additionally, field artillery included two cannoneer, two fusilier, and one bombardier regiments, of 10 companies each. In 1794, there first appeared so-called mounted artillery (5 companies of 14 guns each) where all the gun crews were mounted for greater mobility. In 1798, field artillery was completely revamped with the creation of artillery battalions (1 of guards, 10 of regular artillery, one of mounted artillery, and three of siege artillery) consisting of 5 companies (in siege artillery – 10 companies), each with 12 guns. Meanwhile, former regimental artillery remained in place until 1800. In terms of both technical sophistication and tactical capabilities, Russian artillery remained the world's best throughout the period.

In 1763, the armed forces were broken into 8 territorial divisions (St. Petersburg, Moscow, Finland, Estland, Livonian, Smolensk, Sevsk, and Ukrainian) and 2 corps (Orenburg and Siberian ones) of varying structure and strength (from 2 to 10 infantry and cavalry regiments), but those were not permanent commands. It was only during the second Turkish war, that the principle of dividing armed forces into corps and the latter into divisions was applied more or less consistently. At the same time, Russia led Europe in the creation of major commands (army commands) for specific theaters of war. While Russia switched to that principle in 1768–1774, the first country to follow suit in Europe was France in 1793.

By the late 18th century, Russia's Baltic navy had 45 ships of the line, 19 sailing and 12 rowed frigates, and 132 smaller vessels. Black Sea navy had 15 ships of the line, 6 sailing and 15 rowed frigates, and 72 smaller vessels. Three more frigates and 24 smaller vessels were maintained in the Caspian.

At that time, the overwhelming majority of officers were promoted from lower ranks. As per the directive of 1766, it was a non-commissioned officer's social estate that determined how soon he could get an officer's commission. The fastest track of 3 years was reserved for the nobility, and the slowest of 12 years for those who started as recruits. Guards' regiments remained a major supplier of officer material, since the majority of their soldiers (if no longer all of them as in the first half of the century) were noblemen. In the late 18th century, noblemen started military service as non-commissioned officers (as privates wearing NCO uniforms for the first three months), and were then promoted to warrant officers, which made them eligible to fill vacancies in the first officer rank. Those of common origin had to serve as privates for 4 years before becoming eligible for promotion to NCOs. Further honorable service made possible a promotion to commissioned officer. In 1798, Paul attempted to ban promotion on non-nobility into officers, but had to backtrack the very next year. Catherine II dramatically cut back acceptance of foreign officers into Russian service by establishing discriminatory rules (they had to start in Russian service with reduced rank). Inflow of foreigners increased again late in the century with the enlistment of refugee French royalist officers. The number of officers grew in sync with expansion of the army. While in the mid-1750s the army had about 9 thousand officers, by century's end there were at least 15 thousand.

The system of military education continued to grow under Catherine. In 1762, the Nobility School of Artillery and Engineering was converted into Cadet Artillery and Engineering School, which subsequently supplied almost all artillery and military engineer officers for decades. In the course of 18th century, Ground Forces Cadet School (known from 1800 as simply the 1st Cadet School) graduated 3300 officers, and the Artillery and Engineering Cadet School (known from 1800 as the 2nd Cadet School) – 1600. So-called

Greek Cadet School (which existed from 1775 to 1796) graduated 190 officers (100 of them for the navy). Naval artillery school was opened in 1786. In 1798, the School of Naval Architecture was established in St. Petersburg.

Two more schools for training officers appeared in the late 18th century. In 1778, General Major S. G. Zorich used his private funds to create a college for impoverished nobility in Shklov. Graduates qualified for positions in both military and civil service, and from 1785 many were made commissioned officers right upon graduation. With the accession of Paul, the college was taken over by the government. In November 1799, it was designated a cadet school and soon after moved to Grodno. By 1801, that school graduated 470 officers. In 1795, two Gatchina schools for orphans and the sons of invalided servicemen were merged into the so-called Orphanage House. In 1798, it was relocated to St. Petersburg and rebranded the Imperial Military Orphanage. Its first section catered to 200 orphans of destitute nobility and officers, who graduated as junior warrant officers, while the best got their commissions upon graduation. The second section admitted 800 soldiers' sons who were taught various trades.

Domestic industry continued to supply all that was required by the armed forces. In the late 18th century, there existed about 200 metal smelters and metalworking plants (almost all of them predating the 1760s), and heavy industry employed about 420 thousand (three quarters of whom were bonded 'factory peasants'). Whereas heavy industry was largely inherited from the earlier period, the same can't be said about consumer goods manufacturing, which made major strides. Between the 1760s and the end of the century, the number of large textile mills (some with two to three thousand workers) grew from 231 to 1082 (i.e. increased by 4.5 times). The number of woolen mills grew from 73 to 158, canvas mills from 85 to 318, and silk manufactories from 60 to 357. Overall number of various industrial enterprises increased from 683 to 2094 in this period. Most workers were still bonded labor, yet by the end of the century the number of free hired labor reached 500 thousand (in some state-owned and state-supervised factories the percentage of free labor was as high as 90%).

Catherine consistently encouraged entrepreneurial activity by abolishing government bans on production and export of a number of goods and commodities. Private manufacturing of cotton fabrics was allowed in 1762. Next year, there was promulgated a general principle of freedom to engage in industrial activity. In 1766–1772, there was allowed a tariff-free export of wheat and wheat flour. The freedom of starting private weaving looms was declared in 1769, and in 1775 the right to start private industrial enterprises was extended to all industries without exception, and all government fees and taxes were abolished for small-scale producers. Similar decrees promoting free enterprise were issued in later years as well. Thanks to that, Russian army and navy had no need for any imported goods.

Chapter 6

Russian society in the second half of the 18th century

Annexation of vast areas in the south and the west during the reign of Catherine II helped significant population growth. By the start of her reign, Russia's population stood at 23.2 million, by 1782 it reached 28.4 million, and by the last year of her reign (1796) it grew to 37.4 million. Population density doubled and reached 2.3 persons per square km (7.2 in European Russia). Russia's land area stood at 16.6 million km². By the late 1780s, Russia surged well ahead of other European nations in population numbers. At the time, France had 25.1 million, Austria 20.2, Spain 10, Britain 9.2, Prussia 5.5, and Sweden 2.8 million.

Major territorial acquisitions notwithstanding, the territory inherited from pre-Petrine times still accounted for almost two thirds (63.6%) of the population. Annexation of new lands affected a change in ethnic composition of the population. By the end of the century, Russians (including Little Russians and White Russians) accounted for 77% of the total, while the Poles from new western governorates became the largest minority – 6.2%. The Finns accounted for 2.2%, Lithuanians for 2%, Estonians and Latvians for 3%, the Tatars and Bashkirs for 2.4%. The largest of smaller minorities were the Chuvash (0.9%), Mordvins (0.8%), Moldovans (0.5%), and Kalmyks (0.2%). Two significant new minorities were the Germans (0.6%) invited to colonize newly opened fertile lands in the south, and the Jews (1.4%) who lived on lands gained through partitions of Poland. In 1791, the Jewish *Pale of Settlement* was established. With some exceptions, Jews were forbidden to live outside the Pale, which essentially consisted of all the lands of erstwhile Polish-Lithuanian state and Crimean Khanate.

Important changes occurred in the status of legally recognized estates (i.e. social groups). The key one occurred even before Catherine's rule began. On February 18, 1762, less than two months after ascending the throne, Peter III promulgated the manifesto "On granting liberties and freedoms to all the nobility". The manifesto dramatically changed the condition of that estate. Whereas previously service was an obligation, it now became a privilege and a right. Catherine was opposed to this move, since she believed service to be the main duty of nobility, but considering that she won the throne in a coup widely supported by that same nobility she was hardly in a position to abrogate the manifesto that class obviously liked. A number of her decrees sought to dilute its impact though. Still, in 10 years since the manifesto's promulgation, 6 thousand military officers and civil servants resigned from service, as well as 0.5 thousand private soldiers and non-commissioned officers. In 1766, the nobility was granted the right to constitute itself into local assemblies at the *uezd* level, and in 1775 such assemblies received the right to have their own courts of peers and elect from their ranks local government. Perquisites enjoyed by the serving nobility compared to non-serving members of the class were extended to sometimes trivial matters (thus in 1775 noblemen with ranks below company officer were allowed to use only a one-horse carriage or ride on horseback while in town). Quite importantly, electoral rights of non-serving nobility were curtailed. During triennial elections of heads of local nobility assemblies, local civil servants, and judges, those members of the class who never served or never attained officer rank were not allowed to vote, no matter how much land they owned. Just as the landless nobility, they could attend as observers only.

Corporate institutions of the noble estate took their final shape with the promulgation in 1785 of "The charter of rights, liberties, and privileges granted to the Russian nobility". The charter gave members of the nobility the right to create not only *uezd*-level nobility assemblies, but governorate-level assemblies as well. Furthermore, such corporate bodies were recognized as legal entities and received an important role in local government. To qualify for an elected position, one had to have annual income of at least 100 rubles. The Charter reconfirmed that the nobility were free from taxation, non-tax obligations, and from obligation to serve (noblemen could be called up without consent only at wartime and only by a special imperial decree). It also exempted the nobility from corporal punishment and prescribed some outward trappings of dignified position (the right to a coat of arms, to wearing uniform and the sword, a place of privilege during church service, etc.). Landed estates of condemned criminals in cases where statutory sentence called for forfeiture of estate rights were not confiscated but deeded over to legitimate heirs. Members of the nobility were also given the right to engage in commerce, to own manufactories, and to own real estate in towns and cities. Every governorate was required to maintain books of record of hereditary nobility, with copies kept in the central heraldry office. The books were broken into six parts. Part 1 recorded individuals and lineages whose nobility was bestowed by emperors. Part 2 covered those who gained it through military service, part 3 – those who obtained it through civil service, part 4 listed lineages of foreign extraction, part 5 listed the titled aristocracy, and part 6 covered so-called ancient nobility (families who could prove that their ennoblement preceded the Charter by over a hundred years, i.e. was older than 1685). Persons granted the status of non-hereditary nobility enjoyed the same rights except for the right to own estates with peasants, and they were not recorded in heraldry books.

The award of orders of St. George and St. Vladimir (both instituted during Catherine's reign) meant bestowal of hereditary nobility by default. Besides, the Charter stipulated that hereditary nobility could be granted to those non-hereditary noblemen whose ancestors of three previous generations also served or whose fathers and grandfathers served for at least 20 years each with ranks conveying non-hereditary nobility. Serving the state continued to be the channel for replenishment of the noble estate. In the mid-18th century, 50.2% of civil servants and 16.6% of officers were not of gentle birth. In the second half of 18th century, that proportion among military officers grew to 30%. By 1796, the machinery of state was kept running by 15.5 thousand bureaucrats with rank (and 6 thousand more junior clerks without rank), and the officer corps consisted of about 15 thousand. Even though overall number of nobility grew, and the majority of them were still landlords, the number of landlords grew but little. In 50 years from 1727 to 1777, the number of landlords grew only from 64.5 to 70 thousand (across the same territory). Of that number, the absolute majority (41 thousand or 59%) had small estates with 20 serf peasants or less, another 18 thousand (25%) owned from 20 to 100 souls, and 11 thousand (16% of the total) owned more than a hundred souls. Including family members, the whole noble estate numbered 212 thousand by 1782 (1% of national population), while by 1795 this number stood at 720 thousand (2% of the population). The big difference is partly due to the annexation of Polish lands with their numerous petty nobility, while many of those ennobled in Peter's time subsequently lost their status, left no offspring, or became destitute.

In the second half of 18th century, the clergy became an almost completely self-contained estate. In the 1760s, it was freed from all taxes and service obligations. Its only remaining service to the state was to maintain records of births, deaths, and marriages. In 1764, parish clergy was freed from the tax it previously paid to support senior church hierarchy. In 1765, priests (and in 1771 deacons) were made exempt from corporal punishment. In 1774, the Synod banned outright transition to clergy from tax-paying estates. While in the 1760s other estates supplied 2% of all clergy, by the 1780s–1790s that number fell to 0.8%. At the same time, freely exiting the clerical estate became impossible too. Parish clergy elections by parishioners had long been a formality, but in 1797 they were banned by the Synod. It became universal practice that bishops gave parishes of diseased parish priests to their oldest sons (who usually already served as their fathers' sextons or deacons). If there were no sons, the parish usually went to the husband of diseased priest's daughter. Thus, parishes became in many ways like hereditary estates. The system of seminaries continued to grow with 4.7 thousand students by 1766. Increasingly, students came from within the clerical estate (three quarters or more). While the entry of outsiders into the clerical estate was essentially closed, it supplied its excess members to other social groups through so-called 'clergy reallocations'. Thus, in 1786, 34.5 thousand sons of parish priests (out of the total of 105.8 thousand) were reallocated: 28% were designated as junior clerks, 67% as townsmen, and 5% as peasants.

While at its very top church hierarchy intertwined with that of government (the head of the Synod was appointed by emperors from among secular civil servants), in every other regard the church and clergy were largely autonomous: more divorced from the state and less dependent on it than nobility. In 1756, the organs of diocesan government were dominated by so-called 'black' or celibate clergy (monks and hierarchs), with only 38% representing the 'white' (parish, or marrying) clergy. The bulk of a parish priest's income came straight from the parishioners. Therefore, by late 18th century their annual income (30 to 80 rubles) was below that of junior bureaucrats (who got 100 rubles or more). By 1783, active white clergy numbered 95.3 thousand: 27.3 thousand parish priests (29%), 13.4 thousand deacons (14%), and 54.6 thousand sextons (57%). In 1795, the whole clerical estate (including male children) numbered 216 thousand.

In 1775, townsmen were newly subdivided into merchants, craftsmen guild members, and '*meschane*' (petty traders and artisans, or the lower middle class). Merchants were taxed and classified based on their declared worth. Class one was worth above 10 thousand rubles, class two from one to ten thousand, and class three from 500 rubles to a thousand. The Charter of nobility rights of 1785 was issued simultaneously with the Charter of city rights, which was of no less importance, but to townsmen. That latter Charter defined legal status and corporate bodies of urban communities. Just as there existed nobility books of record, towns were to maintain townsmen lists, which bore proof of one's status as a townsman. Only townsmen were allowed to participate in commerce and industry within city limits. City communities at large had property rights to urban land and were exempt from non-monetary obligations to the state. Annual tax levied on townsmen in the last quarter of 18th century was 1.2 rubles. Every city received a coat of arms.

Merchants enjoyed a special position. Membership of that class was no longer hereditary but depended on one's net worth. Merchants were exempt from poll tax. Instead, they paid as annual tax 1% of their declared worth. Even so, in 1775, tax take from petty (class three) merchants alone was four times that from all non-merchant city residents, and in 1785 – eight times. Merchants were not free from recruit duty, but were allowed to buy personal exemption. In terms of perks and signs of rank, merchants of the first two classes stood largely on par with non-serving nobility. They were also exempt from corporal punishment, and had the right to get around in a carriage (first class in a coach, second class in a calèche with two horses, and third class in a one-horse trap). The charter for cities also identified one more, the highest category, so-called prominent citizens. Those included the wealthiest merchants and entrepreneurs (worth over 50 thousand rubles), bankers (worth over 100 thousand rubles), former members of city government who had served at least two terms, and people of liberal professions (scientists, artists, musicians). If three consecutive generations of one family were prominent citizens, the oldest son in the third generation could claim hereditary nobility at the age of 30.

While cities retained their magistrates, new elected bodies were added: city *duma*, so-called '*duma* of six', and 'community conferences'. *Burgermeisters*, city mayors, and all other city executives were elected by 'community conferences', which included everyone with declared worth of at least 5 thousand rubles. City *duma* (municipal council) was elected by all categories of city residents older than age 25 (1 – home owners, 2 – merchants, 3 – craftsmen and craftsmen guild members, 4 – out-of-towners and foreigners, 5 – prominent citizens, and 6 – everyone else). In turn, the council elected the executive body known as 'the *duma* of six', where each population category had one representative.

Total number of townsmen (males alone) stood at 228.4 thousand in 1762, and reached 336.2 thousand by 1782, and 582.2 thousand by 1795. The number of merchants at the same dates stood at 73, 87, and 118 thousand. In 1764, merchants accounted for 31.9% of city population, in 1775 for 19%, in 1782 for 26%, and in 1795 for 20%.

The condition of peasant estate in this period mostly remained unchanged. Landlords' rights to govern peasant lives were somewhat expanded – in 1765 they received the right to exile their serfs to hard-labor penal colonies for crimes. The decree of 1771 banned sales of serfs without land, but it was often ignored (especially since landed estates fragmented and grew smaller through inheritance, while the government had no real means to monitor compliance). In 1764, with secularization of land owned by monasteries, monastery peasants were transformed into a special class of so-called 'economic' peasants whose status was similar to that of 'state' peasants. In 1797, 'palace' peasants, who were previously jointly owned by the whole ruling family, were distributed between individual members of imperial household and rebranded 'appanage' peasants. When the charters of 1785 were granted to the nobility and townsmen, the original intention was to issue a similar charter for state peasants to confirm their rights as a recognized estate (personal freedom, elected court of peers, self-government, and the right to own property). While state peasants did in fact enjoy those rights, such a charter was never issued in order not to encourage claims of similar rights by privately owned peasant-serfs (who enjoyed none of them). In 1797, the serfs' labor duty (corvée) was limited to three days a week, and corvée work on Sundays and holidays was forbidden. Next year, peasants were allowed to engage in commercial activity in cities. The proportion of well-off peasants in this period is estimated to stand at about 10%, those of average means at 48%, and poor ones at 42%. The migration from peasantry into city estates intensified. In 1782–1811, that transition was made by 25 thousand peasants.

Civil and penal laws underwent no significant change in this period. In 1765, the age of criminal responsibility was raised from 7 to 10 years old, even though the church still insisted that moral responsibility starts at age 7. In 1774, the age of marriage capacity for women was raised from 12 to 13 years old. Private property rights were further strengthened. In 1762–1785, owners' property rights to their landed estates became absolute. The state rescinded its monopoly on some mineral resource development and on the use of certain categories of forests. In criminal law, the trend of gradual relaxation of punishments continued. Capital punishment was used only in exceptional cases of lese majesty, and such cases were heard by newly created Supreme criminal court. Even though most cruel punishments remained on the books, they were used far more sparingly, sentences became far less harsh, and some petty offences were effectively decriminalized and made punishable by administrative penalty. Under the influence of European philosophers of the time, Catherine moved away from viewing punishment as the revenge on the offender emphasizing instead its role in protecting the public at large. Previous vindictive punishments (such as taking one's life, maiming, and seizure of property) began to transform into punishments by incarceration. Accordingly, a system of jails of several types was created, and from 1785 government budgets included allocation for the upkeep of inmates. Workhouses were established for perpetrators of lesser crimes (in 1775 for persons of immoral behavior and in 1781 for those guilty of property crimes). Siberia rather than the remote corners of European Russia became the primary destination for exile. In 1775, the body of laws first included as a general norm the notion of statute of limitations, which applied to any crime that remained unknown for 10 years after it was committed. In 1798, it was stipulated that after age 70 criminals could be exiled but not subjected to corporal punishment.

Catherine's reign saw further efforts to improve public education. By 1765, the number of garrison schools for soldiers' children grew to 108 with about 9 thousand students. In 1764, I. Betskoy was asked to develop a plan for educational reform. As part of that reform, there were established a number of educational institutions, each catering to children from a specific social class. A grammar school was opened in St. Petersburg, a boys' school created under the auspices of Academy of Fine Arts (itself in existence from 1764). Smolny Institute educated girls of gentle birth, and Moscow orphanage school catered to illegitimate children and foundlings. In 1773, there appeared the School of Commerce in Moscow and Mining Institute in St. Petersburg. The latter and Land Surveyors Institute that opened in Moscow in 1779, became Russia's first two specialized institutions of higher learning. Two medical schools of higher learning, both in St. Petersburg, soon joined the list: Clinical Obstetric Institute (1797) and Academy of Surgery (1798, later to become Military Medical Academy).

Transition to the system of public schools in the modern sense of the word began in 1782, when a special commission was tasked with creating a network of standard schools. The commission started with opening several junior (two grades only) and full (four grades) schools in St. Petersburg Governorate, and in 1786 such schools opened in 26 Governorates. That reform extended to governorates of Little Russia as well, where a network of 2-grade, 3-grade, and 4-grade schools was set up. Kiev-Mohyla Academy was transformed with the addition of purely secular subjects to its curriculum (mathematics, natural history, geography, and foreign languages) and switching from Latin to Russian as the primary language of instruction. Three more seminaries operated in Chernigov, Kharkov, and Pereyaslavl. First teacher training colleges appeared in 1783, and the year 1785 even saw the debut of a magazine for children "Reading for Children's Hearts and Minds".

As the 18th century ended, Russia had over 550 various institutions of learning, including about 400 basic public schools, over 60 seminaries and church schools, and roughly the same number of various advanced schools for nobility. Total enrollment stood at about 62 thousand. Lithuanian, White Russian, and Baltic governorates with their mostly Catholic and Protestant populations had their own church-affiliated schools. Western governorates also had a Jesuit Academy in Vilna, 6 schools of the Jesuit order, and several seminaries. Derpt and Reval had grammar schools. Governorates of Estland and Livonia (essentially today's Estonia and Latvia) had a network of elementary schools, while Narva also had a Finnish and a German school.

Progress of education engendered the appearance of many periodicals, which in later years took such a prominent place in Russia's social and cultural scene. While fewer than 10 such periodicals are known to predate 1762, the first 10 years of Catherine's reign alone saw the appearance of 16 new ones. By the end of 1770s, there appeared 19 more, then 30 more in the 1780s and 20 more in the 1790s. This quickened pace of publishing activity was largely due to the 1783 decree that allowed private publishing houses. While literary magazines dominated the firmament of periodicals, some creditable science magazines appeared as well (including the venerable "Annals of the Free Society for Economics").

Chapter 7

Russian Empire under Alexander I

In the opening years of the 19th century, overall situation in Europe remained essentially unchanged. Peace treaties concluded between France and its opponents in 1801 (with Austria in February, Britain in March, and Russia in October) merely delayed resumption of hostilities by a few years. After Napoleon accepted the title of emperor in 1804, France continued to insist on its exceptional position in Europe, and that united all the other major powers against it. Its principal adversaries were still Britain (hostilities resumed in 1803) and Russia, which severed relations with France following the assassination in 1804 of Duke d'Enghien, the last surviving heir to the Prince of Condé (a cadet branch of the royal House of Bourbon). In 1805, there emerged the third anti-French coalition including Britain, Russia, Austria, Sweden, and Kingdom of Naples. It sought the removal of French troops from German and Italian states and restoration of independence for Holland and Switzerland.

Russia took to the field against France with 180 thousand troops. Of that number, the armies of Podolia and Volhynia (each 50 thousand strong) under overall command of M. I. Kutuzov were dispatched to Austria. In October, Russian troops (Kutuzov's army of Podolia) reached Braunau, but earlier that same month the Austrian army of General Mack was wiped out by the French, and therefore Russian troops had to retreat along the Danube valley with significant rearguard engagements fought at Krems (October 30) and Shöngrabern (November 4). By mid-November, allied troops with both emperors in camp amassed in the vicinity of Olmutz. Battle royal was fought on November 20 at Austerlitz (today's Slavkov u Brna in Czech Republic) and lost with major casualties (27 thousand dead or wounded). Following that, Austria disengaged from the war, and Russian troops withdrew back into Russia.

This military campaign resulted in the expansion of Napoleon's sphere of influence to include Austria and 16 German states. The latter, united into the Rhine Confederation, became completely dependent on France. Such a turn of events forced previously neutral Prussia to declare war on France in the autumn of 1806, and thus a new anti-French coalition emerged (Britain, Russia, Prussia, Saxony, and Sweden). Yet, in October of 1806, Prussian troops were defeated in two major battles (at Jena and Auerstedt), and Berlin was taken by the French. For over half a year after that, Russian troops continued to fight hard battles against Napoleon's armies in Eastern Prussia. The biggest battles were those of Preussich-Eylau (January 27, 1807) and Friedland (June 2, 1807). After a defeat in the latter, Russian troops withdrew to the Russian side of Neman River, and soon thereafter (June 25) Russia and France signed the Peace of Tilsit. Peace terms did not include any territorial losses by Russia, but bound it to join the continental blockade against Britain, which was quite hurtful for the Russian economy. Russia found itself in the state of war

84

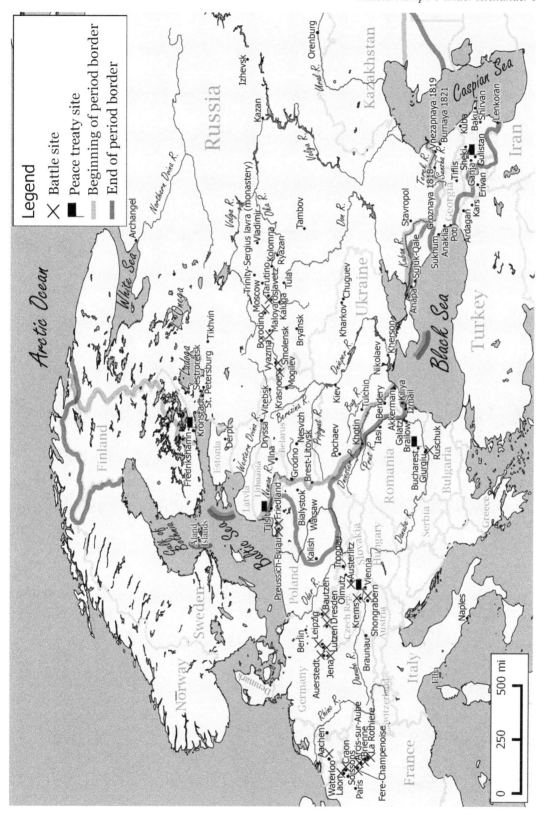

Russian Empire under Alexander I

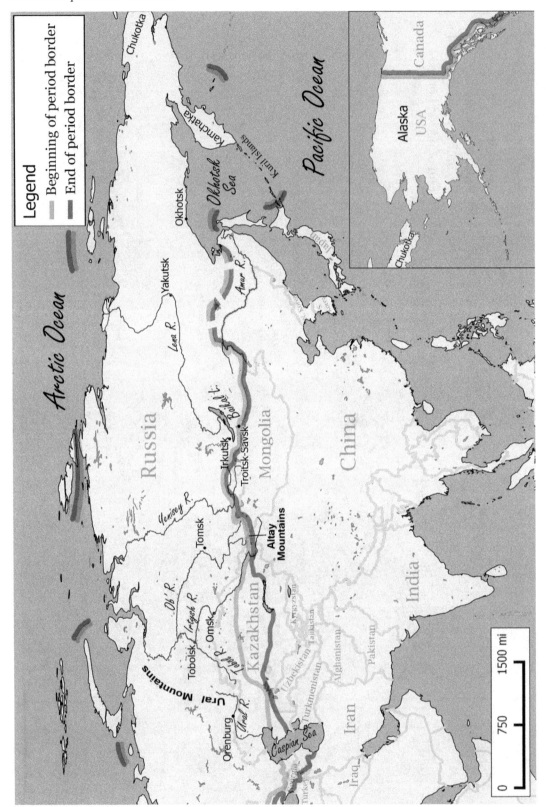

against Britain (this lasted till 1812), and several small engagements were fought between the two country's navies.

Even though in size the Russian army (about half a million men including irregulars and garrison troops) was second only to the French one, Russia could commit to wars in the west only comparatively modest forces since those opening years of the century also brought taxing wars in the south.

In the autumn of 1800, the Shah of Persia demanded complete submission of Georgia. About 20 thousand hill-men led by Omar-Khan of the Avars advanced on Tiflis (Tbilisi), but were defeated by a small Russian detachment under generals Lazarev and Gulyakov. Following that, Georgian King Georgi XII, who was at his deathbed, abdicated in favor of the Russian Emperor, and in February 1801 Eastern Georgia became part of Russia. In March 1803, the ruler of Mingrelia, Prince Dadiani, sent to Tiflis a deputation with a plea for incorporation into Russia, which was made official on December 4 of the same year. On April 25, 1804, Imereti Kingdom followed suit, and so later that year did Guria. Thus, all of Western Georgia acceded to Russia (with the exception of Turkish-held seaports of Poti and Anaklia). In 1806, Russia incorporated Ossetia, and in 1810 Abkhazia (except for Sukhum held by the Turks).

All of these developments caused extreme disgruntlement in Persia and Turkey, and made wars with them unavoidable. War against Persia began in 1804 and lasted until 1813. Military action mostly took place to the south-east of Georgia and along the western shore of the Caspian. As early as January 3, 1804, Russian troops led by Prince Tsitsianov took by assault the city of Ganja (promptly renamed Elizabethpol), that serves as a gateway to northern provinces of Iran. In the summer of 1804, Erivan (today's Yerevan) was besieged, and strategic region of Shuragel (present-day northern Armenia) annexed to provide a protective buffer for Georgia against both Persian advances from Erivan, and Turkish advances from Kars and Ardagan. By 1805, after dealing Persian troops several defeats, the Russians occupied the khanates of Ganja, Karabakh, Shirvan, and Sheki. Next year saw the conquest of Kuba and Baku khanates on the Caspian shores, and in 1813 Talysh Khanate with Lenkoran was taken. Gulistan peace treaty with Persia (1813) transferred all these territories to Russia.

In 1806, Turkey (incited by French diplomacy) launched its own war against Russia. After crossing the Dniester, Russian troops took Iasi, Bendery, Akkerman, Kiliya, Galatz, and Bucharest and reached the Danube. All that remained in Turkish hands on the northern bank of the Danube were the fortresses of Giurgiu, Izmail, and Brailow (Braila). But resumption of war with France meant that Russia could not reinforce its troops in the south and win a decisive turnaround in the war. After the Peace of Tilsit, Napoleon promised to end his backing of Turkey, and in August it had to sign a truce. Yet, Turkey soon violated that truce, and hostilities resumed including action south of Danube and in the Caucasus. In 1807, Russian troops took Anapa on the Caucasian coast, and in 1809–10 they seized the seaports of Poti and Sujuk-Qale (near present-day Novorossiysk). This made possible the subjugation of local Circassian tribes.

In the spring of 1811, M. Kutuzov was appointed commander-in-chief of the Russian army on the Danube. In view of shortly expected new conflict with France, his was a difficult task of concluding the war as soon as possible. On June 22, 1811 near Ruschuk (today's Ruse in Bulgaria), he defeated a Turkish army four times the size of his own. Instead of giving chase, Kutuzov withdrew his troops to the northern bank of the Danube hoping that the Turks will take bait and follow him. The plan worked. Kutuzov encircled the main Turkish force, while a corps of 7.5 thousand under General Markov re-crossed to the southern bank, and in a surprise attack on October 2 routed the Turks by Ruschuk (he lost 9 dead against the Turks' 1.5 thousand) and captured the town. Turkish troops enveloped on the Danube soon capitulated. On May 16, 1812, peace was signed in Bucharest. Its terms gave Russia all of Bessarabia with fortresses of Khotin, Akkerman, Kiliya, Bendery, and Izmail. The new boundary ran along Prut River to its confluence with the Danube. Regarding the status of Moldavia and Wallachia, the terms of earlier Peace of Iasi were reconfirmed. Additionally, Serbia was given autonomy in domestic affairs. At the same time, fortresses captured along the Black Sea coast were returned to Turkey, and the tribes living south of River Kuban reverted to Turkish influence.

Against the backdrop of difficult wars in the south, in 1808–1809 there unfolded a war with Sweden. Hostilities took place in Finland, where Sweden suffered several defeats. The Russian army marched on ice across the frozen Gulf of Bothnia and gained the Swedish shore. That forced Sweden to the negotiating table. Peace treaty signed in Fredrikshamn on September 5, 1809 ceded to Russia all of Finland plus Aland Islands. That last war between Russia and Sweden drew the line under centuries of their rivalry in the Baltic Sea basin. Confined to its western shores, Sweden lost the ability to threaten Russian possessions on land.

After the Peace of Tilsit, French dominance over Europe grew even further. After decisive defeat of Austria in 1809, Napoleon effectively subjugated the whole of continental Europe except Russia (only Portugal was held by British troops). All the other countries were either conquered by France, or were its allies, or else were forced to ally themselves with it following a military defeat (Austria and Prussia). On Polish-speaking lands that he wrested from Prussia, Napoleon created the Duchy of Warsaw, which evolved into his bridgehead for struggles against Russia. For the fervent Polish supporters of Napoleon, that puppet state appeared to be a prefiguration of future revived Poland (which they hoped to restore to its erstwhile boundaries). Another Russian grievance concerned the continental blockade, which was economically quite detrimental to Russia and therefore routinely violated. Little pleased, Napoleon intended to force Russia into compliance with the blockade. From 1810, both sides vigorously prepared for war, but Russia was still obliged to divert a major force to its south.

Napoleon amassed under his command an enormous army of 670 thousand men (including contingents from all subjugated European countries). On June 12, 1812, that army started crossing the Neman River. The first wave of French invasion numbered 450 thousand troops, twice the number of Russian forces (about 220 thousand), which were dispersed between three armies. The first army (127 thousand) commanded by M. Barclay de Tolly was deployed to the north to cover approaches to St. Petersburg, the second army (45 thousand) commanded by Prince P. Bagration was deployed near Bialystok to protect the central vector of advance into Russia's interior, and the third army (46 thousand) under A. Tormasov was staged south of Pripyat River.

From the very beginning, Emperor Alexander I refused to contemplate any compromise with Napoleon, and was prepared to retreat all the way to Siberia if defeated. By contrast, Napoleon was certain that seizure of a significant part of the country including Moscow would force Alexander to conclude a new peace treaty. Therefore, he sought to crush the Russian army piecemeal in the western borderlands and occupy Moscow. In view of Napoleon's great superiority in numbers, Alexander rejected the plan of countering the French with a battle royal by the fortifications of Dryssa camp on Western Dvina River.

The first and second armies started to retreat into the interior and on July 22 they joined forces near Smolensk and fought a rearguard battle with the French. Napoleon's main forces advanced by way of Vilna and Vitebsk, while a smaller force took a southerly route through Nesvizh and Mogilev. The two converged near Smolensk as well. A separate corps under Marshal Udino was deployed toward St. Petersburg where it was opposed by the Russian corps under General Wittgenstein.

On August 8, Kutuzov was appointed commander-in-chief, and on August 17 he arrived in the field. While continuing the retreat, he was forced by public opinion to give Napoleon a battle royal at the approaches to Moscow. The site he chose was Borodino field near Mozhaisk, and the battle took place on August 26. Napoleon had 134 thousand men with 587 artillery pieces, and the Russians had 125 thousand men (plus about 30 thousand militiamen) and 640 guns. The battle's outcome was inconclusive, but its cost in casualties tremendous (up to 40% on both sides). After 12 hours of fighting, the French took most Russian fortifications but failed to break through the Russian lines. At the military council at Fili (now part of Moscow), Kutuzov announced his decision to abandon Moscow and move the army to the south. As the army marched south on Ryazan road, it made an unexpected sharp turn at Kolomna, detached itself from French pursuit and made camp in Tarutino. Napoleon entered Moscow on September 2 and spent 36 days there waiting for Alexander's consent to parley. That never arrived.

Having left Moscow, the French army of 100 thousand marched toward Kaluga, but after October 12 battle at Maloyaroslavetz, it was forced to return to Smolensk road which the French already ravaged during their advance to Moscow. The retreating French were harassed by guerilla attacks and closely pursued by the regular army (fighting at Vyazma on October 22 and at Krasnoe on November 3–6). By the time they reached Smolensk, they lost almost half of their men but still maintained their fighting ability. But following the crossing of Berezina River on November 14–16, the retreat turned into a rout, and only 20 thousand men returned to the border to cross River Neman again. Alexander's manifesto of December 25 declared the country cleared of the enemy.

On January 1, 1813, Russian troops crossed the border and started their European campaign. In February, Prussia rose against Napoleon and made an alliance with Russia. In summer, this new coalition was joined by Britain, Austria, and Sweden. But Napoleon managed to build a new army of 500 thousand and was prepared to continue the war. In April and May of 1813 he defeated Russian and Prussian troops at Lützen and Bautzen, and on August 14 he defeated Russian and Austrian troops at Dresden. But August brought the French setbacks in other places. In the grandiose battle near Leipzig on October 4–7 (it cost 130 thousand lives and has been dubbed 'Battle of the Nations') Napoleon was roundly defeated. After that, he was abandoned by all allied German states, and by December the French retreated behind the Rhine.

The campaign of 1814 unfolded on the French soil. In January, Napoleon defeated the Prussians at Brienne, but next day the allies dealt him a defeat at La Rothière. In some subsequent battles the French won back the initiative. After February battles at Craon and Laon, Napoleon retreated to Soissons, but then went on the offensive again. Yet the allies' numerical superiority forced him to retreat again after March 8 engagement at Arcis-sur-Aube. After March 13 battle at Fère-Champenoise, the allies were at the doorstep of Paris and entered it on March 18 (more than two thirds of 100 thousand allied troops entering Paris were Russian). Napoleon was exiled to the Elba, yet a year later he escaped, landed in

France and entered Paris in triumph. June 1815 battle of Waterloo dealt him the final defeat in the hands of British and Prussian troops.

The future of postwar Europe was decided at the Vienna Congress (September 1814 – June 1815), where Russia played the lead role. In March 1815, Russia, Britain, Austria, and Prussia entered the so-called Quadruple Alliance created as a tool to implement decisions made in the Congress. France lost all its European conquests, and the royal houses of France, Spain, and Italy got their thrones back. For several subsequent decades, the preservation of this 'Vienna system' and 'principle of legitimacy' became the priority of Russian foreign policy. Polish lands that Napoleon made into the Duchy of Warsaw were now reconstituted as Kingdom of Poland which was incorporated in the Russian Empire on the basis of a personal union (Russian Emperor was now also King of Poland). In those years, Russian influence in Europe was at its peak. Victory over Napoleon's France turned Russia into the greatest European power.

In September 1815, Alexander I, Austrian Emperor Francis, and King of Prussia Friedrich-Wilhelm III signed into being the Holy Alliance. The concept was developed by Alexander I who became the alliance's head. In 1818, after withdrawal of foreign troops (at Alexander's insistence), France with its restored Bourbon dynasty joined the Holy Alliance. Alliance congresses in Aachen (1818) and Troppau (1820) hammered out the principle of military defense of legitimate rulers in all European nations. In the 1820s, the Alliance gave Austria permission to suppress rebellions in Naples and Piedmont, while France suppressed a rebellion in Spain.

In the Caucasus, Russia now moved to the systematic policy of preventing depredatory raids by hostile tribes. Pacification of the Northern Caucasus became all the more important since Russia was by then firmly established south of the main range of the Caucasus. It could not tolerate threats to communication lines with those new possessions, of which the Georgian Military Road across the main range was by far the most important one. Besides, most tribes in the Caucasus were Islamized and therefore receptive to any incitement by Ottoman Turkey. In case of a new war, they threatened to tie down Russian forces in the Caucasus which were never large to begin with. In 1816, all the troops in the Caucasus were integrated into a Special Corps of the Caucasus with A. Yermolov as its commander. Knowing full well the mores and values of hill-men tribes who respected nothing but brutal force, he embarked on the policy of systematic pacification while driving deeper into the mountains the most implacable groups. Defensive Line of the Caucasus that followed Kuban and Terek rivers was fortified and settled by the Cossacks and friendly tribes. Clearings were made in forested areas to provide troop access to the strongholds of hostile tribes, the main of which were Circassians on the western segment of the line, Kabardinians and Chechens in the center, and Avars in the east.

In 1817–1818, Yermolov brought to submission Chechen lands between rivers Terek and Sunzha, where he established Fort Redoubtable (*Krepost Groznaya* in Russian, its successor is the present-day Chechen capital Grozny), which became one of Russia's principal strongholds in the region. Following that, he defeated the Avars of Dagestan, where in 1819 he built another key fortress – Fort Sudden (*Krepost Vnezapnaya* near Khasavyurt). The year 1822 saw the final pacification of Kabarda (which was Russia's vassal since 1774), and insurgency in Abkhazia was suppressed in 1823–1824. In 1825, there followed a broad rebellion in Chechnya which was also suppressed. As a result, by the time of a new round of wars with Turkey and Iran, the Line of the Caucasus became a solid bulwark.

At that time, Russia first becomes a blue-water naval power. In 1803–1806, Russia's first round-the-globe expedition led by von Kruzenstern and Lisyansky sailed from Kronstadt to Alaska exploring Pacific islands along the way. In 1811, expedition led by Golovnin explored the Kuriles and Japan (where it was kept in captivity for three years). In 1819–1821, the expedition led by von Bellingshausen and Lazarev discovered the Antarctic continent. Count Litke made a number of discoveries in the Arctic Ocean and surveyed the coasts of Kamchatka and America.

To sum up, the first quarter of the 19th century left Russia with significant new territorial acquisitions. Finland, Poland, and Bessarabia were absorbed on its European flank, the lands of present-day Georgia and Azerbaijan beyond the Caucasus, and in the Northern Caucasus, Ossetia and some lands south of River Terek. In the grasslands beyond River Ural, 1822–1824 saw the final incorporation of the lands of so-called Junior and Middle confederations of Kazakh tribes (who were Russian vassals from 1731–1743).

System of government and military-economic potential

During the first decade of Alexander I rule, the tsar was aided by a supreme advisory body akin to those of 18th century vintage. That body (named the Indispensable Council in March 1801) was called upon to review existing legislation and new draft laws. Of greater importance though was a small circle of Alexander's personal friends that came to be known as the Private Committee and was active from May 1801 to November 1803. It included Prince A. Chartoryzhsky, N. Novosiltsov, V. Kochubei, and P. Stroganov. This circle contemplated reforms in every field of public administration. His Imperial Majesty's Personal Chancellery (headed by Count Arakcheev from 1812 to 1825) continued to operate as well. It served as a conduit for reports from ministers, governors, ambassadors, and other top officials.

By the end of the first decade, there was implemented a thorough reform of government system (especially its central bodies), which then survived essentially unchanged until the early 20th century.

The Council of State established on January 1, 1810 became the supreme advisory body to the emperor. That body enjoyed the exclusive right to review draft legislation and submit it for the emperor's approval. A law approved by the general session of Council of State was submitted for the emperor's signature (until 1842, the standard preamble included the words "having deferred to the opinion of Council of State"). Yet in some cases the Emperor could side with the Council's minority opinion. The Council was made of four departments (law-making, military affairs, matters civilian and spiritual, and economic development), and two commissions (Law-drafting Commission and Commission of Petitions). State Chancellery led by Secretary of State (M. Speransky became the first one) was part of it as well. Council members were appointed by the emperor, and ministers were members by default. The first chairman of Council of State was Count N. Rumyantsev.

Of utmost importance was the introduction in September of 1802 of the ministerial system which remained in place until the end of imperial Russia. The supreme executive body was now known as the Committee of Ministers. From 1810, it included not only the ministers, but also the chairman of Council of State, the heads of the Council's departments and some personal appointees of the emperor. The Council of State and the Committee of Ministers could be headed by the same person. The Committee of Ministers looked at issues that overlapped the jurisdiction of individual ministries, was in charge of supervision of service of the state personnel, and occasionally reviewed draft legislation as well.

With the creation of Committee of Ministers, the Senate lost its function of managing the machinery of state and morphed into a supreme oversight and judicial body. Its first department promulgated laws and had oversight over service of the state system, while the other departments (some of which, namely numbers 6 through 8, were in Moscow), were in fact supreme courts of appeal for groups of governorates. Two of them dealt with criminal cases and the rest with civil ones. The Metes and Bounds Department was also part of the Senate. Department heads were known as senior prosecutors. The head of the Senate was Prosecutor General who was by extension the Justice Minister.

The Holy Synod remained the supreme governing body of the Orthodox church. In 1817–1824, there briefly existed the Ministry for Matters of Faith and Public Education, which incorporated the Synod, the Chief Directorate for Foreign Confessions, and the Ministry of Education, but the model of rolling together matters of faith and education was ruled to be a failure.

In 1802 eight ministries (foreign affairs, army, navy, internal affairs, commerce, finance, public education, justice) and the treasury were established. They subsumed erstwhile collegiate boards, and for a while the minister with his deputy and chancellery were a kind of superstructure piled atop the earlier system. Yet, with the passage in 1810–1811 of the law 'On Allocation of Affairs of State between Ministries' and 'General Incorporation of Ministries' the shape of this reform came into focus. The ministries were given uniform organizational structure (based on the principle of unity of command) and regimented procedures for workflow management. Ministries were broken down into departments, departments into divisions, and divisions into desks. Specialized bodies under ministries could include committees of scientific review, laboratories, and support agencies. Every ministry had a chancellery and a council – a venue bringing together key department heads and some prominent experts. Similar councils (known as assemblies) existed on departmental and division levels. Their meetings were typically attended by invited entrepreneurs, researchers, engineers, etc.

From 1811, the central government included eight ministries. Those were foreign affairs, army, navy, internal affairs, police (created in 1810 but merged into internal affairs in 1819), justice, finance (from 1810 it subsumed Ministry of Commerce), and public education. Three more agencies carried the lesser designation of directorates: that for foreign confessions (established in 1810), audit of public finances, and roads and communications (established in 1809). Other agencies were the Main Treasury (absorbed into Ministry of Finance in 1821) and Department of Imperial Family's Lands and Peasants. Postal department became a separate agency in 1819.

The scope of responsibilities of some ministries was quite wide, especially in the case of Ministry of Internal Affairs. In addition to police functions, it was in charge of charitable institutions, estate-wide courts and estate corporations of the nobility and townsmen, in charge of victualling the military, in charge of foreign settlers, in charge of domestic commerce and industry (it inherited the Board of Manufactories), in charge of public health, in charge of salt monopoly, and briefly also of post service and foreign confessions. The key responsibility of Ministry of Finance was to manage government revenues, but it also dealt with government loans, government properties, management of mining and oversight of private industry. From 1819, it took over oversight of manufactories and domestic commerce (from Internal Affairs Ministry), the treasury, and repayment of state debt. Closely affiliated with this ministry were the Financial Committee (established in 1806) and the Council for State Credit Policy (1818) – two interagency bodies with many representatives of commercial and industrial interests.

There were no significant changes in territorial administration. By 1803, the country had 48 governorates, eight of which were parts of three general-governorates. With the creation of ministries in 1802, all local agencies and officials were put under one ministry or another. Ministry of Internal Affairs played the key role in local government: the governors reported directly to the Minister of Interior. Governors were heads of provincial governments, which were made up of four divisions. The first one was responsible for the promulgation of laws and oversight of compliance with provincial governments' decisions, the second was in charge of police, the third had oversight of the courts of justice, and the fourth had oversight of finances. Like before, *uezds* were administered by police captains and had their *zemstvo* courts.

Some central ministries or agencies used their own groupings of several governorates into service regions. The Directorate of Roads and Communications operated through roads and communications regions, while the Ministry of Public Education carved the country into educational circuits. Six such circuits presided over by trustees were established in 1803: St. Petersburg, Moscow, Vilna, Derpt, Kharkov, and Kazan ones. As per the statute of 1804, each circuit was anchored by a self-governing university, which served as the apex and administrative body for the whole system of non-estate public schools and other institutions of learning within its circuit (governorate directors of public schools were elected by university councils). Until 1826, censorship committees were attached to the universities as well.

Territorial agencies of the Synod were dioceses (usually coinciding with governorates) which, in turn, were divided into *uezd*-level dean's districts, to which individual parishes reported. The bishops and their chancelleries had control over all the elementary and secondary schools of religious education. The most venerable monasteries were known as *lavras* (Trinity-Sergius, Kiev-*Pechersk* ("of the Caves"), Alexander Nevsky, and Pochaev) and controlled directly by the Synod, which also exercised direct control over three divinity academies (in Moscow, Kiev, and Kazan), stauropegic monasteries, and synodal cathedrals.

The Baltic general-governorate (Estland, Livonia, and Courland) retained its own system of estate-based governing bodies and city home rule which evolved prior to annexation by Russia. Poland and Finland (both incorporated during Alexander's reign based on personal union) enjoyed wider autonomy. The Grand Duchy of Finland was divided into small governorates, had its own legislative body (the Sejm, or Diet), its own government (the *Soviet* (Council), from 1816 the Senate) headed by emperor-appointed general-governor, and enjoyed broad home rule rights at local government level. In the Kingdom of Poland, the top official was the viceroy (the emperor's brother, Grand Duke Constantine), but it also had a two-chamber parliament. The upper chamber (the Senate) was appointed by the emperor, while the lower chamber was elected by the nobility and city communities. Its executive bodies were the Council of State and 6 ministries (interior affairs, military, justice, finance, spiritual matters, and education). For administrative purposes, the Kingdom was divided into eight provinces known as *voivodeships*, which consisted of counties (known as *powiats*). The Kingdom of Poland had its own army.

Administrative arrangements in sparsely populated frontier areas with largely non-Russian indigenous population had some special features as well. In the early 19th century, all of Siberia was one general-governorate made up of three governorates (Tobolsk, Tomsk, and Yakutsk). In 1822, it was split into two general-governorates, the West Siberian one (Tobolsk and Tomsk governorates, and Omsk Oblast) and East Siberian one (Irkutsk and Yenisey governorates, Yakutsk Oblast, Okhotsk, Kamchatka, and Troitsk-Savsk border districts). Siberian governorates were divided into units known as *okrug*. An *okrug* was in all essentials the same as *uezd* in European Russia, but of much greater geographic extent. Oblasts were different from governorates in that their top officials were also commanders of troops stationed there. In 1822, 'The Articles on Inorodtsy' (the term *inorodtsy* ("of different descent") applied to non-Russian indigenous populations, mostly those of non-European Russia) divided non-Russian natives into three categories: vagrant, nomadic, and sedentary. Sedentary groups were administered through small districts known as *volosts* (in European Russia such districts which were smaller than *uezds* were used to govern state peasants). Vagrant groups (primarily in the Far North) were administered through their traditional tribal and clan leaders. Nomadic people (the Yakuts, Buryats, Khakassians, Evenks, Khanty, and Mansy) were governed through a mixed system of self-governing clans (15 families or more elected a headman) and local native councils (formed by several related tribal groups or clans electing a council head and assessors for the term of three years) which reported to *okrug* governors. Kazakh tribal confederations (also known as *hordes*) consisted of several *okrugs*, further broken down into 15 to 20 *volosts*, which included 10 to 12 nomad camps of 50 to 70 tents (households) each.

In Georgia, commander-in-chief of the Separate Georgian Corps acted as the chairman of Supreme Government of Georgia. Its departments were equivalent to functional agencies and court chambers of a regular governorate in European Russia. On *uezd* level, the police and *uezd* court were headed by district governors. Cities had city commandants (from the ranks of military officers), police chiefs (from the ranks of local nobility), and magistrates. Former khanates between Georgia and the Caspian were divided into provinces (administered by officer commandants) and smaller districts administered by *naibs* – traditional nobility or elders.

In the first quarter of 19th century, Russia's armed forces remained up to scratch and ensured the country's geopolitical prominence and its leading role in Europe. Detrimental impacts of Paul's brief rule were quickly overcome. By early 1801, Russian army counted 446 thousand men, including 201 thousand in field infantry, 42 thousand in the cavalry, 36.5 thousand artillerymen, and 96.5 thousand garrison troops. In numbers, it was second only to the French army. By 1812, the strength of the army grew to 597 thousand (362 thousand infantrymen, 87 thousand cavalrymen, 52.5 thousand artillerymen, 75 thousand garrison troops, and about 120 thousand irregulars). Three armies in the west included 8 infantry corps, 4 cavalry corps, and 2 Cossack corps. By the end of Napoleonic wars, the army rosters counted about 710 thousand men, and that number hardly went down by 1825.

The new recruit service statute of 1810 introduced the order or recruit call-ups that remained in place until 1874. Each district draft office maintained (and updated every three years) the record of families indicating the number of able-bodied men. During recruit draft campaigns, families with the highest number of such men were the first to part with a recruit. Over the first quarter of the century, there were 28 recruit draft campaigns that yielded about 2 million recruits.

By 1805, the infantry included 117 regiments and several detached battalions (3 regiments of the guards, 13 grenadier regiments, 4 marines' regiments, 20 ranger regiments, and 77 musketeer regiments). Regiments now had three, rather than two battalions, with four companies to a battalion. By 1812, there were 172 regiments (6 regiments of the guards, 14 grenadier regiments, 4 regiments of the marines, 50 ranger regiments, and 98 infantry (former musketeer) regiments). By 1825, the number of regiments grew to 176 (10 of the guards, 15 grenadier, 8 carabineer, 50 ranger and 96 infantry regiments).

In 1803, the cavalry had 41 regiments and some smaller units known as *sotnias*: 4 guards' regiments, 6 cuirassier ones, 22 dragoon, 8 hussar, and one lancer regiment. By 1812, there were 65 regiments: 5 of the guards, 8 of cuirassiers, 36 of dragoons, 11 of hussars, and 5 of the lancers. By 1825, the number of cavalry regiments grew to 77 (10 of the guards, 9 of cuirassiers, 18 of dragoons, 12 of hussars, 20 of lancers, and 8 of mounted rangers).

By 1801, field artillery consisted of one guards' battalion, 10 battalions of regular field artillery and one of mounted artillery, and three siege companies. As per 1803 order of battle, artillery consisted of a guards' battalion, 9 regular artillery regiments and 2 batteries of mounted artillery, as well as 180 siege guns, distributed among three arsenals. In 1816, artillery broke down into 66 battery companies, 66 companies of light artillery, and 33 companies of mounted artillery. In 1825, artillery consisted of 143 companies of regular and 30 companies of mounted artillery. Three companies made up a brigade. Siege artillery consisted of 4 detachments of 22 guns each.

Engineering troops underwent significant expansion. By 1801, there existed one pioneer regiment and two pontoon companies. By 1812 there were two pioneer and one sapper regiments (pioneers prepared roads, bridges, etc. for the main body of the troops, while sappers built field fortifications), one guards' sapper battalion, and a pontoon regiment. By 1825, there were 3 sapper and 7 pioneer battalions, and a mounted pioneers' squadron. In 1819, Russia had 62 fortresses, each with its complement of artillerymen and engineers.

By 1801, garrison troops had 105 battalions. In 1811, there were created home guard (internal security) troops. In 1816, they were integrated into a special Corps of Home Guards which also included so-called invalid details (these were soldiers no longer fit for frontline duty and serving as security and prison guards) and road stage details (providing safety on post roads). These interior security troops were arranged into 12 regions.

Irregular troops were for the most part Cossacks. By 1805, Don Cossack Host quota (to be provided in case of war) ran to 80 mounted regiments, Kuban Host (then known as Black Sea Host) – 10 mounted and 10 infantry regiments, Ural Host – 10 mounted regiments, Bug River Host – 3, and Orenburg, Stavropol-Kalmyk and Chuguev Hosts were to supply one regiment each. Terek, Greben[11], and Siberian Cossacks, as well as the Bashkirs and Mishar Tatars[12] were to provide a stipulated number of men rather than complete regiments.

---

[11] Another distinctive Cossack group located along the Terek River.
[12] The Mishars were a distinctive group of westernmost Tatars, whose historic role in Muscovy was similar to that of Cossacks. They were often relocated in order to garrison Russia's advancing defensive lines in the Volga basin, and were often awarded estates for service, which turned them into petty gentry.

The troops were armed with a variety of rifles and short rifles (each kind of infantry and cavalry had a different type). Those were of 1805–1808 design, came in both smooth-bore and rifled varieties and in two principal calibers. Their projected service life was 40 years. Modernization of artillery systems was completed by 1805. It left field artillery with 7 types of guns (those were copper), and fortress artillery with 13 types of guns (of cast iron). In wars of this period Russian artillery enjoyed an edge over its opponents both in technology and tactics.

The army was distributed between 14 territorial commands known as inspectorates, those of St. Petersburg, Finland, Moscow, Livonia, Smolensk, Lithuania, Brest, Kiev, Ukraine, Dniester, Crimea, Caucasus, Orenburg, and Siberia. In 1806, the field army was divided into divisions of 18 to 20 thousand men. A division included 6 to 7 infantry and 3 cavalry regiments, and an artillery brigade (by 1811, there were 27 such divisions plus individual guards' regiments). Two regiments made up a brigade, and several divisions made up a corps or an army.

By 1812, the Baltic navy had 42 ships of the line, 17 frigates, 4 corvettes, 2 bombardier vessels, 15 brigantines and sloops, 31 small vessels, 127 transport ships, and 500 row galleys. The Black Sea navy had 6 ships of the line, 3 frigates, and 10 other vessels, 3 more ships of the line and one frigate were in foreign seas. At that time, the navy was organized into divisions (3 at the Baltic and 2 at the Black Sea) of three squadrons each. A squadron had one to three fleet companies (all told, by 1816 there were 98 fleet companies, each consisting of 8 troops of a hundred men). By 1825, the Baltic fleet had 111 vessels (15 ships of the line, 12 frigates, 3 steamers, 31 small vessels, and 50 gunboats). The Black Sea fleet had 41 (15 ships of the line, 6 frigates, 2 steamers, and 18 smaller vessels). The Caspian flotilla had 5 small and 6 transport vessels, the White Sea and Okhotsk Sea flotillas had 7 and 11 transports respectively.

At the time, the majority of commissioned army officers were promoted from lower ranks, but almost a quarter of annual replenishment was now accounted for by graduates of military schools and colleges. In 1803, the army had a total of about 12 thousand officers, and on the eve of wars with France (1805–1807) their number reached 14 thousand. In 1809, staff officers alone numbered 2113 (495 colonels, 442 lieutenant-colonels, and 1176 majors). During the war of 1812, the number of officers stood at 15–17 thousand (excluding several hundred in the irregular units).

Early in the 19th century, there opened several new institutions of military education, including preparatory military schools for children aged 8 to 11. The first such school was created in Tula in 1801, the second one in Tambov in 1802, and in 1825 there was formed Orenburg military school (named after Neplyuev) for 80 underage cadets. Grodno Cadet School was relocated to Moscow, and has since been known as Moscow Cadet School. After the annexation of Poland in 1815, Kalish Cadet School (founded in 1793 by King of Prussia in what was then German-controlled part of Poland) supplied with junior warrant officers the Russian army. In 1802, there was created a School of Pages. It was designed along the lines of cadet military school to educate young men appointed as imperial court pages and had a 7-year course of study. In 1807, a military school named Nobility Regiment was established for young noblemen desirous of military careers. It provided only military training per se, and served as a fast track to be graduated as a commissioned officer. In 1819, the Topography School in Fredrikshamn (itself established in 1812) was expanded into Finland Cadet School. In 1823, a School of Guards Warrant Officers with 2-year course of study was set up to supply guards' troops with commissioned officers. Over the period of 1801–1825, the 1st and the 2nd Cadet Schools and School of Pages graduated the total of 4845 officers, another 721 were supplied by the Imperial Military Orphanage.

An Artillery College with a 5-year course of study was opened in 1820. In 1804, in St. Petersburg there opened an engineering school, and in 1810 it was converted into Engineering College. In 1819, it was further expanded into the Main Engineering College with a 4-year course of study for both warrant and commissioned officers. Topographic Surveyor School was opened in 1822.

That aside, for a period of about 10 years some field army headquarters had their own schools for training of junior warrant officers, so-called *junker* schools (from German *junger herr* – young sir). From 1820, such a 2-year school with enrollment of 120 existed at the 1st army headquarters at Mogilev. From 1818, a 3-year *junker* school operated at the 2nd army headquarters at Tulchin. For a brief period, such schools (funded through unallocated part of army budgets) existed even at the headquarters of individual 1st army corps. But overall, *junker* schools did not quite take off at that period.

Military needs were still fully satisfied by domestic industry. Mining and metallurgical industries of the time were mostly concentrated in the Urals, the Altay mountains, and beyond Lake Baikal, while metalworking and textile industries clustered in St. Petersburg, Tula, and Moscow and Vladimir governorates. Small arms were manufactured at the arsenal mills in Tula, Sestroretsk, and (from 1811) Izhevsk. Copper artillery pieces (both field and siege) were manufactured in the arsenals of St. Petersburg, Kiev, Bryansk, and Kazan, while iron pieces for fortresses and coastal defense works were cast at Mining Ministry mills. Russia had several centers of naval shipbuilding. The Baltic fleet was supplied by navy yards in St. Petersburg, Kronstadt, and Archangel, and the Black Sea fleet by those in Kherson and Nikolaev. All new ships at that time were built domestically. In the first decade of 19th century, there were built 99 warships and vessels (including 30 ships of the line and 18 frigates), and in the following decade 90 more (including 30 ships of the line and 29 frigates). In 1805, the government mill at Alexandrovsk (near St. Petersburg) commissioned Russia's first steam engine. In 1815, Charles Baird's works in St. Petersburg built the first passenger steamer (he was the second man in Russia after Robert Fulton to receive the exclusive royal patent to build steamers, but Fulton never built one). By 1820, 4 steamers were in operation, and then steamer construction expanded to Archangel and Volga shipyards. In 1817, Okhta (now part of St. Petersburg) shipyard built the world's first combat steamer '*Skory*' (Swift), and 4 more followed by 1825. Mariinsky (after Empress Maria, Paul I spouse) and Tikhvin systems of inland canals (built in 1808–1811) provided a navigable link between the Baltic and Caspian seas.

Chapter 8

Russian Empire during the reign of Nicholas I

The enthronement of Emperor Nicholas was marred by an army rebellion. The two secret societies behind it emerged in the early 1820s, the Northern Society in St. Petersburg and the Southern Society in Ukraine. They were inspired by various ideas for constitutional reform of the monarchy, and their membership numbered several dozen army officers and officials. Following the death of Alexander I on November 19, 1825, there was uncertainty about the succession. The next oldest brother, Constantine (viceroy of Kingdom of Poland) abdicated (in fact, according to the law on succession passed under Paul, he had no right to succeed to the throne due to his marriage to a social inferior). Alexander bequeathed the throne to his younger brother Nicholas, but that bequest was not promulgated, and the troops swore allegiance to Constantine (the latter remained in Warsaw and confirmed his abdication in the letters to Nicholas, but never made a public statement). The conspirators decided to exploit that ambiguity.

On December 13, the Council of State and the Senate swore allegiance to Nicholas, and the next day was scheduled for the swearing of allegiance by the troops. The soldiers were understandably confused by having to swear a new oath of allegiance, and several Northern Society members (who were guards' officers) seized the opportunity. In the morning of December 14, they led into the Senate Square two regiments of the guards (Moscow and Grenadier) and the guards' fleet company (the total of about 3 thousand men). There they were surrounded by troops loyal to Nicholas, and after the conspirators killed the military governor of St. Petersburg, General Miloradovich (who remonstrated with the rebels), they were dispersed by artillery fire. In the south, the conspirators managed to rally several companies of Chernigov regiment, but on January 3, 1826 those were dispersed as well. The investigation into the case of 'Decembrists' (as they became known) showed some degree of onetime involvement with the two secret societies of about 600 individuals, but the punishment meted to them was quite lenient. Only five lead conspirators (who planned extermination of the whole ruling family) were executed, several dozen were sent to forced-labor camps in Siberia, and the rest (out of only 121 punished) got away with exile or being stripped of officer rank.

The first five years of Nicholas' reign were marked by non-stop wars. The first of them was the war against Persia in 1826–1828. It started in July 1826 with the invasion of Karabakh by 60 thousand strong Persian army led by the Shah's heir Abbas-Mirza. Simultaneously, Russian border was crossed by the troops of provincial ruler of Erivan. There were also rebellions in Muslim khanates annexed under the previous reign, all of which again exposed Georgia to danger. After besieging but failing to take Shusha, Abbas-Mirza marched on Elizabethpol, but near Shamkhor his 10 thousand strong vanguard was defeated by a detachment under Prince Madatov and lost over 2 thousand men. On

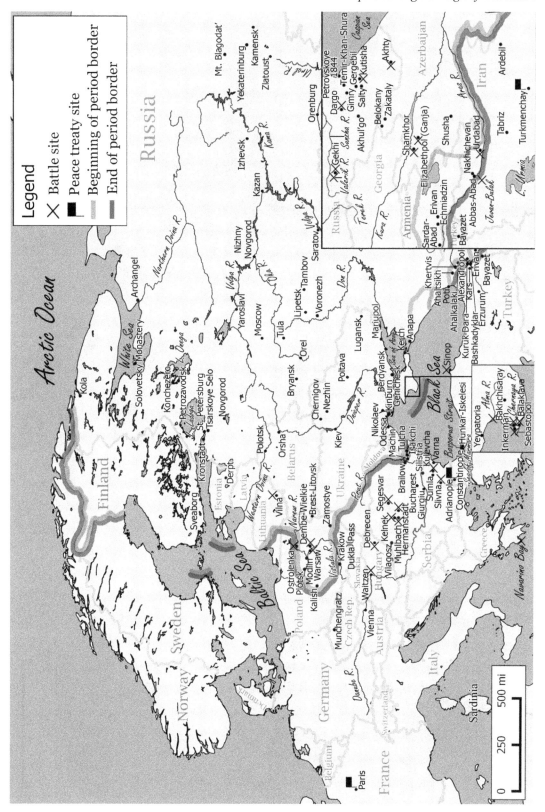

Russian Empire during the reign of Nicholas I

99

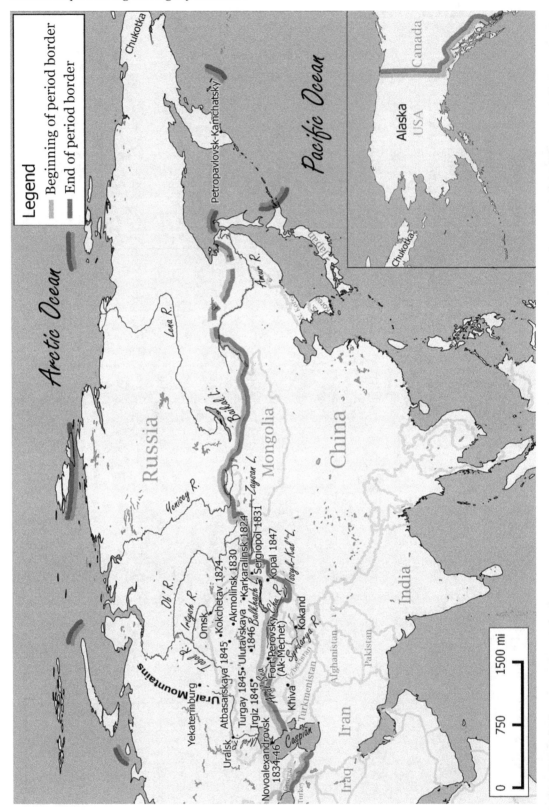

Russian Empire during the reign of Nicholas I

September 13, by Elizabethpol, the rest of the Persian army (35 thousand men) was trounced by Russian troops under I. Paskevich. Following that, rebellious khanates were brought to heel, as well as rebellious Jar-Belokany Muslim communities (in the area of Zakataly and Belokany).

In March 1827, Paskevich succeeded Yermolov as the commander of Special Corps of the Caucasus, and the Russian troops took the fight to the enemy by seizing Echmiadzin and laying siege to Erivan. Moving into Nakhichevan Khanate, on June 26 Russian troops seized Nakhichevan, and on July 4 defeated the Persians by Jevan-Bulak (a creek near Abbas-Abad fortress). The fortress of Abbas-Abad fell on July 7, and on August 7 the Persians were defeated at Urdabad. Although Abbas-Mirza succeeded in moving hostilities back to Erivan Khanate where he laid siege to Echmiadzin, on September 19 Russian troops seized Sardar-Abad and on October 1 they took Erivan itself. In the autumn of 1827, Russian troops crossed the Aras River and advanced on Tabriz, which fell on October 13. On January 25, 1828, Ardebil was taken, and the whole swath of territory from Ardebil to Lake Urmia in the west was now in Russian hands. The Shah capitulated. The treaty of Turkmenchay (February 1828) gave Russia Erivan and Nakhichevan khanates, which were now governed as Armenian Oblast. Iran was to pay Russia 20 million rubles as war indemnity and lost the right to maintain military vessels in the Caspian. This was Russia's last war with Iran, and the boundary along River Aras stood unchanged to the last days of empire.

During the reign of Nicholas I, the biggest foreign policy objective for Russia was to resolve what was referred to as the 'Eastern Question'. Christian populations in the Ottoman Empire increasingly strove to get rid of Ottoman rule and pinned their hopes on Russia. Yet, since both Alexander I and Nicholas I positioned themselves as guarantors of the principle of sanctity of legitimate rule in Europe, they could hardly openly support such aspirations. When the great Greek rebellion flared up in 1821 and was ruthlessly suppressed by Turkey, Russia along with Britain and France tried to give the Greeks diplomatic cover, but Turkey remained resolute to crush the rebellion for good. Moreover, it violated existing agreements by moving troops into the principalities of Moldavia and Wallachia. Having failed to extract any concessions from Turkey on the Greek issue, the three powers concluded a treaty that recognized Greece's right to autonomy. After Turkey refused to grant such an autonomy, the allied squadron (dominated by the Russian squadron under Count Heiden), wiped out the Turkish fleet stationed at Navarino Bay (October 8, 1827). On April 14 of the next year, Russia declared war on Turkey.

On April 26, 1828, Russian troops crossed Prut River. Bucharest fell in four days, and in a few more days the Russians controlled the whole of Danubian principalities. Brailow was besieged by mid-May and surrendered in early June. By late May, all of Northern Dobruja was taken, and in summer, Sumla, Varna, and Silistria were sealed off. The campaign culminated in the seizure of Varna on September 29. The campaign of 1829 (led by the new commander, I. Dibich, who replaced P. Wittgenstein) began with the siege of Silistria (made possible by several previous victories). In mid-May, a Turkish army of 40 thousand set out to relieve Varna, but Dibich with 30 thousand troops (the rest were left to continue the siege of Silistria) maneuvered to hit the Turkish rear, and trounced the Turks at Kulevcha. On June 19, Silistria surrendered. After that (on July 2) the Russian army (leaving one corps by Sumla) started its crossing of the main Balkans range in Bulgaria. Having crossed the Balkans, the army (suffering major losses to heat exhaustion and fevers) headed for Adrianople. On July 31 at Slivna, the Turks were again routed (with minimal

Russian losses), Adrianople fell on August 8, and Russian troops stood within sight of Constantinople.

On the Black Sea, seaborne assault of June 12 seized Anapa. South of the Caucasus, Paskevich took the Turkish stronghold of Kars on June 23, 1828, and a month later he took the fortresses of Ahalkalaki and Khertvis. In early August, the Russians pushed back Turkish troops and besieged Ahaltsikh, which was taken by storm on August 15. The capture of Ardagan and Bayazet followed. In February and March of 1829, several Turkish attempts to retake Ahaltsikh were repulsed, and following more Turkish defeats in June, Paskevich advanced on Erzurum, a crucially important Ottoman stronghold in Asia Minor. Erzurum fell on June 27, and Turkish counterattacks on Bayazet were repulsed.

Peace treaty signed on September 2 in Adrianople ceded to Russia the Black Sea coast with fortresses of Poti and Anapa, Ahaltsikh district with the fortresses of Ahaltsikh and Ahalkalaki, and the mouth of the Danube. The war cost Russia about 80 thousand casualties. Even though combat losses were light, the army was badly battered by illness and heat exhaustion. Yet, Russia's gains under the peace treaty were extremely modest, especially considering that Turkey was left with almost no army and would have had to swallow any terms. But the principle of the sanctity of legitimate rule then prevalent in European politics disallowed a complete destruction or dismemberment of Ottoman Empire. That is why all the other captured territories were returned. Greek autonomy was now guaranteed though, and in 1830 Greece became fully independent.

In the autumn of 1830, revolutions in France and Belgium inspired a revolt in Poland. On November 17, the crowds attacked the residence of Grand Prince Constantine, and the Sejm declared Romanov dynasty deposed. Constantine with a detachment of guardsmen left Poland leaving behind even those Polish troops that stayed loyal. The situation was much exacerbated by Poland having its own sizable army (of 130 thousand) which now became an instrument of the rebellion. In late January of 1831, Russian troops (114 thousand) commanded by Count Dibich-Zabalkansky crossed the River Narew. On February 13, there unfolded a slaughterous battle of Grochow (now part of Warsaw) (9.4 thousand Russian and 12 thousand Polish casualties). Having spent his ammunition, Dibich did not risk the storming of Warsaw. On March 20, the corps under Baron Rozen was defeated by the Poles at Dembe-Wielkie, while on April 7 the detachment under General Rudiger defeated the Poles in Volhynia. On May 14, the principal Polish forces were defeated by Dibich at Ostrolenka, and Polish troops operating in Lithuania were defeated near Vilna in June and retreated into Prussia. An epidemic of cholera that broke in the Russian army ended the lives of both Dibich and Grand Duke Constantine.

On August 6, the new commander-in-chief, Count Paskevich-Erivansky besieged Warsaw and took it by storm on August 26. Surrendering Poles were allowed to keep their arms with the promise that they retreat to Plotsk and cease hostilities, yet they soon resumed the fighting. On September 20, they were forced to escape into Prussia, where they put down their arms. The fortress of Modlin (renamed Novogeorgievsk in 1834) surrendered on September 25, and Zamostye fortress on October 9. That ended the rebellion. After the rebellion, the constitution was abrogated, the Sejm dissolved, and Polish army disbanded. Kingdom of Poland was turned into a general-governorate with the same administrative arrangements as in Russia proper.

By the early 1830s, there were significant shifts in European situation. The revolution of July 1830 in France and the assumption of power in Britain by liberal Whig government took those two countries out of the Holy Alliance. That pushed the remaining members (Russia, Austria, and Prussia) even closer together. Their new closeness was solemnized at the 1833 meeting of three monarchs in Münchengrätz. In 1835, Russia and Prussia even conducted joint military games culminating in joint troop review in Kalish.

All of that gave Russia a free hand in the south. In 1831, Russian troops were sent into Turkish vassal states of Moldavia and Wallachia. Their commander, Count Kiselev penned the so-called 'Organic Statute' which became the foundation stone of Romanian nationhood. In 1832, Turkey was faced with the invasion by Egypt's rebellious ruler Muhammad Ali. When Egyptian troops advanced on Constantinople, the Ottoman Empire teetered on the brink of collapse. In February 1833, Nicholas interfered by sending to the Sultan's rescue the Black Sea fleet and a landing party. Its mere appearance in the Bosporus forced Muhammad Ali to withdraw. The price Turkey had to pay for this aid was its 1833 Hunkar-Iskelesi treaty of alliance with Russia. The treaty denied passage through the straits into the Black Sea to foreign nations' warships, while Russian warships enjoyed freedom of passage into the Mediterranean. That was a major but short-lived Russian success. In 1839, Muhammad Ali sought complete independence from the Ottomans, and his army threatened Constantinople again. This time, when the Sultan again appealed for Russian help, European powers interfered. In the face of intense British pressure, 1840–1841 London conference replaced Russian-Turkish treaty with a new regime of international control over the straits, which were made closed (in peacetime) for the passage of any nation's warships. During Nicholas' private visit to London in 1844, he tried to talk Britain into partitioning the Ottoman Empire (which he referred to as 'the sick man'), but met with no success.

In the early 1830s, Russia's position in the Northern Caucasus had seriously worsened with the spread among local tribes of Sufi Islam movement of Mourides (meaning followers). Mullah Gazi Muhammad used that religious enthusiasm to rally around himself hill-men tribes and declare 'holy war' on Russia. In 1831, the Mourides ravaged Kizlyar, but were repulsed at fortresses Burnaya and Vnezapnaya. On December 1, Russian troops entered Gazi Muhammad's headquarters at Temir-Khan-Shura (present-day Buynaksk in Dagestan), while he escaped to the mountain village of Gimry. On October 17, 1832, Gimry was taken by storm and the mullah killed. Yet, the movement continued under the leadership of his follower, Shamil, who established a stronghold in another mountain village, Akhul'go. May 1837 expedition to defeat him failed, but after several assaults in July of 1839 the village was taken and Shamil fled. But unrest flared anew in February 1840 with the general uprising of all Circassian and Lezgin tribes, while Shamil incited a new rebellion in Chechnya. On July 11, he was defeated by Valerik River, but escaped to invade Avar Khanate (in present-day Dagestan), where the ruler switched to his side. In 1842, the Russians took fortified mountain village of Gergebil, but their expedition against Shamil's stronghold in Chechnya, Dargo, was routed and suffered heavy casualties. In 1843, Shamil seized a number of forts, retook Gergebil in November and established his rule over lands of the Avars. In July of 1845, the new commander-in-chief, Prince M. Vorontzov led an expedition against Dargo. The village was taken, but on their way back the troops were ambushed and lost 3 thousand men. In 1846, Shamil suffered a defeat at Kutisha. Vorontzov launched a systematic campaign of cutting down forest thickets or cutting clearings through them with concomitant construction of forts and roads, which seriously complicated the resistance by hill-men. In 1847, Russian troops took Salty and put up to 3 thousand hill-men to the sword, and in 1848 they took Gergebil and defeated Shamil by Akhty. In 1850–1852, a number of tribes were pacified, while Shamil suffered defeats in Dagestan and at Gekhi heights. Mouride movement began to fizzle out.

In the eastern part of the empire, the 1820s and 1830s saw the steady advance south of the forward forts of Siberian Line. After advancing by 600–700 kilometers, the line reached the drylands of Betpak-Dala (north-west of Lake Balkhash). The 'Middle' confederation of Kazakh tribes fully accepted allegiance to Russia. New fortresses built in Kazakh grasslands were Kokchetav and Karkaralinsk (1824), Akmolinsk (in 1830, today's Nur-Sultan, the capital of Kazakhstan), Sergiopol' (1831), Atbasarskaya (1845), Ulutavskaya (1846), and Kopal (1847). The situation along the Siberian Line was calm. By contrast, to the west of it, along the Orenburg Line, late 1830s witnessed attacks on Russian forts from rebellious 'Junior' Kazakh confederation backed and incited by Khiva Khanate. In December 1839, the governor of Orenburg, Count Perovsky with a detachment of 3 thousand set out to attack Khiva, but severe weather and illnesses forced him to turn around a little bit short of the Aral Sea. In 1845, the Orenburg Line was pushed further south to the rivers of Irgiz and Turgay where eponymous fortresses were built, and the Aral Sea flotilla was built in 1847. At this time, Russian border ran (moving east to west) from Lake Zaysan to Lake Issyk-Kul', River Chu, and thence to the Aral Sea and to Fort Novoalexandrovsk on the Caspian coast (built in 1834–1846). In late May 1853, Count Perovsky with 5 thousand men and 36 guns advanced on the fortress of Ak-Mechet (today's Kyzyl-Orda in Kazakhstan). Located close to where Syrdarya River empties into the Aral, the fortress held key to routes deep into Central Asia proper. After a five-day assault, the fortress fell on July 28. Renamed Fort Perovsky, this fortress anchored the new Syrdarya defense line, which ran along the northern bank of Syrdarya River. On December 18, its garrison of a thousand men repelled the 12 thousand strong party of attackers from Kokand. Finally, in the Far East, Amur expedition of 1849–1854 under admiral Nevelskoy reached the mouth of Amur River, where Russian flag was planted on August 1, 1850.

1848 was the year of multiple European revolutions which threatened the very foundations on which the Holy Alliance was built. Nicholas remained true to the principle of inviolability of legitimate rule. In the autumn of 1848, he put the army on the war footing in expectation of forthcoming struggles with Europe's revolutionaries. Austria found itself in a particularly critical situation: while conducting war with the Kingdom of Sardinia in Italy, it was shaken by revolutionary events and faced a real threat of secession by Hungary (which declared its independence). Emperor Ferdinand abdicated, and the new emperor, Francis-Joseph pleaded for Russian help. True to his obligations as an ally, Nicholas sent an army of 120 thousand to the rescue.

In April 1849, a railway was used to move from Krakow to Vienna general Panyutin's division, which became the crack part of Austrian troops. In summer, Russian troops under Paskevich marched overland, crossed the Dukla Pass and entered Hungary. On July 3, his vanguard clashed with Hungarians at Waitzen. On July 21 in the vicinity of Debrecen, the vanguard of Hungarian army was crushed, but the main forces slipped away into Banat chased by General Rudiger's corps. On August 1, 1849, a Hungarian army of 31 thousand capitulated at Vilagosz (now Siria in Romania). In Transylvania, Russian troops under General Luders (using Wallachia as operational base) defeated Hungarians in June and took Hermannstadt (today's Sibiu in Romania). On July 19 and 20, the Hungarians were defeated again at Segesvar and Kelnek (Calnic). After a series of battles by Hermannstadt (July 25) and Mühlbach (present-day Sebes in Romania) (July 30), Hungarian army led by Bem was wiped out, its remnants surrendering on August 6.

The Hungarian campaign involved the total of 170 thousand Russian troops. While battlefield casualties were negligible (708 dead), the epidemic of cholera took the heavy toll of 11 thousand dead. Yet, the chivalrous act by the Russian emperor and his faithfulness as an ally were hardly appreciated by Austria. Even though Russia saved the Austrian Empire from dissolution, in a mere four years it was repaid with a monstrous ingratitude. Ever since that time, Austria was unfailingly hostile to Russian moves in the Balkans and often thwarted Russia's search for a favorable solution to the Eastern Question. It was that stance by Austria that created the fateful alignment of powers in Europe which sixty-something years later was to erupt in World War I.

In 1850, a conflict flared up between the Orthodox and Catholic churches regarding the use of holy places in Jerusalem and Bethlehem (in Ottoman-ruled Palestine). The Orthodox were backed by Russia and the Catholics by France. The Sultan chose to back France which has always been far more friendly to the Ottomans and had no unresolved territorial issues with them. At the same time, following the turbulent European events in the 1840s, Russia lost the lead position on the continent that it enjoyed after 1815, nor did it have the same leverage against Turkey as in the early 1830s. The mission to Turkey under Prince Menshikov was sent to make them recognize Russia's right to be the protector of Orthodox communities in the Ottoman Empire and to recognize Russian Orthodox church privileges in the Holy Land. It failed. Nicholas hoped that in this standoff with France and Turkey he could count on Britain (in view of its traditional hostility to France that was recently compounded with the assumption of power by Napoleon III). Yet, Britain was far more concerned with the tangible prospect of partition of Ottoman Empire – something that could only tremendously strengthen Russia's hand in the Near East. That is why it preferred to join forces with France against Russia. When Russia moved its troops into the Danubian principalities, Anglo-French navy sailed into the Sea of Marmara. Emboldened by this open support, on September 14, 1853, Turkey declared war on Russia in the bid to regain all the territories it lost. So began what came to be known as the Crimean War.

In late 1853, hostilities unfolded along the Danube without either side prevailing. But on November 18 the Russian fleet under P. Nakhimov roundly defeated the Turkish fleet in the Bay of Sinop. In the Caucasus, the Turks' main force of 40 thousand advanced from Kars on Alexandropol, where it was opposed by a detachment of 11 thousand under Prince Bebutov. Following the battle on November 2, the Turks retreated beyond the Arpachay River (left tributary of Aras). Another Turkish force of 18 thousand advanced against Ahaltsikh (defended by 7 thousand Russians under Prince Andronikov) but it was routed on November 12. On November 19, Bebutov dealt the final blow to the Turkish army at Bashkadyklar. In the Northern Caucasus, Shamil found new heart with the start of the war and tried to break through into Georgia, but was repulsed and could do no more harm.

By the start of 1854 campaign, the Army of the Danube under Prince M. Gorchakov was reinforced to 140 thousand men. Another 120 thousand were deployed in the Caucasus, 45 thousand protected the Black Sea coasts, 105 thousand were deployed in Poland, and 125 thousand protected the Baltic coast. It was increasingly clear that a large-scale war will now develop in the west. Russia rejected Anglo-French ultimatum to withdraw troops from Danubian principalities. On March 14, Russian troops crossed the Danube and took Isakchi, Tulcha, and Machin. On May 6, they laid siege to Silistria, but withdrew back beyond the Danube in June. In turn, 30 thousand Turks crossed from their side of the Danube by Giurgiu and planned to march on Bucharest, but were defeated by the force under General Soimonov. By that time, the events took a very poor turn for Russia, and the window of opportunity for decisive operations in the Danube basin was lost. Britain and France declared war on Russia on March 15–16 and started moving their troops to the Balkans, while their fleets entered the Black Sea. Austria took an openly hostile stance by amassing troops along its border with Danubian principalities, in the rear of Russian troops.

These circumstances forced Russia to withdraw from Moldavia and Wallachia in July and August, and those principalities were duly occupied by the Austrians. For the first time in a century and a half Russia found itself isolated in Europe and forced to stand up to the coalition of Turkey, Britain, France, and Sardinia alone. In summer, Anglo-French fleet blocked naval fortresses of Kronstadt and Sveaborg in the Baltic. In the White Sea, the British shelled Solovetsky monastery, and on the Murman Coast they burned down the town of Kola. In August, Anglo-French squadron put ashore a landing party and shelled Petropavlovsk-Kamchatsky, but was repulsed. In May and July of 1854, the Turks suffered several defeats in Abkhazia and near Bayazet where they threatened Erivan. The big battle between the main Turkish (57 thousand) and Russian (18 thousand) forces took place on July 24 at Kuruk-Dara, and the Turks were roundly defeated.

On September 4, Anglo-French (55 thousand) and Turkish (7 thousand) troops landed by Yevpatoria in the Crimea. What Prince Menshikov had in the Crimea was the 6th corps of 33 thousand men. In September 8 battle at river Alma they were defeated and retreated to Bakhchisaray. Allied troops approached Sebastopol, and on September 28 they started building siege works. After the ships of Black Sea fleet were scuttled to prevent the enemy access to inner harbor, the fortress garrison grew to 16 thousand, and later to 32 thousand men. The defense of Sebastopol was led by Vice Admiral V. Kornilov and Admiral P. Nakhimov, while E. Totleben was in charge of defensive works. In early October, reinforcements from the Army of the Danube started arriving to the Crimea. In the battle by Balaklava on October 13, the outcome favored the Russians, but in a big battle by Inkerman on October 24 Russian troops were defeated and failed to relieve the siege of Sebastopol. By early 1855, Russian troops in the Crimea were brought up to 100 thousand men, and those of the allies to 120 thousand (80 thousand French, 15 thousand British, and 25 thousand Turkish). In February, Prince M. Gorchakov replaced Menshikov as commander-in-chief. But on February 19, 1855, Emperor Nicholas passed away, and his death largely predetermined the outcome of the war.

By early May, allied forces grew to 170 thousand (100 thousand French, 25 thousand British, 28 thousand Turkish, and 15 thousand from the Kingdom of Sardinia) opposed by 110 thousand Russians (46 thousand of them in besieged Sebastopol). In May, the allies' landing parties seized Kerch and laid waste to Anapa, Genichesk, Berdyansk, and Mariupol. Repeated assaults on Sebastopol on May 10, 22, and 26 succeeded in seizing some defensive works. On June 6, the allies attacked in force (40 thousand men), but were repulsed. On August 4, Gorchakov sent some of his forces (31 thousand men) to attack 40 thousand French and Sardinian troops by Chernaya Rechka (Black River) but they were beaten back and suffered heavy casualties. On August 27, Anglo-French troops unleashed a new all-out assault on Sebastopol. They were repulsed everywhere except the heights of Malakoff (seized by the French), but the city's garrison lost over a quarter of its strength. After that, Gorchakov decided to abandon Sebastopol, and on August 28–29 Russian troops crossed the harbor over floating bridges to the northern side. On October 3, the French seized Kinburn fortress at the mouth of the Dnieper. With that, hostilities in the Crimea ended. In the Caucasus, the new commander-in-chief General N. Muraviev besieged Kars (August 1). The assault on September 17 failed, but the fortress surrendered on November 12.

Peace treaty was signed in Paris on March 18, 1856. Russia suffered almost no territorial losses (with the exception of the Danube's delta and the coastal strip of Bessarabia), but it lost its status of the official protector of Serbia and Danubian principalities as well as the right to have military ships, fortresses, and arsenals on the Black Sea.

System of government and military-economic potential

During the reign of Nicholas I, the system of government underwent only partial changes. One important step was the transformation of His Majesty's Own Chancellery. In 1826, it became just one more body of central government. The chancellery was divided into four sections (the fifth was added in 1836 and the sixth in 1842). Section 1 inherited the functions of the erstwhile chancellery. It handled the ministers' reports, prepared draft decrees, and from 1830s it served as civil service personnel department – in 1846–1858, a special Inspectorate that operated as part of this section handled hiring and firing, and service promotions of all civil servants.

Section 2 dealt with codification of laws. By the 1830s, the team led by Count M. Speransky completed the enormous work of compilation and chronological arrangement of all the official acts issued from 1649 to December of 1825. That's how Russia's first 'Complete Digest of Laws' was born. It was published in 45 volumes (31 thousand acts). Volumes of the second 'Complete Digest' covered the period from 1825 and were published annually (the final, 55th volume came out in 1883 and covered acts promulgated through February 1881). That aside, in 1832 there was published the 'Code of Laws of the Russian Empire' that included only the legislation still in effect. Its updated editions came out in 1842 and 1857, and annual compilations were published in between editions. Other similar publications were the 'Code of Military Statutes' (1838) and the 'Code of Criminal Penalties and Correctional Punishment' (adopted in 1845).

Section 3 dealt with safeguarding the system of government and assumed the functions of several predecessor agencies. Its remit included cases of lese majesty, cases involving religious schismatics, cases of abuse of office, and complaints by peasants against their owners. It also acted as counterintelligence office responsible for surveillance of foreigners, investigation of accidents, review of various complaints of alleged persecution, and censorship. Attached to this section was the special Corps of Gendarmes commanded by section chief (during Nicholas' reign this position was held by Count A. Benkendorf and Count A. Orlov, and the Corps headquarters chief from 1839 to 1856 was L. Dubelt). The country was divided into 8 gendarmerie circuits.

The other sections dealt with more specific issues. Section 4 was in charge of charities and women's education (it was built on the foundation of personal chancellery of Empress Maria Feodorovna, the wife of Paul I). Section 5 prepared the reform of state peasants' status and section 6 worked on the administrative reform for the Caucasus.

That aside, special 'supreme committees' were set up to prepare some particularly important statutes, to govern specific peripheral areas, or to develop solutions to the 'peasant issue' (i.e. the abolition of serfdom). The committees were temporary but led by the empire's highest officials and endowed with very wide authority. Such was the Special Secret Committee (1826–1832) which dealt with demarcation of jurisdiction between government bodies, the Permanent Secret Committee (responsible for censorship from 1848), and the Secret Committee on Schismatics and Apostates from Orthodoxy (1817–

1855). Some others administered frontier areas: the Siberian Committee (1821–1838 and 1852–1864), the Caucasus Committee (1840–1882), the Committee on Kingdom of Poland (1831–1841), and the Committee of Western Governorates (1831–1838). Among committee chairmen there were such grandees as D. Buturlin, Prince I. Vasilchikov, Prince A. Golitsyn, Count P. Kiselev, Baron M. Korf, Prince V. Kochubey, Prince A. Menshikov, Count M. Speransky, and Count A. Chernyshov.

In 1841, the Senate added two more departments located in Warsaw (one for civil and another for criminal cases). In 1848, what used to be a Senate office was expanded into Department of Heraldry dealing with cases of conferring nobility and nobility registers. The Synod acquired the directorate for facility management, directorate for religious education, and chief prosecutor's chancellery. As to the central executive agencies, the remit of the Main Directorate of Roads and Communications was expanded to include management of public buildings, and in 1837 the Directorate for Revision of Government Accounts became simply the State Inspection (with the status of a ministry). In 1826, there was created the Ministry of Imperial Court and Properties (since 1842 it included the Chancellery of Honors), which was also in charge of the Academy of Fine Arts, theaters, museums, and some research institutions. In 1837, there was created the Ministry of State Properties that was in charge of state lands (part of it was a Forestry Department with its corps of forest wardens). In 1843, there was created the Main Directorate of Government Stud Farms (in 1848–56 it was part of the Ministry of State Properties). State Commercial Bank was set up in 1847.

Local government system saw no substantial changes. The number of general-governorates grew to 10 in 1850 (they covered 12 'regular' governorates). The decree of 1837 enhanced governors' powers. A new practice was to replace civilian governors with military ones who commanded troops stationed in their governorates as well.

Russia's armed forces remained Europe's largest. Early in this reign, the army (including irregulars) had 1055 thousand men, and by 1850 – 1317 thousand. By the end of Crimean War, the number of men under arms reached 2190 thousand plus 370 thousand in militias. According to 1831 Order of Recruitment, the country was divided into two parts with annual recruit drafts alternated between them. The usual quota was up to 7 recruits per thousand men, and in years of stepped-up recruitment that ratio reached 7 to 10 men (with recruitment pool of 6.5 million men, that translates into annual recruitment of 45 to 65 thousand). In 1834, the term of service was reduced from 25 to 20 years, after which a soldier was considered to be in reserve for 5 more years. In 1839, the term of service was reduced to 19 years.

A wide-ranging military reform was launched in 1833. In place of 33 divisions with 194 regiments the army now had 30 divisions (of two brigades each) and the total of 110 regiments (10 guards', 16 grenadiers, and 84 infantry). The regiments remained with those same divisions until 1917. Divisions numbered from 1 through 18 made up six infantry corps (of 3 divisions each), divisions numbered 19 through 21 were the Corps of the Caucasus. Additionally, there was a Guards' Corps and a Grenadier Corps. The remaining divisions were not assigned to any corps. Divisions stationed in some borderlands (number 22 through 24) consisted of combat battalions rather than regiments. By the late 1840s, there were 96 such battalions, five to eight of which made up a brigade (18 Georgian, 16 Black Sea, 13 Caucasus, 22 Finnish, 16 Siberian, and 11 Orenburg battalions). From the 1830s, there were introduced riflemen battalions distributed between corps. Smoothbore capsule percussion rifles were adopted by the army in 1845, but some troops were still armed with flintlocks. Riflemen were armed with short rifled rifles.

In 1833, the number of cavalry regiments was reduced from 75 to 52 (8 cuirassier, 8 dragoon, 22 lancer, and 14 hussar). They were grouped into 7 light cavalry divisions (each of two lancer and two hussar regiments), 2 lancer divisions, 2 dragoon, and 2 cuirassier divisions. The guards retained one cuirassier and one light cavalry division. Thus, there was a total of 13 divisions and one special brigade. In turn, those were grouped into 3 cavalry corps and a guards' cavalry corps. By 1853, there were 59 regiments (12 cuirassier, 11 dragoon, 20 lancer, and 16 hussar), which were grouped into 15 divisions of 4 regiments each. Two cuirassier divisions formed the 1st reserve cavalry corps, two dragoon ones made up the 2nd corps, and two guards' divisions – the 3rd corps. The other nine divisions were attached to infantry corps. The cavalry numbered 95–110 thousand men.

Prior to 1831–1833 reforms, the artillery had 4 grenadier and 21 field brigades (185.5 batteries of 8 pieces each). In 1833, they were rearranged into 21 brigades of regular artillery and 7 brigades of mounted artillery for the total of 10 artillery divisions attached to army corps (6 infantry, 3 cavalry, and one of the grenadiers). Another 3 brigades (in Finland and the Caucasus) were not made part of divisions. A battery had 12 guns. Equipment included 6-pounder and 12-pounder guns and 1838 type 'unicorn' howitzers. In peacetime, the army's summary firepower amounted to 1140 guns and in wartime to 1446. Siege artillery had 286 guns. The artillery numbered 80–100 thousand men. Engineering troops (17–20 thousand men) consisted of 9 sapper battalions (made into 3 brigades) and 2 battalions of mounted pioneers.

By the early 1850s, there were 10 Cossack hosts. The biggest, Don Host had to raise 34 mounted regiments and 4.5 batteries in peacetime and 58 regiments and 14 batteries in wartime. Kuban (Black Sea) Host's obligation was 4 infantry battalions, an artillery company and a battery (12 infantry regiments, 1 artillery battalion and 4 batteries in wartime). Cossacks of the Caucasus Line owed 18 cavalry regiments and 3 batteries, Orenburg Host – 10 regiments, the Ural Host – 1 artillery battalion and 12 cavalry regiments. All the other Cossack groups (Danubian, Azov, Astrakhan, of the Siberian Line, Trans-Baikal, and Siberian town regiments) taken together owed 28 regiments. Ethnically non-Russian units included Balaklava Greek battalion, Georgian infantry force, 4 cavalry regiments and a squadron of Caucasus hill-men, a cavalry squadron of Crimean Tatars, 12 *sotnias* of Dagestan's standing militia, and a force of Bashkirs and Mishar Tatars (the total of 37.5 thousand).

Border Guard was established in 1837 under the aegis of Ministry of Finance. By the 1850s, it numbered 11 brigades (3.6 thousand men). An important step was the transformation in 1832 of His Majesty's Quartermaster Train into the new group of officers of the General Staff (about 300 men) who were trained in the special academy created for the purpose.

Immediately upon his accession, Nicholas declared that Russia must have the third largest navy (after Britain and France). From 1827 to 1844, there were built 41 ships of the line, 33 frigates, 38 brigantines, and 42 transports. Steamships were being built as well, but they were paddlewheels with poor seaworthiness (reliable naval steamships appeared with screw-propelled designs). Nonetheless, in 1843–1853 there were built 20 steamer-frigates alone. The first screw-propelled steamers appeared in Europe in 1844 and in Russia in 1848. By 1853, the Navy had 457 vessels: 42 ships of the line, 24 frigates, 16 steamer-frigates, 46 small steamers, 38 brigantines, 44 transports, 105 row galleys, and 142 others

(20 more ships were under construction). The navy had 48 fleet companies (including one of the guards) of 10 units each (thus one fleet company had a thousand men). Three fleet companies added up to a brigade, and 3 brigades to a division (the Baltic fleet had three divisions, and Black Sea fleet had two).

The number of army officers stood at about 30 thousand. In 1831, it was reduced to 25 thousand, but by late 1840s it regained its former strength (by the end of Crimean War, there were 40.4 thousand officers plus 5.6 thousand in the militia).

The system of military education changed significantly under Nicholas. In the 1830s and 1840s, the network of cadet schools was much expanded. A new Cadet School for Young Orphans (named after Alexander I) was opened in 1830 at Tsarskoye Selo (Tsar's Village in Russian) to serve as a prep school for future admission into a regular cadet school. That same year, Tula and Tambov military colleges were converted into cadet schools. There also appeared military colleges of Cossack Hosts (for Ural Host in 1832 in Uralsk and for the Cossacks of the Siberian Line in 1826 in Omsk), and Orenburg Neplyuev military college (established in 1825) was converted into a cadet school in 1844. Novgorod cadet school named after Count Arakcheev was created in 1834. More new cadet schools soon followed: Polotsk in 1835, Poltava (named after Peter the Great) in 1840, Brest (named after Crown Prince Alexander) in 1841, Orel (named after Bakhtin) in 1843, Voronezh (named after Grand Duke Mikhail) in 1845, and Moscow 2nd cadet school in 1849. Alexander's Orphanage Institute in Moscow was transformed into the Cadet School for Orphans. Finally, Kiev Cadet School for Young Children (named after Grand Duke Vladimir) opened in January 1852. As early as 1836, all the cadet schools received a uniform curriculum and organizational structure. All the courses were broken down into preparatory-level ones (1 year of study), general military education (5 years), and specialized training (3 years).

All cadet schools belonged to one of two categories: class one schools (with a 9-year course of study) graduated commissioned officers, while those of class two (with a 5-year course of study) prepared entrants for class one schools.[13] In 1825–1856, all the cadet schools graduated 17653 officers. By 1854, total enrollment in all these military schools stood at 8288 (in the School of Pages – 150, in School of Guards Warrant Officers and Cavalry *Junkers* – 228, in Nobility Regiment – 1000). College of Military Auditors was established in 1832 and graduated 201 officers by 1850. Artillery College (known from 1849 as Mikhail's Artillery College) graduated 300 officers in 1826–1855. The Main Engineering College (bearing the name of Nicholas I from 1855) graduated 1036 officers from 1819 to 1855.

---

[13] Class one schools were the 1st and 2nd Cadet Schools in St.Petersburg , the 1st and 2nd Moscow Cadet Schools, Finland Cadet School, Pavel's Cadet School (rebranded from the Imperial Military Orphanage and named after Paul I) in St.Petersburg, Cadet School for Orphans named after Alexander in Moscow, Novgorod Cadet School named after Count Arakcheev, Orel Cadet School named after Bakhtin, Voronezh Cadet School named after Mikhail, Polotsk Cadet School, Poltava Cadet School named after Peter, Brest Cadet School named after Alexander, Orenburg Cadet School named after Neplyuev, and Siberian Cadet School in Omsk. Other class one schools that graduated officers were the School of Pages, Nobility Regiment, School of Guards Warrant Officers and Cavalry *Junkers*. Class two schools were Cadet School for Young Children in Tsarskoye Selo, Tula Cadet School named after Alexander I, Tambov Cadet School, Kiev Cadet School named after Vladimir and young children section at the 1st Moscow Cadet School.

Finally, military academies were first created as the pinnacle of military education system. They provided continuing education for the most promising serving officers, especially those groomed for staff positions. The Emperor's Military Academy was opened in 1832 to train senior field commanders and staff officers. In 1855, it was renamed Nicholas General Staff Academy. In 1855, officer classes of Mikhail's Artillery College were transformed into Mikhail's Artillery Academy. At the same time, officer classes of Nicholas Engineering College were transformed into Nicholas Engineering Academy. Both had a two-year course of study and the same admission and graduation rules. In 1827, the Naval School added a 2-year course of study for serving officers (from 1831 the course lasted three years and officer classes later became Nicholas Naval Academy). In 1844, the College of Naval Architects was transformed into Naval Engineering College.

Even though the Industrial Revolution in Russia unfolded later than in the most advanced European nations, domestic industry still almost completely satisfied the needs of the armed forces. By the mid-century, Russia had about 15 thousand industrial enterprises, seven times more than at the start of the century. That number included some major privately-owned metallurgical and metalworking plants. Thus, the first plant (by brothers Butenop) of farm machinery and implements opened in Moscow as early as 1831. Mining industry continued to rely primarily on bonded and serf labor, but in manufacturing industries free hired labor accounted for 82% of the total. In 1844, production of flintlock rifles was discontinued, and new percussion action rifles (both smoothbore and rifled) of uniform 7.1 caliber were manufactured exclusively within Russia. By the early 1850s, the troops had enough of these new generation rifles, but the rifled (as opposed to smoothbore) kind were relatively few (by 1856, about 209 thousand were manufactured domestically and 9 thousand more imported). Just as in the French army, those were given to riflemen battalions. In the second quarter of 19th century, government mills in Tula, Sestroretsk, and Izhevsk manufactured the total of 1536 thousand rifles (including 267 thousand percussive action ones) and 40.5 thousand handguns. Production of field guns at this period was concentrated in St. Petersburg arsenal (the ones in Bryansk and Kiev repaired damaged guns, and the one in Kazan was shut down). From 1825 to 1850, 3181 guns were manufactured or restored, and a further 523 from 1852 to 1855. Iron guns and all artillery ordnance were manufactured at Mining Ministry mills: Alexandrovsky mill near Petrozavodsk, in Konchezero, Lugansk, Lipetsk, Kamensk, Yekaterinburg, Zlatoust, and around Mount Blagodat' (in the Urals). Ship guns came from Alexandrovsky mill, which produced 9093 of them from 1830 to 1850. A special Rocketry Manufactory was set up in St. Petersburg in 1826 (rocket artillery was widely used at the time), and in 1845–1855 it made 75 thousand rockets. Steamships were built at the shipping yards in St. Petersburg, Archangel, and Nikolaev. By the early 1850s, 46 steamers were built and 35 more purchased abroad. Their steam engines were built at Baird and Nobel plants in St. Petersburg.

Transportation system of the time consisted of pretty basic trunk roads connecting the country's key centers: St. Petersburg to Moscow and Warsaw, and Moscow to Yaroslavl and Nizhny Novgorod. The first railway (between St. Petersburg and Tsarskoye Selo) appeared in 1837. Construction of strategically important Warsaw–Vienna railway began in 1839, and the railway between Moscow and St. Petersburg was completed in 1843–1851. By 1855, Russia had 1045 kilometers of railways. Inland water transportation was quite important: by mid-century Russian rivers were plied by about 100 steamers. In 1843, Russia's first telegraph line (between St. Petersburg and Tsarskoye Selo) came into operation. Russian financial system was bolstered by monetary reform of 1839–1844 carried out by finance minister, Count Kankrin. The system centered on the silver ruble. Since there was too much paper money in circulation, it was recalled to be exchanged for new bank notes (3.5 to 1), which in turn, were freely interchangeable with silver coin. Russia consistently maintained a positive balance of foreign trade as its exports exceeded imports. European nations accounted for 90% of external trade, with Britain alone responsible for over a third of all exports and imports.

Chapter 9

Russian society in the first half of the 19th century

Throughout the first half of the century, there continued a rapid population growth sustained both by natural increase and annexation of new territories, especially the Kingdom of Poland and Grand Duchy of Finland. By 1815, the population stood at 46.3 million and by 1858 at 74.5 million. The majority still lived on the lands that were part of Russia even in mid-17th century (61.8% in 1815 and 54.8% in 1858). Russia's advantage in population size compared to major European countries became even more pronounced as it was now almost twice that of the next largest country, France (27.3 million at the start of the century and 34.9 at its midpoint). For Britain, the corresponding numbers are 11 and 21 million, for Spain 10.5 and 14.4 million, for Sweden 2.3 and 3.5 million. Population density steadily grew as well. From 2.7 persons per km^2 in 1815, it climbed to 4.1 in 1858 (from 8.7 to 12.4 in European Russia). Yet, in this regard Russia still dramatically differed from other European nations where population densities were higher by an order of magnitude (in 1820, it stood at 66 persons per km^2 in Britain, 57 in France, 48 in Prussia, and 38 in Austria). The same contrast applies to the percentage of urban population. While in 1800 Russia's level of urbanization (8.5%) was comparable to that of Western Europe (9.5% in France, 4.4% in Austria, 21.3% in Britain), by 1850 it even shrank somewhat to 7.2%, just as it climbed steeply elsewhere (to 14.4% in France, 26.5% in Prussia, 39.5% in Britain). Only Austria fared worse than Russia (5.8%).

Following the annexation of new lands in the west, in the Caucasus and in the drylands beyond the Urals, ethnic composition of the population showed a further decline of the proportion of Russians (including Little Russians and White Russians), even though it still exceeded two thirds of the total – 68.3% in 1857. The Poles remained the largest minority (5.2%), followed by the Jews (2.7%), Finns (2.2%), Estonians and Latvians (2.2%), Lithuanians (1.6%), Germans (1.1%), Moldovans (1%), Tatars and Bashkirs (3.4%), Kazakhs (2.2%), the Chuvash (0.7%), and Mordvins (0.9%).

Social structure of Russian society experienced further changes driven by continued expansion of the machinery of state administration and the armed forces. While the number of nobility grew significantly, the number of landowning nobility remained essentially unchanged. If the comparison is made for the same territory, between the late 1770s and 1833 their number grew from 70 to 72.1 thousand (with essentially the same breakdown by social strata: 54% owned less than 20 serf peasants ('souls' in the parlance of the time), 28% owned 20 to 100 souls, and 18% more than 100 souls). By contrast, the number of nobility in civil service grew severalfold: while in 1804 ranking bureaucrats numbered 13.2 thousand, by 1847 they numbered 61.5 thousand. The officer class grew more than twofold as well: from 12–15 thousand at the start of the century to about 30 thousand by its middle. It is these two occupational groups that were responsible for the growth of nobility numbers. In the first half of 19th century, about 26% of officers were not of gentle birth, while among the bureaucracy that proportion stood at 60%.

Other than climbing through service ranks, one more path to nobility lay through bestowal of any Russian order (decoration with an order was not an exclusive privilege of the serving class, members of the clergy and merchants qualified as well). The oldest two orders were those of St. George and St. Vladimir. A new order of St. Anne (which was considered junior to the original two) was added in the late 18th century. After the incorporation of Kingdom of Poland, two Polish orders were added: order of the White Eagle and order of St. Stanislaus (while the former was awarded only to the highest aristocracy and therefore did not help expand nobility ranks, the latter – the most junior in the hierarchy of orders – was awarded quite generously).

As a result, the inflow of commoners into the noble estate was quite high. From 1836 to 1843, almost two thirds (64.7%) of those who reached class 8 of the Table of Ranks (which conferred hereditary nobility) were commoners by birth. In the period from 1825 to 1845 alone, service or award of an order created 20 thousand new hereditary nobility members. It was felt that inflow of commoners into the nobility became excessive and should be curtailed. The manifesto of June 11, 1845 raised the plank for gaining hereditary nobility (even though Nicholas I long vacillated on this decision which he saw as an infringement on the privileges of the officer class that he so loved and considered to be 'his own people'). From then on, in the military service hereditary nobility was conferred with gaining the first staff officer rank (class 8 of the Table of Ranks, or major), while in the civil service it was that of state councilor (class 5). Officer ranks from 14 to 9 now conferred only personal (that is to say, non-hereditary) nobility (still, the basic principle of all officer class being nobility was not violated). Similarly, civil service ranks from 9 to 6 now brought personal nobility only, while lower ranks (14 through 10) gave one the status of 'citizen of honor'. It was also decided that only the order of St. Anne 1st class confers hereditary nobility (in 1855 the same ruling was made regarding the order of St. Stanislaus). Therefore, after 1845, only the lowest three civil service ranks (three because the practice of that time was to skip classes 13 and 11 altogether) did not confer any nobility (but made one a citizen of honor). But as a practical matter, these junior civil servants and the next higher strata of non-hereditary nobility were the same social group. Since the length of service for climbing to class 9 was typically from 9 to 12 years, eventually almost every civil servant gained it. (Also, while personal nobility gave fewer privileges than hereditary, the legislation specifically emphasized that both are part of one noble estate). The measures described above did not reduce the inflow of commoners by much though.

Only less than a half of the noble estate could afford the lifestyle traditionally considered proper for a nobleman's dignity. In the first half of the century, such 'proper' lifestyle required an annual income of 300–400 rubles (and twice that in the capital cities). That was the income of only senior bureaucrats and officers of class 8 and above (if all bonus payments, food and housing allowances, etc. are included), who accounted for less than a third of the total serving class. For landowning nobility, 'proper' income (of 400–800 rubles) required having a midsize estate, and such landowners were fewer than half of the total. The incomes of junior civil servants and small landowners were half of that required threshold or less. Family size of petty landowning nobility was typically the same as in peasant households, while junior bureaucrats were for the most part single or had few children. Material well-being of most non-serving noblemen was not significantly different from that of an average peasant family. Agricultural productivity of the time was such that

114

'value added' could support one non-working person per ten working peasants. Yet, according to the census of 1834, 45.9% of landowning nobility had fewer than 20 'souls', while another 14% had no landed estate as such. By 1850, out of the total number of 253 thousand hereditary nobility, 148.7 thousand had no serfs at all, 24 thousand had fewer than 10 'souls', and 109.4 thousand tilled the land themselves. The latter group included even some descendants of ancient princely lineages. From that, one can say that already by mid-century there was a clear trend of the nobility evolving into an 'honorable' estate. By 1853, the absolute majority of civil servants owned no land. That was true even of a half of senior bureaucrats of rank 5 and of 32% of top bureaucrats with ranks 1 through 4.

In 1831, qualification requirements for voting in nobility assembly elections were raised. Although all nobility (including non-hereditary) had the right to attend, to be elected as officials, or to vote on procedural matters, the right of electing officials was restricted to those who had at least 100 'souls' or over 3300 hectares of land without peasants. That meant the topmost stratum of landowners. Smaller nobility had to form pools that collectively met those qualification requirements, so that a pool could appoint one voting representative.

By the mid-century, clergy remained a closed estate little changed from before. By 1830, 47% of all priests were sons of priests, 20% – sons of deacons, and 33% – sons of sextons. The breakdown for deacons was 24%, 22%, and 54%, and for sextons 21%, 9%, and 70%. Surplus children of clerical estates spilled into secular lives (they accounted for 20% of all bureaucrats, 35% of teachers and professors, and 30% of medical doctors). From the start of the century and until the end of the empire, the composition of the Synod remained unchanged: it included up to 10 senior clerics from the 'black' (i.e celibate) clergy and 2 representatives of the 'white' (or marrying) clergy (senior chaplain of the army and navy and the emperor's confessor). Diocesan governments came to be dominated by 'white' clergy. The level of educational attainment of the clergy had significantly improved. As early as 1808, the number of students in the seminaries reached 29 thousand, so that by 1835, 42.5% of priests and 4.2% of deacons had theological education. Yet, parish priests remained unsalaried, and their incomes were about half of those of junior officers and bureaucrats. The composition of parish clergy remained unchanged throughout the period: 31% were priests, 14% deacons, and 55% sextons. In absolute numbers, they were about 110 thousand.[14] In 1850, the whole clerical estate (black and white clergy and their male children) numbered 281 thousand. In this period, the clergy was made eligible for decoration with imperial orders for their ministering service, and those awarded became hereditary nobility while remaining in clerical estate and continuing service as clergy. In 1801, priests and deacons were made exempt from corporal punishment in the sentencing by secular courts (previously, such exemption existed only for penalties imposed by the church itself).

This period witnessed significant changes in the status of urban population. In 1832, the category of 'prominent citizens' was abolished (by 1820, they were only 28 persons, and about 150 including family members), while there was instituted a new estate of 'citizens of honor' defined on a different principle. Just as nobility status, honorable citizenship could be both hereditary and personal. Children of non-hereditary nobility and

---

[14] In 1824, there were 34.1 thousand priests, 15.1 thousand deacons, and 59.7 thousand sextons. In 1836 the corresponding numbers were 32.4 thousand, 15.2 thousand, and 58.7 thousand for the total of 106.3 thousand.

of the clergy with seminary or academy education became hereditary citizens of honor by default. Another group eligible to become citizens of honor were merchants of the 1st and 2nd ranks who were members of their merchant ranks for, respectively, 10 and 20 years (without interruptions), or were decorated with an order (from 1826, award of an order no longer gave merchants hereditary nobility). This privilege extended to the merchants' children, and such professionals as performers, artists, and scientists. Personal honorable citizenship was enjoyed by default by children of the clergy without a seminarian education and by all graduates of the institutions of higher learning. Citizens of honor paid no direct taxes, were not subject to recruit duty, and were exempt from corporal punishment. For decades, their numbers remained quite small: by 1840 there were 2.4 thousand such citizens, and by 1850 – 7.2 thousand. On those two dates, they made up only 0.2% and 0.4% of urban population respectively.

The number of all townsmen taken together grew fast and steadily throughout the first half of the century. With Poland and Finland excluded, it stood at 776.5 thousand (males only) in 1811, 1110.5 thousand in 1825, 1378.7 thousand in 1835, 1592.8 thousand in 1840, and 1887.1 thousand in 1850. Yet, the number of merchants declined sharply between 1812 and 1825 due both to many bankruptcies during the war of 1812, and to the granting of the right to engage in trade to peasants. While in 1811 there were 122.9 thousand merchants, in 1815 there were only 81.4 thousand, and in 1824 – 52 thousand. Even in 1835 they were fewer than before the war – 119.3 thousand. By 1840, the number of merchants rose to 136.4 thousand, and by 1850 to 175.5 thousand. Percentage of merchants in all urban population was estimated at 16% in 1811 (only 1.5% for those of the top two ranks), at 12% in 1815, at 5.6% in 1824, at 8.6% in 1835 (0.7% for the two top ranks), 9.2% (0.5%) in 1840, and 7% (0.5%) in 1850. In the middle of 1820s, townsmen lost their exclusive right to engage in commerce and industry in full. People of all estates now acquired that right by simply buying a license. By the early 1830s, peasants already made up 7% of the holders of such licenses and noblemen 0.4%, and by 1850 those proportions stood at 14% and 0.6%.

By the middle of the century, the composition of peasantry underwent significant change. According to the census of 1857, the proportion of state peasants grew substantially at the expense of all other categories. Even by 1811, 'economic' (former monastery) peasants accounted for only 8.5% of the total, and in 1815 they were relisted as state peasants. Appanage peasants accounted for only 3.9%, landowners' serf peasants and bonded factory peasants together accounted for 47.3%, and state peasants became the largest group – 48.8%. The migration from peasant estate into merchants and other townsmen groups intensified, in 1816–1842 it was achieved by 450 thousand peasants.

Starting early in the century, there were issued many decrees that expanded the peasants' rights. In December 1801, all commoners and peasants, except landowners' serfs, were allowed to freely buy and sell unsettled land. February 1803 decree 'On the Free Tillers of the Soil' allowed landowners to manumit their serfs based on mutual agreement (by 1825, 47 thousand were manumitted under that decree). In 1804, peasants in Baltic governorates received their land allotments as full hereditary property, while tax and other obligations were made proportionate to the income from those allotments. Market sales of serfs were banned in 1808, in 1809–1822 landowners lost the right to exile serfs to Siberia, in 1816 it was forbidden to buy serfs for work in factories, mills, and mines, and in 1816–1819 serfdom was altogether abolished in the Baltic governorates. In 1812, the peasants were granted the right to engage in commerce, in 1818 the right to engage in industry, and in 1827 the right to own their own houses in cities. Sales of serfs without land or sales splitting family households were banned in 1833. In 1840, the owners of mills and factories were allowed to manumit their bonded peasants. The decree of 1843 offered government support to peasants who were willing to resettle in Siberia. In 1845–1847, peasant obligations in western governorates were fixed at set levels, and landowners' rights vis-à-vis their peasants were restricted. In 1848, all landowners' peasants were allowed to buy land (with landowner's permission and in his name). In the course of the first half of the century, the percentage of well-off peasants grew from 10 to 23%, the proportion of poor one's went down from 42 to 24%, and of those of average means grew from 48 to 53%.

The period witnessed systematization and further development in all areas of law. Published under Nicholas I in 1832, the 'Code of Laws of the Russian Empire' regimented all aspects of life in Russian society. For the most part, it confirmed preexisting laws and acts, or gave legal validity to already established practices. But the 'Code' also ushered in changes in various areas of the law. The age of civil legal capacity was raised to 21 years. The 'Code' finally enshrined the right of full, exclusive, and hereditary private ownership of all forms of real estate (first and foremost, land). By that time, such a right was already enjoyed by all social groups except bonded peasants. Length of ownership was added as a legitimate way of acquiring property: a person who owned a given thing for 10 years became its proprietor regardless of how it was initially acquired.

In the area of obligations law, it was defined what agreements and contracts were acceptable only in written form. Four ways of contract enforcement were defined as well (suretyship, forfeiture, and pledging as security of real estate or movable property). Real estate swaps were forbidden. Lease of real estate was allowed for the term not to exceed 12 years. Annualized interest rate on loans was capped at 6%. The first legal definition of agreement to sell (or forward contract) was of importance to commerce, especially foreign trade (one side took on the obligation to sell some goods or property to another at a preset price, with various forfeiture penalties in case of a violation).

In the area of laws on inheritance, the 'Code' of 1832 further broadened the discretion of a testator by allowing the bequest of any property (with the exception of primogeniture estates and nature preserve estates specifically defined in imperial decrees). Last wills and testaments made by the insane, underage persons, monks, those who committed suicide, and those stripped of estate rights were recognized legally invalid. Marriage age was raised from 15 to 18 for men and from 13 to 16 for women. Women received the right to freely dispose (sell, gift, etc.) of property received as dowry without a husband's consent. Entering marriage still required parental agreement (or that of trustees). For the serving class, it required permission from one's higher-ups, and for privately owned peasants – that of their owners. In 1845, a husband's right to inflict corporal punishment on his wife was abolished, and criminal penalties were introduced for parents inflicting bodily harm on their children.

In 1833, a new notion of 'conditional competency' was added to criminal law: criminals of ages 10 to 17 had their sentences reduced proportionate to 'degree of their competency'. With the enactment in 1845 of 'Code of Criminal Penalties and Correctional Punishment', the age of 'conditional competency' was limited to 10–13 years, but offenders of ages 14 through 20 still qualified for reduced sentences (provided they were not repeat offenders). The 'Code' classified all legally defined crimes into 150 varieties (out of 2035 articles in the Code, 32 were devoted to crimes against the faith, 19 to crimes against the state (lese majesty), 74 – to crimes against the system of government, 175 to abuses of office, 1415 to offences 'against the interests of the state and treasury', and 320 to crimes endangering individuals' lives, health, and rights).

The 'Code' of 1832 classified all punishments into 10 types by their severity and mode: capital punishment, political death, stripping of rights, corporal punishment, forced labor, exile, being made a recruit soldier, incarceration, monetary fine, and church penance. As per the 'Code' of 1845, 11 types of punishment (each further broken down by severity and length of term to be served) were subdivided into two categories: 4 were labeled 'criminal' punishments (meaning those where the offender was removed from society forever), and 7 were labeled 'correctional' punishments (where the removal from society was only temporary). All criminal punishments entailed stripping of rights. In the order of decreasing severity, the four types of 'criminal' punishment were execution, hard penal labor, exile to Siberia, and exile to the Caucasus. In 'correctional' punishments, type 1 involved Siberian exile (or whipping and service in a penal battalion in case of lower classes), type 2 – exile into other parts remote (or a term in the workhouse for the lower classes), type 3 – incarceration in a fortress (military brig), type 4 – incarceration in a 'house of correction', type 5 – exile (prison term in case of the lower classes), type 6 – short-term detention, type 7 – a reprimand, admonishment, and/or fines. For the privileged estates (nobility, clergy, and the top two classes of merchants), the first two kinds of correctional punishment also meant the loss of all special privileges (rank, decorations, the right to state service), the 3rd and 4th – some of them.

The Code of 1832 allowed capital punishment for crimes against the state and military crimes, as well as for looting during epidemics. The Code of 1845 abolished capital punishment for military crimes. Throughout the period, capital punishment was used very sparingly. Whipping came out of general use early in the century. In 1845, the limit for whipping and horsewhipping was set at 100 strokes (from 1851 a doctor's presence was mandatory). Hard penal servitude was a relatively rare sentence too: in 1834–1844 such sentences averaged 1320, and in 1846–1860 – 974 per year. Incarceration could take place in prisons, workhouses, and houses of correction, in temporary detention wards (founded in governorate seats in 1827), in penal battalions, and in military custody, or fortress brigs (if the crime did not impugn one's honor or suggest a dishonorable intent). Prisoners worked for 10–11 hours a day, were paid for their work, and were allowed to mess separately and have additional food brought to them. Total prison population of Russia stood at about 14 thousand in 1804 and 17 thousand in 1840. Of all the sentences in the years 1834–1845, criminal punishments were used in only 9% of the cases (3.6% hard penal labor and 5.4% exile). Out of 91% of sentences of correctional punishment, 44% were detention or lighter punishment. In 1846–1860, criminal punishments were prescribed in 8% of the cases (3% hard labor and 5% exile), while of the remaining 92% that were correctional punishments 50% were of the lighter kind. It should be kept in mind that in 1803–1860 fully 52% of all those on trial were exonerated, and the absolute majority of those convicted got off without incarceration.

Incidence of crime was extremely low in the first half of the century. In 1803–1808, the incidence of crimes (most of them petty) was 593 per 100 thousand population, in 1825–1830 it stood at 652, in 1831–1840 at 594, in 1841–1850 at 563, and in 1851–1860 at 516. During the first third of the century, it was 4 times lower than in France and 7.6 times lower than in Britain. Average annual number of the more common crimes in 1846–1857 stood at 109.6 thousand, including 4.2 thousand murders, 1.7 thousand cases of bodily harm, 0.6 thousand sex crimes, 1.6 thousand cases of robbery and banditry, 18.6 thousand cases of theft, and 3.3 thousand cases of fraud. In other words, crimes against individuals and personal property were very few, and the statistics were fully dominated by crimes against the state: 14.4 thousand against the system of government, 47 thousand against state property, 7.4 thousand abuses of office, 6.8 thousand offences against the faith, and almost no cases of lese majesty (10 cases per year). Russia of that period also had a notably low incidence of suicides – only 2.6 per 100 thousand population in 1831–1840. That compared to 5.4 in France, 6.3 in Britain, 7 in Prussia, and 3.2 in Austria.

On January 24, 1803, there was promulgated a general reform of educational system. Undertaken in tandem with administrative reform (creation of ministries), it had a huge impact on the future of public education in the country. All subsequent development of education was guided by the newly created Ministry of Public Education. The reform envisaged a fully integrated system of elementary, secondary and higher education relying on uniformity of educational institutions within each level. A significant proportion of urban population were literate at the time, but literate peasants were only 5% of the total.

Universities were not only the pinnacle of educational attainment, but were also given broad executive authority over secondary and elementary schools. In 1803, the whole country was divided into educational circuits, each anchored by a university. Standard university charter adopted on November 5, 1804 gave universities a broad autonomy (professor faculty elected the president, deans, inspectors, and facility managers). In a few brief years, several new universities were created in addition to the one in Moscow. Derpt (Yur'ev) university was restored in 1802 (it operated from 1632 to 1710 when Estland was annexed by Russia), Vilna university was restored in 1803 (previously, it operated from 1579 to 1773), Kazan university opened in 1804, and Kharkov university in 1805. Somewhat later, universities were opened in Warsaw (1816), St. Petersburg (in 1819 on the foundation of the Main Teacher College founded in 1804), Helsingfors (on the foundation of the Royal Academy of Abo relocated in 1827), and Kiev (1834, its official name was St. Vladimir university). Moscow University was much expanded with student body going from 215 in 1811 to 814 in 1831. In 1832, Vilna University was closed (in the aftermath of Polish rebellion) and converted into a Medical and Surgery Academy (relocated to Kiev in 1842, where it became the school of medicine at Kiev University) and Academy of Divinity (relocated to St. Petersburg in 1842).

In this period, there opened a number of specialized institutions of higher education, both in humanities and sciences. Tsarskoye Selo Lyceum (opened in 1811) was a privileged school, the best Ivy League humanities college of its time. Many top officials of the empire were its graduates. Demidov Lyceum of Law in Yaroslavl opened as early as 1803, Prince Bezborodko Lyceum opened in 1820 in Nezhin. The College of Law established in St. Petersburg in 1835 was another privileged school with a 10-year course of study[15] (a blend of secondary school and university-level courses). Just like the lyceum at Tsarskoye Selo, it became a supplier of cadre for the top bureaucracy. Lazarev Institute of Oriental Languages opened in Moscow in 1815, and in 1832 there was created Moscow College of Painting, Sculpture, and Architecture. Richelieu Lyceum opened in Odessa in 1817, St. Petersburg Main Teacher College reopened in 1828. Forestry Institute was established in St. Petersburg in 1803, and the Institute of Transport Engineers in 1810. More new institutes of higher learning were established under Nicholas, who highly valued engineering knowledge: Petersburg Institute of Technology in 1828, Moscow Engineering

---

[15] One of its graduates was the famous composer Tchaikovsky

College in 1830, the College of Construction (later known as Civil Engineering College) in St. Petersburg in 1842. Gory-Goretsky Agricultural College (opened in 1840 in Orsha *uezd* of Mogilev Governorate) and Derpt (Yur'ev) Veterinary School (1848) were Russia's first in their field.

According to its charter of 1803, the Academy of Sciences no longer had to have a teaching responsibility, and its scope now included humanities. In 1841, what was known until then as the Russian Academy was made part of the Academy of Sciences (as its Russian language and literature section; the other two sections were physics and mathematics, and history and philology). In 1839, there opened Pulkovo Observatory near St. Petersburg (the Russian equivalent of Greenwich), and Russian Geographical Society was founded in 1845.

According to the reform of 1803, every governorate seat was to have 4-year schools (known as gymnasiums and meant to be comprehensive schools), and *uezd* seats were to have 2-year schools and 1-year parish schools. In 1824, Russia had 49 gymnasiums, and by 1854 they were 77 (including 3 in Siberia: in Tobolsk, Tomsk, and Irkutsk). The reform of December 1828 removed *uezd* schools and gymnasiums from the control of their region's university. In 1856, the whole system of institutions of general education (i.e. without engineering and other specialized colleges) enrolled 119 thousand, of whom 2.3 thousand attended universities and lyceums, 19 thousand were in gymnasium schools, and 95 thousand in *uezd*, parish, and private schools.

Alongside the standard types of public elementary and secondary schools, there existed a number of special schools at various levels. Those included institutes for the nobility and private boarding schools (on par with gymnasium schools in level), which mostly educated girls. Well-known Smolny Institute aside, similar institutions of learning were opened in Moscow, Nizhny Novgorod, Kazan, Astrakhan, Saratov, Irkutsk, and some other cities. Rabbinate schools for Jews (equal in status to gymnasiums) were established in 1844. Elementary schools were started by the church, individual landowners, and some ministries, especially the Ministry of State Properties that had oversight of state peasants.

Expansion of the network of secondary schools and higher learning brought forth a profusion of new magazines and newspapers. Only in the first decade of the century, there appeared 58 new periodicals (including 'Herald of Europe' published by N. Karamzin with circulation of 1.5 thousand), 44 more appeared in the second decade (including a widely read literary magazine 'Fatherland's Son' and the newspaper 'Russian Invalid', which remained the military ministry's paper of record until 1917). In the 1820s, there appeared 73 new periodicals (including the magazine 'Moscow's Telegraph' published by N. Polevoy and the newspaper 'Northern Bee' published by F. Bulgarin). In the 1830s, there were added 117 more periodicals (including the justly famous 'Contemporary' and 'Annals of the Fatherland'). In 1838, it was decided that a local newspaper must be published in each governorate seat, and 43 different 'News of the Governorate' came about. In 1841–1855, there appeared 62 more new periodicals. Overall, 350 new periodicals were started in this period. By 1840, the number of newspapers was comparable to that in West European nations: 204 in Russia, 132 in Austria, 305 in Prussia, 493 in Britain. In terms of book publishing, the period 1828–1832 saw 764 new titles published in Russia, not much less than in Britain (1060), although several times less than in France (4640) and Prussia (5530).

Chapter 10

Russian Empire under Alexander II

The new emperor, who was enthroned on February 19, 1855, was well-prepared for his role. During his father's reign, he was long involved with various affairs of state, served as the member of Council of State and Committee of Ministers, and chaired the secret committee on peasant reform. While broadly and thoroughly educated under the tutorship of renowned poet V. Zhukovsky, he was also very knowledgeable about military matters as he served in the army from his youth and had a general's rank. Desirous of focusing on domestic reforms, he accepted the Treaty of Paris (concluding the Crimean War) even though the treaty was unfavorable to Russia, and all the allied troops managed to do by then was to seize Sebastopol, while their prospects of invading the Russian mainland were nil.

Nonetheless, this setback, the first in a century and a half, only confirmed the trend of Russia losing the position of dominance in international affairs that it enjoyed after 1815. That shift was being felt from the early 1840s. Therefore, the struggle to overturn the Treaty of Paris became the leitmotif of Russia's foreign policy. In turn, that objective ushered in the irreconcilable standoff between Russia and Britain which lasted until early in the 20th century. It never exploded into a military conflict, but became a constant current in international affairs.

Russia's foreign policy (directed by the new foreign minister, Count A. Gorchakov) was based on exploiting the antagonisms between European powers, most of which had far greater grounds for conflict with each other than with Russia. Russian public opinion was incensed about Austria's treachery during the Crimean War (even though Russia saved that empire from collapse only four years prior). Accordingly, during the Franco-Austrian War of 1859 that ended with Austrian defeat and loss of its possessions in Italy, Russian sympathies leaned to France. An alliance between France and Russia was concluded in 1859, but proved disappointing to Russia as France preferred the status quo and wished to prevent Russia's strengthening in the east. When the new Polish rebellion flared up in 1863, French hostility became quite obvious.

In 1859, the amnestied rebels from the previous rebellion of 1831 were allowed to return from exile to Poland. They celebrated the return by unleashing a war of terror against the Russian officials and the military, over 5 thousand of whom perished. On January 10, 1863, an open armed rebellion began and spilled to the Lithuanian and Byelorussian governorates. Large rebel bands numbering thousands hid in the forests and avoided battle preferring guerilla tactics. In Lithuania and Byelorussia, the bulk of their forces was dispersed, and rebel commander, Serakowsky captured by April. In the course of May, Vilna governor M. Muraviev completely pacified that part of the theater of rebellion. By summer, 163 thousand troops were deployed in the Kingdom of Poland and put on combat alert due to the hostility displayed by Austria and France. In April and May, rebels with

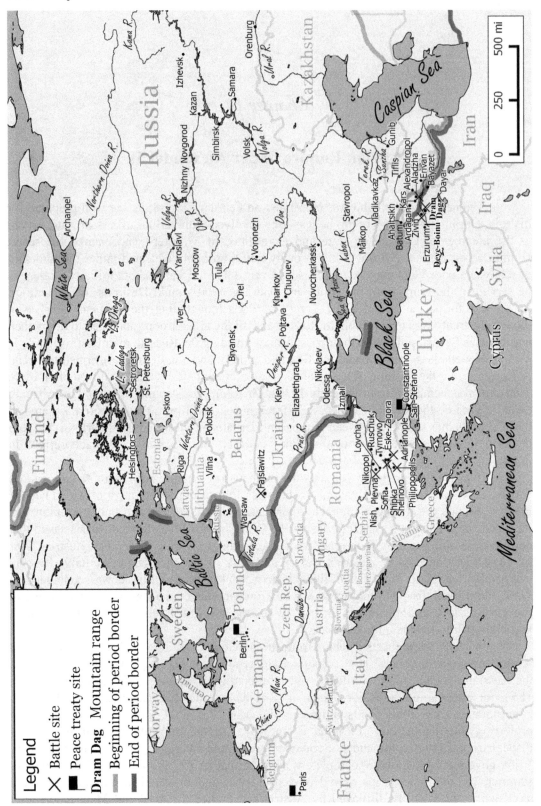

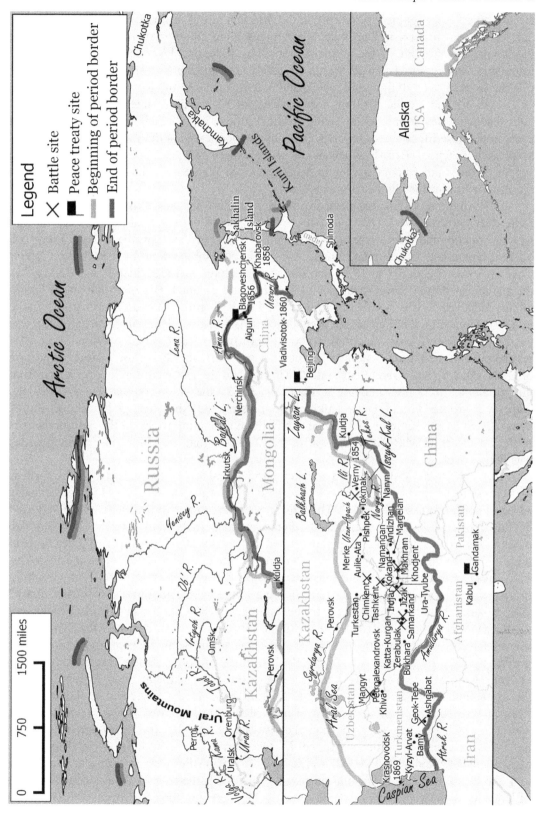

military experience (gained by serving in the Prussian army) infiltrated Poland from Prussia but were soon dispersed. The main rebel forces were finally defeated on August 12 at Fajslawitz. By the end of the year, the rebellion started to lose steam, and its political leadership was captured in late March of 1864. Overall, numerous armed confrontations cost the lives of over 30 thousand rebels, and at least 1.2 thousand Russians.

In the end, neither Britain, nor Austria, nor France dared interfere in that conflict, but subsequent developments involving Russian moves in the south and east, gave Britain even more cause for concern. In 1863, Russian navy appeared at the shores of United States to prevent potential British blockade of the northern states. Since Britain and France supported the southern confederacy in American Civil War, Russia duly supported the north against her former foes in the Crimean War.

By the late 1850s, the new commander in the Caucasus, Prince Baryatinsky won some decisive successes. The right flank of the Line of the Caucasus was pushed all the way to Maikop, and the Cossacks were settled in the newly won swathe of land. From late 1856, preparations were being made for the final subjugation of Chechnya. Lesser Chechnya was conquered in 1857, and Greater Chechnya in 1858. Shamil was defeated in the canyon of Argun River (tributary of Sunzha) and escaped. His final hideout in Gunib village in Dagestan was stormed in August 1859 with Shamil captured. With that, the whole eastern segment of the Caucasus (from the Caspian Sea to Georgian Military road) was pacified for good. Circassian tribes in the western part of the Caucasus continued to offer resistance, and their suppression took several more years. In 1861–1862 a large proportion of Circassians was allowed to emigrate to Turkey, and the rest were forcibly relocated from the mountains into the plains. In February 1863, the new commander-in-chief, the emperor's brother Grand Duke Mikhail, suppressed the Shapsugs (a branch of Adyge people), and by the summer of 1864 he pacified the remaining tribes on the northern slopes of the Caucasus. In May 1864, the war in the Caucasus that lasted for quite a few decades was finally over.

By the mid-1850s, Russian advance into Central Asia was anchored by the fortress of Perovsk near the Aral Sea and the fortress of Verny (founded in 1854, present-day Almaty) north of Lake Issyk-Kul'. The huge gap between the two was undefended and used by the troops of Khanate of Kokand (then ascendant in Central Asia) to raid Russian possessions in the drylands. The gap needed to be closed with a fortified line, both to prevent further inroads and to cut short Kokand's subversive influence upon the Kazakhs. Yet, Russian forces across this huge area were spread very thin: Ural and Orenburg Cossacks and 11 Orenburg battalions of the line in the west, and Siberian Cossacks and 12 West Siberian battalions in the east. In the summer of 1860, the Khan of Kokand amassed 22 thousand men and prepared to raze down the fortress of Verny, devastate the Semirechye (Seven Rivers) region (south of Lake Balkhash in present-day Kazakhstan) and incite a general uprising by the Kazakhs. Yet, a Russian force of only a thousand men with 8 guns under G. Kolpakovsky routed Kokand troops in a three-day battle at Uzun-Agach River. At the same time, another Russian force took from Kokand the fortresses of Tokmak and Pishpek (present-day capital of Kyrgyzstan). Merke fortress was seized in 1862. In the spring of 1864, two Russian forces marched towards each other from the opposite sides of the Syrdarya gap: a force under Colonel M. Chernyaev (1.5 thousand) set off from Verny and that under Colonel N. Verevkin (1.2 thousand) from Perovsk. On June 4, Chernyaev took the fortress of Aulie-Ata, and on July 22 he gave battle to a 25 thousand strong army of Kokand by the walls of Chimkent. On July 12, Verevkin took the fortress of Turkestan and was joined by Chernyaev there. On September 22, Chernyaev (a General Major by then) seized Chimkent (defended by 10 thousand Kokand troops). On October 1, he attempted the storming of Tashkent but was beaten back and retreated to Turkestan fortress. In December, 12 thousand troops from Kokand advanced on Turkestan fortress, but after a clash with a small detachment of the Cossacks they retreated before meeting the main Russian force.

In the spring of 1865, Chernyaev was appointed governor-general of the newly established Turkestan Oblast. On May 9, his force of 1.8 thousand men and 12 guns defeated Kokand's army in the vicinity of Tashkent. The city of Tashkent decided to ask for protection from the Emir of Bukhara, but it was too late. On June 15, Chernyaev stormed and seized Tashkent with its garrison of 30 thousand (himself losing 123 men). In the spring of 1864, the Emir of Bukhara assembled up to 43 thousand troops in a bid to retake Tashkent, but the force of 3 thousand men and 20 guns under General Romanovsky defeated Bukhara troops near Irdjar (May 8). On May 24, Romanovsky took Khodjent, on July 20 he seized Ura-Tyube, and on October 18 Jizak. The whole campaign cost the Russians 500 casualties, while Bukhara troops lost about 12 thousand and escaped to Samarkand.

In 1867, Turkestan Oblast was transformed into a governorate-general (under General Kaufman) made up of two oblasts: Semirechenskaya (Seven Rivers) Oblast with the center in Verny and Syrdarya Oblast with the center in Tashkent. In April of 1868, General von Kaufman with a force of 4 thousand men and 20 guns advanced on Samarkand, which fell on May 2. On May 18, Bukhara forces were defeated at Katta-Kurgan, and on June 2 Bukhara's army of 35 thousand was decisively trounced (with 10 thousand dead) at Zerabulak heights by the Russian force of only 2 thousand (which lost 63 men). On the same day, Samarkand rose in rebellion, and Russian garrison of 700 holed up in the citadel, but by June 7 the rebels were dispersed as Kaufman's troops arrived. The Emir of Bukhara had to accept Russian protectorate and cede to Russia the lands extending to Zerabulak River (with Samarkand, Ura-Tyube, Khodjent, Jizak, and Katta-Kurgan).

The area surrounding Lake Zaysan was annexed by Russia in 1864, and in 1868 Russia occupied the lands south of Lake Issyk-Kul' (where Naryn fort was built). In 1869, G. Kolpakovsky led the expedition into Chinese Turkestan, where the rebellion by the Dungans (Chinese Muslims) threatened to spread into Russian possessions. In 1871, he annexed to Russia the territory west of Kuldja (Yining in China today) along the rivers Ili and Tekes (Kuldja itself and lands to the east of it were returned to China in 1881). In 1869, General N. Stoletov landed on the eastern shore of the Caspian and built the port and fort of Krasnovodsk. By 1874, Russia controlled all the Caspian coast down to Atrek River (present-day border between Turkmenistan and Iran), and that territory was officially designated as the Trans-Caspian section of the Caucasus Military District. With that, the hostile Khanate of Khiva was surrounded on almost all sides.

In 1873, four separate Russian forces advanced on Khiva from different directions (Verevkin from Orenburg, Kaufman from Turkestan, and the force under colonels Lomakin and Markozov from the Caspian – the total of 14.5 thousand men and 44 guns). After the extreme hardship of crossing the desert and the defeat of 3 thousand Khivan troops by Mangyt, the troops approached Khiva on May 26. On May 29, the city was captured, and the Khan of Khiva (just as the Khan of Bukhara a bit earlier) recognized himself Russia's vassal and ceded lands on the right bank of Amudarya River where Fort Petroalexandrovsk was built. After that, Kaufman marched against Yomut tribe of the Turkmens who occupied the eastern shore of the Caspian and ensured their submission.

That left the Khanate of Kokand. On August 8, 1875, its ruler, Khan Pulat (who recently usurped power) attacked Khodjent with a force of 15 thousand but was repulsed. Kaufman immediately took to the field. On August 11, a small force under General Golovachev defeated 6 thousand Kokand troops at Zyulfagar (half-way between Tashkent and Khodjent), while Kaufman's main force (4 thousand men with 20 guns) advanced on Khodjent. Khan Pulat with an army of about 60 thousand met them by Makhram and was completely routed (the Russians lost only 5 men). On August 29, they entered Kokand without a battle. Kokand Khanate ceded to Russia lands on the right bank of Naryn River (which were made into Namangan district). But the moment the Russian troops left Kokand, the Khanate rebelled again and declared holy war against Russia. On October 1, an all-out assault led by General V. Trotzky seized Andizhan, but after the troops withdrew Khan Pulat (who holed up in Margelan) rose in rebellion again, and so did the city of Namangan. On December 31, General M. Skobelev defeated a Kokand force of 20 thousand, on January 4, 1876 he retook Andizhan, and on February 12 he took Kokand. The khanate was abolished and annexed to Russia as Fergana Oblast.

In the aftermath of G. Nevelskoy expedition to the mouth of Amur River, there arose the issue of settling Russia's boundary with China in the Far East. Its eastern segment was left ambiguous in the Peace of Nerchinsk of 1689. As China was dramatically weakened by Opium wars, the new, Aigun Treaty signed in 1858, ceded to Russia all the lands on Amur's left bank (the cities of Blagoveshchensk and Khabarovsk were founded there), but left in limbo the ownership of lands between Ussuri River and the Pacific. Another treaty signed in Beijing in 1860 gave that region (known in Russian as *Primorsky* (Maritime) *Krai* (region)) to Russia. On June 20, 1860, the foundations of Vladivostok were laid on the shore of Golden Horn Bay. That city and base were destined to become Russia's major stronghold in the Far East. Shimoda Treaty with Japan (1855) confirmed Russia's rights to the northern half of Kuril Islands, while Sakhalin Island (which Russia considered its own from 1853) was declared to be a condominium. St. Petersburg treaty of 1875 recognized Sakhalin to be exclusively Russian, while Japan got the whole of Kuril Islands chain. In 1867, Russia (which following the end of American Civil War enjoyed a honeymoon of friendship with the United States) ceded to the United States the huge but largely empty expanse of Alaska. Even though Alaska was colonized by Russia from the earliest years of 19th century, the land appeared to have little value, while logistical and communications challenges were enormous. The colony was actually sold for 7.2 million dollars, the price that seemed fair at the time but ludicrously low later when Alaska's wealth in gold and oil was discovered.

Russia's acquisition of vast and geopolitically important territories in the Far East which firmly planted it in the Pacific, the removal of that permanent thorn of irritation in the Northern Caucasus, and especially the annexations in Central Asia (that brought Russia so close to British India), all incited extreme unease in Britain and made it view Russia as the greatest threat to Britain's global standing. Given that, Britain was willing to ally with anybody as long as it was against Russia. Following the Crimean War, Austria turned into another implacable foe of Russia. And France displayed its hostility by the stance it took during the Polish rebellion of 1863–1864. In other words, Russia was opposed by the same set of great powers as in 1853. The only great power not hostile to Russia was Prussia, which stayed friendly to Russia ever since 1813. Prussian foreign policy at the time was largely the doing of one man, Otto von Bismarck, who well understood the importance of staying on Russia's good side for his own country and knew that Russia can never be brought down for good. Yet, he was also aware that excessive strengthening of Russia poses a threat to his country. That explains why the king of Prussia Wilhelm I (who was Alexander's uncle) listened to Bismarck and turned down Russian invitation to join forces in a war against Britain, Austria, and France. Were those powers defeated, Russia would come to dominate the world with Prussia merely its junior partner.

Nonetheless, in 1863–1875, the relations between Russia and Prussia could hardly be improved upon. Pretty soon, two of Russia's enemies will be defeated and humiliated by Prussia. In a brief and brilliant war of 1866, Prussia has thoroughly trounced Austria and eliminated its influence over smaller German states (especially Bavaria and others in the south). All of Germany north of Main River was brought into Prussia-dominated North German Union. Only four years later, Germany triumphed in Franco-Prussian War of 1870–1871. Russia's stance was that of friendly neutrality, and Austria was warned that Russia would not tolerate Austrian interference on the side of France (as early as 1868, Alexander promised Prussia that his army would invade Austria should that happen). Russia took full advantage of Prussian victory. Napoleon III surrendered to the Germans on September 2, 1870, and just two months later Russia notified all the nations that it no longer considered itself bound by the articles of Paris Treaty devoted to military 'neutralization' of the Black Sea. Naturally, that provoked a furious response in Britain and Austria, and the conference to discuss the issue was convened in London in January 1871, yet it was clear that under the circumstances no one could oppose Russia's stance. The conference meekly reconfirmed the principle that Turkey has the right to close the straits to foreign ships of hostile nations. The legacy of the Crimean War was put behind.

While Prussia had reasons to feel jealous of the prospect of excessive strengthening of Russia, Russia had equally legitimate concerns about excessive strengthening of Prussia. After the French defeat in 1871, Wilhelm I of Prussia became the emperor of unified German Empire strongly dominated by Prussia. In order to avoid the scenario where Germany and Austria would have a rapprochement and leave it sidelined, Russia moved to create the alliance of three powers. In 1873, Alexander II, Wilhelm I, and Frances-Joseph agreed to resolve their differences through consultations and undertake joint action should any of the three face the threat of attack from another nation. The alliance was not exactly sincere (mutual animosity between Russia and Austria remained, and there was mutual wariness between Russia and Germany), but it proved a lasting one since it genuinely maintained stability in Europe. An advantage for Russia was that it fenced it in against trouble from the principal enemy, Britain, and also hamstrung through 'friendship' the lesser foe, Austria. Relations between Russia and Germany noticeably cooled for the first time in 1875 when Germany raised the prospect of a new war with France intended to finish it off for good. Russia (with a favorable understanding in Austria) made it known that it would not stand for such a war. Britain defended France stridently too, and Germany had to back down.

In the mid-1870s, tensions in the Balkans heightened again and put the Eastern Question back on Russia's agenda. In 1875, the uprising of Ottoman Empire's Christian subjects began in Bosnia and Herzegovina and quickly spread to Bulgaria. Serbia and Montenegro declared war on Turkey but suffered a series of defeats. In Russia, there was a groundswell of sympathy for the Serbs, and a stream of volunteers left to fight alongside them (including the popular hero of Central Asian campaigns M. Chernyaev). In a bloodbath in Bulgaria, the Turks butchered about 30 thousand Christian Bulgarians. Feeling the pressure of public opinion, which demanded that Russia interfere to protect the Slavs in the Balkans, Alexander II demanded from the Sultan the end to the massacres and negotiated peace with Serbia. In April 1877, after Turkey rejected those demands, Russia declared war.

In May, Russian troops numbering up to 185 thousand entered Romania (which joined Russia in the war effort and fielded 45 thousand men). To protect the border along the Danube, the Turks assembled a force of about 200 thousand. Unlike in the previous wars, the Turkish army now had a much better discipline and was very well armed. In June, Russian troops forced the Danubian crossings and took Tyrnovo. After that, troops in the center of the front (under generals I. Gurko and F. Radetzky) crossed the Balkans and seized the crucial Shipka Pass on July 7, while on the left flank Nikopol was taken by the Ruschuk force of the Russian army on July 4. On the right flank, troops under General N. Kridener undertook their first assault on the fortifications of Plevna (July 8), but were beaten back with heavy losses. After disappointing engagements by Eske-Zagora in July 17–19, troops under Gurko retreated to the Shipka Pass. On July 18, Kridener assaulted Plevna again and suffered another defeat with the loss of over 7 thousand men. On August 7, the army of 40 thousand commanded by Suleiman Pasha began its assault on Shipka Pass defended by only 4 thousand men, but they stood their ground. At the same time, Mehmed-Ali with the main force (92 thousand) attacked the Ruschuk force, but was thrown back.

The Russian command decided that Plevna with its strategic location must be seized as soon as possible. Lovcha was taken on August 22, and the third assault on Plevna was launched on August 30. It failed again but became the bloodiest battle of the whole war (Russian casualties were about 13 thousand, and the Romanians and Turks both lost 3 thousand men). On September 5, Suleiman Pasha attacked Shipka Pass again but failed to take it, while Mehmed-Ali launched another futile attack on the Ruschuk force. From October, Plevna was completely encircled by the Russian army of 170 thousand. On November 28, Osman Pasha attempted to break out of encircled fortress but was defeated and capitulated. The fall of Plevna gave the freedom of movement to the Russian forces, which by then were beefed up to 310 thousand men (plus 40 thousand Romanians). Serbia renewed its war effort too with an army of 82 thousand advancing on Nish. On December 13, in fierce cold and driving snow, the troops under Gurko crossed the Balkans, threw back Turkish troops and on December 23 took Sofia. Following that, all Russian forces went on the offensive. On December 24–28, the Turkish army under Wessel Pasha was completely routed in engagements around Shipka-Sheinovo. On January 3–5, 1878, the Turkish army under Suleiman Pasha was defeated again near Philippopolis (Plovdiv). On January 19, truce was signed in Adrianople, and on February 19 peace treaty was signed in San-Stephano (now part of Istanbul) near Constantinople (today's Istanbul).

In another theater of war, the Caucasus, Russian troops operated in three groups: the main force under M. Loris-Melikov amassed around Alexandropol (present-day Gyumri in Armenia), while Ahaltsikh force formed the right flank of the front and Erivan force the left flank. On May 5, Ahaltsikh force successfully stormed Ardagan, and soon afterwards the main force besieged Kars. Yet, in late June after a lost engagement by Zivin on June 13, the main force retreated to the border. The Erivan force defeated the Turks on June 4 and 9 by Dram-Dag and Dayar, but once it was learned that the main force retreated they had to retreat as well. Bayazet (taken by the Russians) was invested by the Turks, but a 24-day long siege was relieved on June 28 by Russian troops. In July, the Turks went on the offensive. Following heavy fighting around Aladzha on August 13 and September 20–22, Turkish forces retreated to their initial positions. On October 2–3, battle royal unfolded on the heights of Aladzha, and the Turks were roundly defeated suffering 22 thousand casualties. On October 23, by Deve-Boinu they suffered another serious defeat. On October 28, Russian troops undertook a failed assault on Erzerum, but the storming of Kars on November 6 was a success. From then and to the signing of truce, the only hostilities were in the area of Batum (today's Batumi in Georgia).

Turkey was completely defeated, and Russian troops were encamped half a day's march from Constantinople, but never entered the city because the international situation became quite difficult for Russia (Austria-Hungary and Britain assumed an openly hostile stance, and British fleet entered the Sea of Marmara). Moreover, Russia was soon to part with some of the prizes won in this war. Under the Treaty of San-Stefano, Serbia, Romania, and Montenegro received complete independence (while previously they were self-ruling dependencies) and more territory. Bulgaria and Bosnia-Herzegovina were to become autonomous. Russia was to get back southern Bessarabia with Izmail and receive new territories in the Caucasus, the hinterlands of Batum and Kars with important fortresses of Kars, Ardagan, and Batum, as well as Bayazet district and some adjacent lands with Armenian population. Temporary Russian administration developed the draft constitution for Bulgaria (adopted by the Constitutional Assembly in Tyrnovo in April of 1879).

Yet, Britain and Austria-Hungary saw the creation of a large Bulgarian state with predominance of Russian influence as quite impossible and insisted on the revision of Treaty of San-Stefano. At the June 1878 Berlin Congress (the participants were Turkey, Russia, Britain, Austria-Hungary, France, and Germany), Russia found itself completely isolated and was forced to make major concessions. Bayazet district with adjacent Armenian lands went back to Turkey. Southern Bulgaria was to remain under Turkish rule (with autonomous principality including only northern Bulgaria), territorial gains of Serbia and Montenegro were much reduced, while Bosnia-Herzegovina was to be occupied by Austria. By favoring Austrian claims during Berlin Congress Germany created a foundation for lasting friendship between the two countries that persisted until World War I. In 1879, Germany and Austria-Hungary entered into a secret alliance directed against Russia and France. After Italy joined it in 1882, it became known as the Triple Alliance. By betraying Russia in the Congress, Germany paid back for what it saw as Russian betrayal in 1875. Just as the powers prevented Germany from finishing off France in 1875, so now they prevented Russia from finishing off Turkey. Quietly, the biggest winner was Britain. The secret Cyprus Convention of 1878 between Britain and Turkey gave Britain Cyprus and also made it a de facto mistress of the straits since the Convention allowed for British interference in Turkey.

Nonetheless, the war had significantly improved Russia's position both in the Balkans (where Russia now wielded much more influence) and in the Caucasus (where new boundaries remained unchanged until 1917). It also strengthened Russia's hand in its confrontation with Britain (from the spring of 1878, the two countries hovered on the brink of war). In March 1878, Britain announced the call-up of reservists. In response, Russia amassed troops at Amudarya River and in Alay valley in Central Asia, and sent a military mission under General N. Stoletov to Afghanistan. By that time, Afghanistan was semi-enveloped by the British who seized Baluchistan in 1876. In November 1878, the British troops attacked Afghanistan. The Emir decided to seek asylum in Russia and left Kabul with the Russian mission, but early in 1879 he died. In May 1879, Britain forced

Afghanistan to sign Gandamak Treaty which turned it into a British protectorate and adjusted the border in favor of British India. All of that was in direct contravention of past agreements with Russia on mutual guarantees of Afghanistan's independence and territorial integrity. Russia responded by declaring that it now considered itself free to act in Central Asia.

After the Trans-Caspian Oblast was created in 1874, further Russian advance along that direction was checked by the resistance of militant Teke tribes from hard-to-reach Akhal-Teke oasis. An expedition of 1877 managed to annex only its outskirts in Kyzyl-Arvat and was forced to return due to lack of forage and victualling. In August 1879, it was decided that more decisive action is needed in view of developments in Afghanistan. On August 28, the force of 3 thousand Russian troops stormed Geok-Tepe but was beaten back with the loss of 445 men. On May 23, 1880, troops commanded by M. Skobelev (8 thousand with 64 guns) occupied Bami (beyond Kyzyl-Arvat) from where they reconnoitered Geok-Tepe fortress and besieged it on December 23. On January 12, 1881, Geok-Tepe was taken by assault. Defenders of the fortress lost up to 8 thousand men, but Russian losses were also the highest in the history of Central Asian campaigns (more than 800 men). The district around present-day Ashgabat was occupied in February, and Akhal-Teke elders swore allegiance to Russia. Thus, almost the whole Trans-Caspian territory bordering on Iran was annexed.

System of government and military-economic potential

Even though the reign of Alexander II became the time of far-reaching reforms in many areas, administrative machinery of central government of the empire changed but little. Just as before, high-level ad hoc committees were created to address specific issues and then disbanded. In 1861, the Main Committee on Peasant Issues was transformed into the Main Committee on Organization of Farming (chaired by Grand Duke Constantine). It oversaw the execution of peasant reform (abolition of serfdom) proclaimed by His Majesty's Manifesto on February 19, 1861. In 1862–1865, there existed the so-called Western Committee that dealt with the aftermath of Polish rebellion. In 1864–1881, Polish issues were handled by the Committee on Kingdom of Poland Affairs. The Siberian Committee was disbanded in 1864, and the Committee on the Caucasus in 1882. In 1859–1874, there existed a Railway Committee. While the Committee of Ministers dealt with matters of daily administration, in November of 1861 there was created a Council of Ministers (chaired by the emperor himself and including ministers and some other top administrators) designed to deliberate on major measures affecting the country as a whole and initiated by the emperor. In 1866, there were created criminal and civil cassation departments within the Senate. They looked into complaints and appeals against local courts' decisions. All agencies of central government retained their functions and changed but little in structure. With the rapid expansion of railway network, a special directorate for oversight of railway construction and operation was added to the Chief Administration of Communications and Public Buildings, and in 1865 it was transformed into the Ministry of Transport.

The system of territorial administration did not change much either. The scope of governors' powers was somewhat restricted, and territorial directorates of some agencies no longer reported to them. Police reform of 1862 merged hitherto separate police departments of cities and towns with *uezd* rural police into a single *uezd* police department commanded by a governor's appointee (chosen from the ranks of local nobility). From 1878, the boroughs (smaller subdivisions making up an *uezd*) received their own police sergeants, who in turn commanded village policemen elected by village communities. Also, the governorates now had two public reception offices, *prisutstviya* (meaning 'presence' in Russian) where a person could meet local officials. One was known as the public reception office for peasant affairs (established in 1861), and another was devoted to townsmen affairs (established in 1870). As part of the military reform of 1874, there additionally appeared governorate and *uezd*-level public reception offices on the matters of military duty.

Following the abolition of serfdom in 1861, new local representative bodies were created for the peasantry. Every rural commune (consisting of one or several villages) held periodic village assemblies (gatherings) which elected the commune elder, village policemen, and the tax collector. Next higher level was a borough assembly attended by electors, each of whom represented 10 peasant households. This assembly elected borough chairman (for a 3-year term) and other borough-level officials, as well as borough representatives for *uezd*-level assembly. The latter elected *uezd* councilmen representing the constellation of rural communes. Borough chairman presided over the borough administration (which included all elders, tax collectors, one or two assessors, and a clerk). Borough court (of 4 to 12 members) was also elected by annual borough assembly and had jurisdiction in small claims suits (involving sums lower than 100 rubles) and petty criminal offences. In 1861–1874, village communes also had arbitrators who looked into disputes about land between the peasants and landowners. In 1874, those functions were handed over to *uezd* and governorate public reception offices (*prisutstviya*) for peasant affairs.

An extremely important innovation of the time was the creation on January 1, 1864 of the institution known as *zemstvo* (local council). *Zemstvo* was put in charge of local administrative and economic matters, of local schools, clinics, roads, food supply and relief in years of failed harvest, charities, provision of credit secured by land, gathering statistics, etc. Such local councils existed at both governorate and *uezd* levels and had their own executive branch – *zemstvo* executive boards. *Zemstvo* bodies were elected for a 3-year term. *Uezd*-level *zemstvo* councilmen were elected by three *curiae* (groups) at three separate assemblies: 1) landowners (qualification requirement varied, generally from 200 to 800 hectares), 2) townsmen (to qualify one had to own real estate valued at over 500 rubles, or have a guild license, or own a business with annual turnover over 6000 rubles), and 3) villagers (elected at *uezd* assemblies of borough representatives).

The reform of city government (1870) abolished the former system of separate administrative bodies for each estate. They were replaced with *zemstvo*-type city councils known as *dumas*. City *dumas* were elected by three constituencies, each electing the same number of councilmen. The constituencies were defined by the size of one's tax obligation. The *dumas* elected executive boards, and general oversight of their activities was vested in governorate *prisutstviya* for city matters.

Courts of justice reform of 1864 overhauled all lower courts coming under the Ministry of Justice. Rural parts of an *uezd* combined with its *uezd* seat (or sometimes just a large city alone) now constituted a district court jurisdiction, which further broke down into wards. A ward had two justices of peace (a regular and honorary one). Justices were elected for 3-year terms either by *zemstvo* councils or by city *dumas*. To qualify, a prospective judge had to meet certain age, educational, and property requirements (real estate worth at least 15 000 rubles). Justices of peace had jurisdiction in cases of civil claims of 500 rubles

131

or less and in criminal cases where sentencing guidelines called for fines of 300 rubles or less, 3 months of detention, or 1.5 years of incarceration. *Uezd* assembly of justices of peace with an elected chairman acted as the court of appeal.

Several *uezds* combined constituted a court circuit. Circuit courts consisted of a chairman, his deputy, and members, while its staff included a prosecutor and deputy prosecutor. All of those were appointee positions. In criminal cases, the verdict of guilt was established by jurors. Jurors were elected from all estates based on qualifications of age, local residence, and property ownership (the latter was quite permissive: 10 hectares of land or real estate worth at least 500 rubles). The court of appeal for circuit courts was known as court chamber (only for cases tried without jurors; jury decisions could be challenged only through a cassation petition to the Senate). In some kinds of cases (involving government property, officials, the media), the chambers acted as trial courts. The staff of chambers was divided into criminal and civil departments, and the general session included the chairman, his deputy and all the assessors. A chamber's prosecutor had a staff of major case investigators. Solicitors in circuit courts and court chambers were known as attorneys-at-law and differed from private practice lawyers in being civil servants.

As far as the Ministry of Finance is concerned, in 1861 there were instituted governorate excise boards (with district excise boards and supervisors under them). In 1864, there were created governorate treasuries as well. State Inspection (ministry) was enhanced with the addition in 1865 of governorate inspection chambers. The Ministry of State Properties also added directorates in governorates (1866). As to the public education, in 1864–1874, there were created governorate and *uezd*-level school boards and school inspectors.

After the position of viceroy for the Kingdom of Poland was abolished in 1874, Poland (10 governorates with standard imperial administrative system) was administered by Warsaw governor-general. In the Caucasus, the creation of the system of military districts in 1865 resulted in the disbandment of Army of the Caucasus headquarters (although the viceroy persisted until 1883). Former large districts (*okrugs*) were replaced with regular *uezds*. While the reforms of justice system and city government applied to the Caucasus, policing functions there remained under the Military (Army) Ministry. The Baltic general-governorate was abolished in 1867. From 1867, Central Asia was constituted as the general-governorship of Turkestan consisting of Fergana, Semirechenskaya, and Syrdaya oblasts administered by military governors. The oblasts had streamlined government structure, a crossbreed of governorate administration and chamber of inspections and public properties. *Uezds* were administered by *uezd* superintendents and smaller boroughs by police captains. All the officialdom of Turkestan fell under the jurisdiction of Military Ministry. Indigenous component in the administration of cities was represented by chief elders and the elders of each city ward. Rural borough administrators and village elders were popularly elected to the term of 3 years.

The armed forces underwent a dramatic transformation during the reign of Alexander II. The reforms are firmly linked with the name of military minister, D. Milyutin who assumed the position in 1861. In the second half of 1850s, the size of the army was reduced, but the Polish rebellion of 1863 led to a temporary expansion to 1076 thousand. Then the army was downsized again and stayed at about 750 thousand until mid-1870s, but in 1876–1881 it ballooned to 900–1030 thousand (at the peak of the war with Turkey – to more than 1500 thousand). That army was the world's largest: as per 1869, it stood at 837 thousand, the next largest was the French army with half that much – 404 thousand, Germany had 380 thousand, Austria-Hungary 190 thousand, Britain 180 thousand, and Italy 120 thousand.

Until 1874, the army was manned by the old system of recruit draws (briefly suspended in 1856–1862, when only those on extended leave were called up). The new Charter on Military Duty of 1874 introduced the principle of universal military duty as the new basis for manning. Every man who reached 20 years of age by January 1 was eligible for the draft. New draftees were selected by casting lots (the remainder of this age cohort were automatically listed as militia). The term of army service was set at 6 years with subsequent 9 years in the reserve (7 and 3 years respectively in the navy). Men with college education had to serve on active duty for only 6 months, and were then listed as members of the reserve (for up to 15 years). For those with secondary education, active duty was limited to 1.5 years, those with incomplete secondary education to 3 years, and for those with elementary education to 4 years. All men capable of bearing arms and under age 40 were listed as militia (the four youngest age brackets in the militia could be drafted into the regular army). The Cossacks served for 3 years as soldiers-in-training, then for 12 years on active duty, and stayed on reservist rolls for 5 years. Non-Russian ethnic groups were not subject to military duty. In 1874–1879, the annual draft under new rules stood at 148–213 thousand men. Military registration and enlistment offices were set up in *uezds* and bigger regions.

By 1861, the infantry consisted of 10 regiments of guards, 16 of grenadiers, and 84 of infantry. A regiment had 3 battalions (5 in those stationed in the Caucasus). The regiments were grouped into 3 divisions of guards, 4 of grenadiers, and 21 of the infantry, 29 riflemen battalions (3 of the guards, 3 of grenadiers, 18 of the army, 4 of the Caucasus, and 1 Finnish), and 77 battalions of the line[16] (10 in Finland, 2 in Kronstadt, 37 in the Caucasus, 10 on the Orenburg line, 12 in western Siberia and 6 in eastern Siberia). Under a new organizational scheme introduced by 1877, there were 48 divisions (3 of the guards, 4 of grenadiers, and 41 of the infantry with a total of 192 regiments, each named after a city), which further divided into 2 brigades of 2 regiments each. Riflemen brigades (1 guards', 5 riflemen, the Caucasus, Turkestan, and East Siberian brigade) consisted of 4 battalions each. Of the battalions of the line only 26 remained in the remote districts. Additionally, there were 165 army reserve battalions. From 1870, the infantry was armed with Berdan No.2 rifle. The infantry numbered 550–600 thousand men.

As to the cavalry, in 1860, army cuirassier regiments were transformed into dragoons. By 1866, the cavalry had 2 guards' divisions, 7 army divisions, and a division of the Caucasus, each consisting of three brigades made up of two regiments. Those were 4 regiments of cuirassiers, 20 of dragoons, 16 of lancers, and 16 of hussars, each consisting of 5 squadrons, one of which was in reserve. By 1877, the divisions were reorganized to consist of 2 brigades, and army divisions included one regiment each of dragoons, lancers, hussars, and the Cossacks. All told, there were 3 divisions of the guards, 14 army divisions, division of the Caucasus, and the Cossack division. On average, the cavalry numbered 60–70 thousand men.

By 1856, the artillery had 9 divisions consisting of the total of 24 regular and 7 mounted artillery brigades, which, in turn, broke down into 114 regular and 30 mounted

---

[16] These were garrison duty battalions stationed in remote and borderland parts of the empire. 'Of the line' here refers to the old defensive lines.

batteries. By 1863, it consisted of 28 brigades (made up of 3 batteries), the Trans-Baikal brigade, and 6 detached batteries. Mounted artillery had 8 brigades of 2 batteries each. By 1869, the number of regular brigades reached 49 and mounted brigades were 7. By 1877, the artillery consisted of 48 regular brigades, 3 special brigades, 27 brigades of mounted artillery, and 29 Cossack batteries. The artillery numbered 75–90 thousand men.

According to 1857 tables of organization and equipment, engineering troops had 10 sapper battalions and 1 sapper semi-battalion. From 1864, they had one guards' battalion, one grenadier, 7 army, 3 of the Caucasus, 3 of reserve, and 6 pontoon. By 1876, the structure of engineering troops changed again into that of 15 sapper battalions, 6 sapper semi-battalions, 3 railroad battalions, 6 military telegraph depots and 4 field engineering depots, as well as 5 companies of the line and 2 depots of siege engineering equipment. On average, these troops numbered 16–19 thousand men.

Home guard troops (136.4 thousand men in 1880) were made up of locally stationed battalions and smaller detachments (inherited from the Corps of Home Guards abolished in 1864), plus another 93 thousand auxiliaries (construction and other non-combat units). Another component was special Finnish units. Military obligation of the Cossacks (as of 1856) added up to 389 cavalry *sotnias*, 5 infantry battalions, and 14 batteries. In 1862, it was 475 *sotnias*, 8.5 battalions, and 17 batteries. By 1881, Alexander's overhaul of the Cossack hosts left the hosts of Don, Kuban, Terek, Astrakhan, Ural, Orenburg, Semirechye, Amur, Siberia, Trans-Baikal, and Ussuri. Taken together, they had to field 51.5 regiments, 4 battalions, and 2 semi-battalions, consisting of 290 mounted *sotnias*, 37.5 infantry *sotnias* and detachments, and 118 guns. In 1862–1876, the units made of several non-Russian ethnic groups added up another 4.5–5.5 thousand men.

By the end of 1856, the Baltic fleet had 53 sailing ships (including 22 ships of the line and 15 frigates), 30 steamships, 40 screw-propelled ships, and 126 rowed gunboats. The Black Sea fleet had 22 sailing ships, 12 steamships, and 37 gunboats. There were 2 steamships in the White Sea, 8 in the Caspian, and 4 in the Far East. Strictly speaking, the country needed a new navy of screw-propelled and armor-clad ships that had to be built from scratch. As early as 1857–1858, the navy received 62 screw-propelled ships of various types, 45 paddlewheel steamships, and 75 gunboats (1198 guns in total). The program of building armor-clads was launched in 1862, and by 1870 Russia had 23 armor-clad battleships. Only Britain and France had more (42 and 40), while Prussia and Sweden lagged far behind with 5 each. The Black Sea fleet was rebuilt after 1870, and by 1875 it had two armor-clad battleships, 5 screw-propelled corvettes, 14 schooners, 1 yacht, and 7 steamships. The Caspian flotilla had 3 screw-propelled schooners, 3 gunboats, 7 steamships and 15 ships of other classes. The Siberian flotilla had a clipper, 5 gunboats, 2 transport ships, 4 schooners, 3 steamships, and 7 ships of other classes. The White Sea flotilla consisted of a total of 5 vessels. By 1877, the Baltic fleet had 24 armor-clad battleships, 3 partially armor-plated cruisers, and 20 other vessels.

Another significant change affected the army command structure. As before, the armed forces came under the Military (Army) and Navy ministries. The Military Ministry included the Military Council, General Headquarters, the Emperor's Field Chancellery, the Main Court of Military Justice and a number of directorates, inspectorates, and committees. In 1864, the country was divided into 10 (and later 14) military command regions (of several governorates each): St. Petersburg, Finland, Riga, Vilna, Warsaw, Kiev, Odessa, Kharkov, Kazan, Moscow, Caucasus, Orenburg, West Siberia, and East Siberia. Every region had a military council, a court of military justice, the headquarters (with quartermaster, communications, and on-duty general's sections) and specialized directorates: quartermasters, artillery, engineering, and medical. The old division of the army into corps was first abolished, and then reinstituted in the mid-1870s. By 1880, there were 19 army corps: the guards' corps, grenadier corps, army corps numbered 1 through 15, and the 1st and 2nd corps of the Caucasus (5 divisions were not incorporated into any corps). A corps consisted of 2 infantry and one cavalry divisions, a sapper battalion, and a mobile depot of artillery and engineering equipment. An infantry division included 2 brigades of 2 regiments each and an artillery brigade of 6 batteries: 3 of 9-pounders and 3 of 4-pounders. A cavalry division included 2 brigades of 2 regiments each and 2 mounted batteries.

In the 1860s and 1870s, the number of officers stood at 28–32 thousand (in 1878 it reached 37.2 thousand because of the war with Turkey). The system of military education was dramatically reformed in the 1860s. The principal innovation was to separate general military education from advanced specialized training. Former cadet schools were split into military gymnasiums (which provided the general education), and military colleges (for specialized education). Following this reform, only graduates with military education could be commissioned.

In 1863, the senior grades (devoted to specialized training) of cadet schools (except for the School of Pages, Finland, Orenburg and Siberian) were reorganized into three military colleges with a 2-year course of study: the 1st named after Paul I, the 2nd named after Grand Duke Constantine in St. Petersburg, and the 3rd named after Alexander II in Moscow. In 1865, the College of Guards *Junkers* named after Nicholas I (former School of Guards Warrant Officers and Cavalry *Junkers*) was transformed into Nicholas Cavalry College. The School of Pages and Finland Cadet School retained their old organization: their senior grades were the equivalent of a military college, and junior grades – of a military gymnasium. By 1871, the total enrollment of military colleges and senior grades in the Schools of Pages and Finland stood at 1188, and in 1880 at 1360.

Junker colleges with a 2-year course of study were intended to give military education to the so-called 'volunteer'[17] *junkers* and non-commissioned officers. Upon graduation, they became commissioned officers. These colleges admitted graduates of either military progymnasiums[18] or of qualifying civilian schools. Late in 1864, such *junker* colleges opened in Vilna and Moscow, in 1865 in Helsingfors, Warsaw, Kiev, Odessa, Chuguev, and Riga and cavalry *junker* colleges in Tver and Elizabethgrad, in 1866 – in Kazan and Tiflis, and in 1867 in Orenburg. Two more were added in 1869 (Petersburg Infantry College and Novocherkassk Cossack College), then one in 1870 (Stavropol) and one in 1872 (Irkutsk). In 1878, Stavropol and Orenburg colleges were transformed into the Cossack ones. By 1879 (when the Helsingfors college closed), there were 16 *junker* colleges with total enrollment of 4500. Total number of *junker* college graduates in 1866–1879 added up to 16731.

Military gymnasiums first appeared in 1863 through reorganization of cadet schools. By 1871, there were 12 military gymnasiums: the 1st and 2nd of St. Petersburg, the 1st and 2nd of Moscow, Orel (named after Bakhtin), Voronezh (named after Grand Duke

[17] Since military duty became universal in 1874, these servicemen were not strictly speaking volunteers. This was an option available to those with some educational attainment allowing them to avoid the blind luck of the draft, serve a shorter term, and enjoy privileges, such as the path to officer status described here.
[18] These were in effect junior gymnasiums with the curriculum of 4 junior grades of a 'full' gymnasium.

Mikhail), Poltava (named after Peter the Great), Kiev (named after Grand Duke Vladimir), Polotsk, Nizhny Novgorod (named after Arakcheev), Orenburg (named after Neplyuev), and the Siberian one, plus the preparatory boarding school at Nicholas Cavalry College and the junior classes of unrestructured Schools of Pages and Finland. Their total enrollment stood at 3782 students. In 1873, military gymnasiums switched from a 6-year to 7-year course of study, and two more military gymnasiums were added for non-boarding students: the 3rd one in St. Petersburg and one in Simbirsk. In 1874, there opened the 3rd Moscow gymnasium, in 1875 one in Tiflis, and in 1876 Moscow's 4th and Pskov gymnasiums (transformed from progymnasiums). In 1871–1879, all military gymnasiums and other schools of equivalent level supplied military colleges with 4347 graduates. Accordingly, the proportion of military gymnasium graduates in military college enrollment went up from 50% in 1871 to 75% in 1879.

Military progymnasiums were first formed in 1858 out of elementary military schools[19] and were intended to educate the children of destitute noblemen and of well-deserving lower ranks of the army. They groomed their wards to be admitted into *junker* colleges or (for the less studious) into special schools run by the Military (Army) Ministry to prepare non-commissioned officers for non-combat positions. In 1867, 8 military-elementary schools were transformed into progymnasiums with a 4-year course of study: in Moscow, Pskov, Yaroslavl, Kiev, Volsk, Orenburg, Omsk and Irkutsk. The ones in St. Petersburg (a transformed draughtsman school) and in Perm followed. By early 1871, there were 10 progymnasiums with combined enrollment of 2700 students. In 1871, a military progymnasium was established in Tiflis, and in 1875 it was converted into a full gymnasium. In 1876, Moscow and Pskov progymnasiums became full gymnasiums too. After more reorganizations, 8 progymnasiums with a total enrollment of 1735 were left by 1881. They were in Yaroslavl, Orenburg, Elizabethgrad, St. Petersburg, Omsk, Volsk, Irkutsk and Vladikavkaz. In the period of 1867–1870, military progymnasiums trained 10850 graduates, and further 6730 in 1871–1880. Yet, they could not become the principal supplier of entrants into *junker* colleges: from 1867 to 1871, *junker* colleges admitted 3120 graduates of military progymnasiums compared to almost 5000 'volunteer' servicemen.

Specialized military colleges and academies remained in place. Mikhail's Artillery College graduated 1428 officers in 1861–1880, and Nicholas Engineering College graduated 791 officers in 1866–1880. In 1865, the course of study in both was extended to 3 years. The College of Military Auditors was transformed into the College of Military Justice in 1868. In 1878, that college (that produced 1298 graduates by then) was closed and replaced with the Military Law Academy with a 3-year course of study. In 1856, Naval Engineering College was transformed into Naval Engineering and Artillery College which trained artillerymen, ship mechanics, and ship engineers. In 1872, the College of Navigators was merged with the Engineering and Artillery College into what became known as Naval Ministry's Engineering College with a 3-year course of study. In 1862, officer classes of the Naval Cadet School were transformed into what was first named the Academic Course in Naval Sciences and in 1877 became the Naval Academy (with a 2-year course of study).

---

[19] Those were the schools in military settlements, where soldiers' children were considered enlisted from birth and therefore their elementary education and military training were rolled into one. Military settlements existed in Russia on a limited scale in 1810–1857 and represented an effort (by Alexander I) to let soldiers live with their families and till the land in peacetime, so that they would have some safety net for their old age. The system proved costly for the treasury and was much maligned by the 'cantonment' settlers themselves.

Small arms continued to be manufactured at the arsenal mills in Sestroretsk, Tula, and Izhevsk. After the upgrades in the early 1870s, they significantly raised their output. In 1873–1879, they produced almost 2 million rifles, exceeding target numbers by 100 thousand and making certain that the army rearmed with new Berdan rifles (which replaced Krnka rifles). From 1859, rifled field guns of bronze were made at the arsenals in St. Petersburg, Kiev, and Bryansk. With 4287 guns manufactured between 1869 and 1880, they fully met the army's requirements. Obukhov mill in St. Petersburg manufactured steel guns and ammunition. The first phase of that strategically important plant, which was on par with the best foreign counterparts, was commissioned in 1864. In 1867–1880, it produced 153 thousand rifle barrels, 4696 steel artillery shells for the navy, 530 naval guns and 731 army guns. It became the world's first mill to manufacture 12-inch guns capable of piercing 14–15 inches of armor plate. In 1879, the fleet had 573 guns of Obukhov mill manufacture and 188 guns made by Krupp in Germany. Armor plate was made at Izhora mills near St. Petersburg. Armor-clad ships were built at the New Admiralty shipyard, and two private shipyards in St. Petersburg: Carr and MacPherson's and Semyannikov and Poletika's, as well as at the shipyards in Nikolaev on the Black Sea.

Throughout this period, supplying the needs of the military domestically still posed no problems. The abolition of serfdom in 1861 dealt a serious but temporary blow to some heavy industries, especially the metallurgical one and particularly in the Urals with its historic dependence on the labor of bonded 'factory' peasants. Output of iron regained its 1860 level only in 1870. But with the expansion of free labor market, the slump was overcome and rapid industrial growth resumed on a completely new foundation. From the 1860s, entrepreneurship of all kinds expanded at a never before seen pace. Some money-losing government mills were shut down or privatized. While the heavy industry in the Urals was relatively slow to overcome the doldrums, in the South, primarily in the Donbass (where there was no historic legacy of serf labor), coal mining and metallurgical sector experienced boom times. By the early 1880s, the south caught up with the Urals in the scale of iron and steel industry. St. Petersburg and surrounding region became the major cluster of machine-building and metalworking. The industrial region centered on Moscow (with its strong legacy of artisanal and cottage industry) became the major focus of textile and other consumer-goods industries, which fully met domestic demand. In 1860–1880, per capita output of cotton fabrics doubled. Railway construction continued and accelerated, with Moscow evolving into the main hub. Moscow to Nizhny Novgorod railway (opened in 1862) provided a direct link to foreign markets for the famous huge fair in Nizhny Novgorod. In 1869, the railway connected Moscow to Samara and the Urals. Although Russia's industrial revolution started only in the mid-1850s and thus lagged by 20 to 30 years behind the leading European nations, it proceeded apace, and the wealth of Russia's resources made its prospects brighter than in other countries.

While the reign of Nicholas I faced almost no domestic seditious forces deserving of the government's concern, and after the troubles of 1825 the opposition was restricted to a number of literary salons (the only truly secret and militant group was Petrashevsky's circle of 1849), in the 1860s the nature of domestic opposition changed dramatically and forever. It took the form of revolutionary movement aimed at doing away with the established political and social order.

When the early crop of revolutionaries who fled abroad when Nicholas was still alive (M. Bakunin, A. Herzen, N. Ogarev) arranged a campaign to support Polish revolt, the public had little patience for it. Of far greater danger to the powers that be was the

'*Narodnik*' (People's) movement that evolved from the late 1860s. By the early 1870s, that mix of utopian socialism and populist sentiment (its multiple strands were inspired by M. Bakunin, P. Lavrov, and P. Tkachev) was well-organized into a number of 'circles' and operated inside the country. The 'Land and Freedom' organization of over 150 members emerged in 1876 and arranged its first public manifestation in St. Petersburg the same year, but then moved to terrorist methods. Soon, it split into the more moderate faction known as 'Black Repartition' (led by G. Plekhanov) and a radical-terrorist faction that named itself 'The People's Freedom' (led by A. Zhelyabov). Agents of the latter penetrated even the army and created several circles among officers, but their preferred technique was to hunt down top imperial officials and the emperor himself. After 1879, there were several attempts on his life, and on March 1, 1881, Emperor Alexander II was killed by the bomb thrown by terrorists.

Chapter 11

Russian Empire under Alexander III and Nicholas II

Newly enthroned emperor, Alexander III faced the imperative of quelling the revolutionary turmoil in the country. Even though the terrorist-minded 'People's Freedom' was destroyed within a month, and five assassins executed, the new emperor made it clear that he intended to nip in the bud the full spectrum of revolutionary movements and reject various projects for constitutional reform that his predecessor toyed with. On April 29, 1881, he drove the point home with the promulgation of the manifesto on inviolability of autocratic rule.

Initially, Russia's foreign policy continued the course of cooperation with Germany. On June 6, 1881, there was signed a secret treaty that appeared to reconfirm the 'Alliance of Three Emperors' of 1873. Yet, it was not a full-fledged treaty of alliance. All that Russia, Germany, and Austria-Hungary promised each other was to maintain a benevolent neutrality should any of them have an armed conflict with some fourth great power. In other words, Russia guaranteed its neutrality in case of a new Franco-German war, and Austria and Germany promised neutrality should Russia be at war with Britain (or with Turkey for that matter, but with the proviso that there must be a preliminary agreement on sharing the spoils of war, which really meant the safeguarding of Austrian interests). The treaty also rejected Britain's right to send warships through the straits with Turkey's concurrence, and secured the primacy of Austria's interests in Bosnia-Herzegovina and Macedonia, and of Russia's in Bulgaria. In 1884, the treaty was extended to another three years.

That mattered because Anglo-Russian relations soon deteriorated again. In 1882–1884, the Trans-Caspian railway was extended from Krasnovodsk to the oasis of Merv. On January 1, 1884, the population of Merv oasis swore allegiance to Russia. The southern part of the oasis (Panjdeh), which directly abuts on Afghanistan, was left alone lest its annexation provoke Britain. That leftover territory was promptly snatched by Emir of Afghanistan who was backed by Britain and postured defiantly against Russia. On March 18, 1885, the commander of Trans-Caspian Oblast, General A. Komarov with 1.8 thousand infantrymen and 4 guns trounced 4.7 thousand Afghan troops at Tash-Kepri on Kushka River, and drove them back into Afghanistan. After that, the southern part of the oasis was annexed to Russia as well. Britain threatened war, but eventually had to swallow the pill (especially since Germany, Austria, and Italy pressured Turkey to stay true to the principle of closing the straits to foreign navies). While Bismarck (who was still at the helm of German foreign policy) believed an Anglo-Russian war to be beneficial to Germany, he had an overriding concern that finding itself abandoned Russia would ally itself with Britain and France and thus realize Germany's worst nightmare. A protocol signed in London on

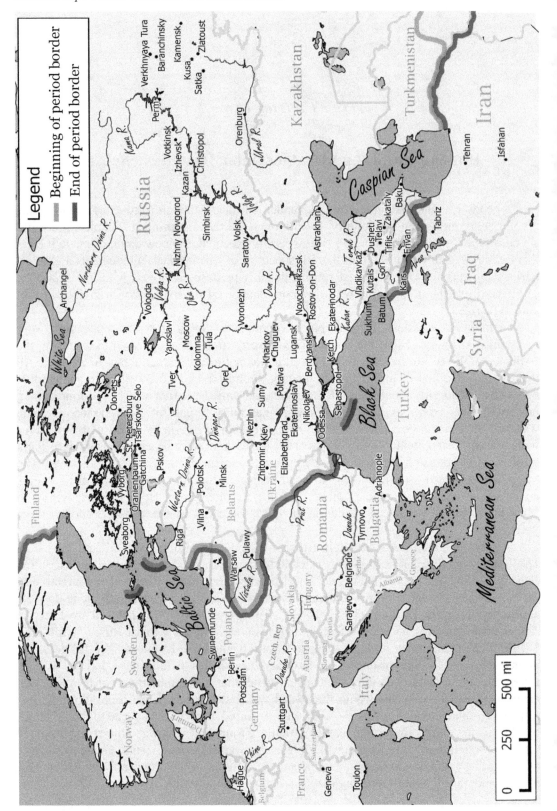

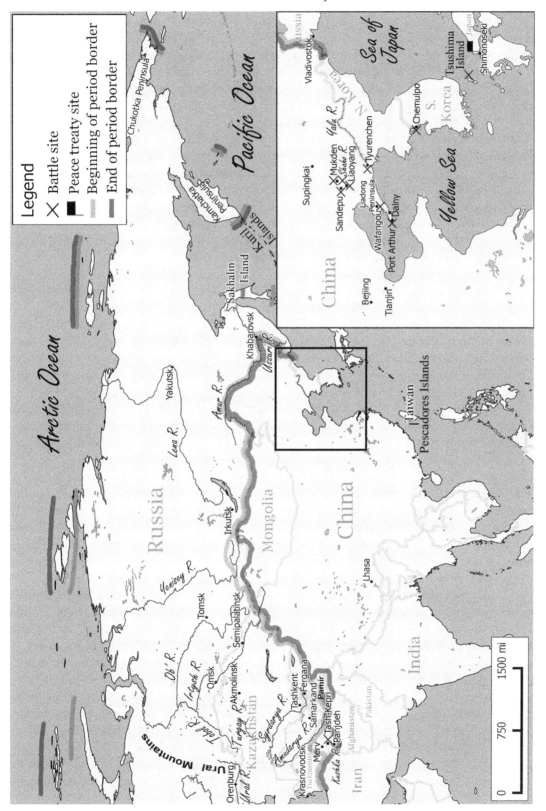

Legend

✕ Battle site
■ Peace treaty site
▨ Beginning of period border
▨ End of period border

September 10 recognized Russian possession of Panjdeh. By that time, Anglo-Turkish relations badly deteriorated over the British occupation (in 1882) of Egypt (an Ottoman vassal state), while German influence over Turkey was in the ascendant.

Back in 1879, while jockeying for influence in Bulgaria, Russia placed its bets on Bulgaria's first ruling prince, Alexander of Battenberg (who was the nephew of Russian empress). Yet, in May 1881, he revoked the Tyrnovo constitution and aligned his country with Austria while taking a hostile anti-Russian stance. In 1885, all Russian officers were recalled from the Bulgarian army (prior to that, all military ministers of Bulgaria were Russian generals). In August of 1886, Battenberg was deposed, but days later another coup brought to power pro-Austrian government of Stambulov that was even more hostile to Russia. In 1886, Austria formally declared that any entry of Russian troops into Bulgaria would make Austria go to war. It was against this background (and a serious row with Germany over customs duties) that Russian public opinion led by influential opinion journalist, M. Katkov launched the campaign against pro-German orientation of Russia's foreign policy arguing for rapprochement with France instead.

Early in 1887, another Franco-German war was brewing, and Germany was keen to get a green light from Russia. It did not succeed. In June of 1887, Russia and Germany signed only the so-called 'hedging treaty' which promised benevolent neutrality of the two parties should they be at war with a third power, unless that third power was Austria or France and the attacker was Russia or Germany. Germany was disappointed with Russia's stance, and relations deteriorated even further when Germany supported the election of Ferdinand of Coburg as the new king of Bulgaria. Seen as Austria's catspaw, Ferdinand was completely unacceptable to Russia.

Gradually, there began a Franco-Russian rapprochement. In summer of that same year (1887) Russia backed the French position on Egypt, and after their joint protest the Sultan of Egypt refused to ratify a convention with Britain which would have legitimized British occupation of his country. Russia also started to redirect its foreign financial dealings to France (obtaining foreign loans and placing Russian government bonds). Besides, anti-Russian sentiment gained the upper hand in Germany. German general headquarters did not share Bismarck's fear of war on the two fronts, planned for exactly such a war, and in 1887 even insisted on a preemptive war against Russia. The new emperor, Wilhelm II (enthroned in 1888) detested Bismarck and was under the sway of army HQ thinking. In March of 1890, Bismarck was sent into retirement, and the 'hedging treaty' was not extended.

By the summer of 1891, the Triple Alliance of Germany, Austria, and Italy was rather ostentatiously extended for a new term, and there were some indications that Britain gets drawn closer to its members. The circumstances made France to strongly promote the idea of a Franco-Russian alliance, and Alexander III increasingly leaned in its favor. In August of 1891, the two countries signed a secret preliminary agreement on mutual consultations in case of a threat to one of them, and the French navy paid a friendship visit to Kronstadt. In August of 1892, they signed a draft military convention which called for Russia's entry into the war should France be attacked by Germany or Italy, and French entry into the war should Russia be attacked by Austria or Germany. France promised to field an army of 1300 thousand against Germany, and Russia an army of 700–800 thousand. In 1893, a Russian navy squadron was feted on a visit to Toulon, and in December Alexander III approved the convention making Franco-Russian alliance a fact. It became a counterweight to German-Austrian alliance of 1879 that became a Triple Alliance of Central Powers in 1882.

In October of 1894, Emperor Alexander III passed away, and his son Nicholas II acceded to the throne. That same year, he married Princess Alice of Hessen. The new empress (baptized as Alexandra Feodorovna upon conversion to Orthodoxy) was the granddaughter of queen Victoria of England, who played mother to her in early childhood. While that marriage in itself could not directly impact relations between the powers, it contained some potential for eventual patching up of relations with Britain. Overall, the new emperor consistently followed his father's policy of strengthening Franco-Russian alliance while remaining as friendly as possible with the other powers. As German might and global influence continued to grow, they were becoming a threat not only to France, but to Britain as well. Germany made an attempt to revive a rapprochement with Russia, but Russia proved not receptive and remained firmly committed to the alliance with France. While it tried to remain neighborly with Germany, Russia avoided anything that might hurt its alliance with France, and Nicholas II refused to have any written agreements with Wilhelm II.

In 1895, Russia's expansion in Central Asia ended with the annexation of eastern Pamir Mountains. It now shared a border only with Afghanistan and China. Only a thin strip of Afghan territory in the Pamirs now separated Russia from British India. In 1897, Russia and Austria signed the agreement to maintain the status quo in the Balkans. Britain was alarmed, but the agreement gave the Balkans ten more years of peace. Another cause for British concern was Russia's shipbuilding program adopted in 1898. It called for doubling Russia's Baltic fleet of 10 new armor-clads. On January 31, 1899, Britain made Russia the offer to divide China and Turkey into spheres of influence. Upon refusal, in March, it offered an alliance to Germany, which was also turned down (even if Germany tried to blackmail Russia with such a prospect). When Britain went to war with the Boer republics in 1899, Russian public opinion was entirely on the Boer side, and many volunteers sailed to South Africa to fight the British.

It was becoming fairly obvious that an arms race between the powers got underway, and Nicholas attempted to put an end to it by convening an international peace conference. The note calling for a big international conference was circulated in August of 1898. While the powers were mostly skeptical, the conference attended by 27 countries was still held in Hague in the summer of 1899. That was the world's first such forum. The conference did adopt international conventions on the issues of war and peace: the declaration on peaceful resolution of conflicts, and on the laws and customs of war on land and sea. It also founded the International Court in Hague.

Thanks to the international agreements concluded after the Russo-Turkish war of 1877–1878, overall situation in Europe by the end of 19th century was fairly stable. At this time, great power rivalries were mostly played out in Asia and Africa (which then fell prey to the race for overseas colonies). Control of overseas empires required ocean sea-lanes. To Russia, the oceans were freely accessible only in the Far East: its Black Sea fleet was boxed in by Turkey's control of the straits, and the straits leading out of the Baltic could be easily sealed by a strong British of German navy. That explains the special importance of the Far East for Russia.

Dominance of the Far East was claimed by Japan. Following the dramatic reforms of the 1870s, it made a quantum leap in development and created a modern army modelled on European ones. Enormous China ruled by Qing dynasty had no industry or combatworthy modern army, which doomed it to depredations by stronger powers. Korea (which was a Chinese vassal and the country nearest Japan) became the first objective of Japanese expansion. Sino-Japanese war of 1894–1895 dealt China a crushing defeat, and Japanese troops occupied Korea and installed a puppet government. Shimonoseki peace treaty (1895) stipulated independence for Korea, and Japanese possession of Taiwan, Pescadores Islands, and Liaodong Peninsula.

With the support of Germany and France, Russia forced Japan to drop the demand for Liaodong Peninsula. In 1896, Russian mission in Korea provided asylum for Korean ruler (the Wan) who fled there from his palace (where he was effectively a prisoner). The Wan disbanded his pro-Japanese cabinet. That undermined fledgling Japanese influence in the country, while the group of Russian military advisers arrived and stayed until 1898. That same year, Russia and China entered into the treaty of mutual defense against Japan and concluded the agreement on the construction of a major segment of the great Trans-Siberian railway across Chinese Manchuria (it was a shortcut compared to the much longer route if the railway stayed completely on Russian territory). Russia also received a 25-year lease on Liaodong Peninsula (with the seaport of Port Arthur and soon to be built Russian city of Dalny (meaning 'the remote one' in Russian)), where it was granted the right to build fortifications and maintain armed forces. By that time, Britain and Germany also had their own footholds on Chinese coast. While they advocated the partition of China, Russia preferred to see the country whole, but with the government under a Russian sway.

In the spring of 1900, China was engulfed by the infamous Boxer Rebellion (the symbol of one of the sects that launched it was a clenched fist). The rebellion sought to wipe out western presence and influences in China and was quietly supported by the government. Thousands of foreigners and Chinese Christians were put to the sword. The embassy quarter in Beijing was besieged. European powers and Japan dispatched troops to China. Their joint force (12 thousand Japanese, 8 thousand Russians, and several thousand from other nations) marched inland from Tianjin. On August 2, Russian troops under General N. Linevich entered Beijing, while another force under General von Rennenkampf was crossing Manchuria from the north to south. Early in 1901, the rebellion was suppressed, and Russia decided to take the most China-friendly stance of all the powers by advocating rapid withdrawal of foreign troops. Russia offered to forego its part of war indemnity and extend China a large loan in exchange for Chinese guarantees of Russia's exclusive position in Manchuria, where no other powers would be given leases and concessions. Naturally, Japan was bitterly opposed. It viewed both Korea and Manchuria as its priority sphere of interest in the Far East.

Britain, which in 1902 concluded a treaty of alliance with Japan, fully supported it in this confrontation with Russia. Britain built ships for the Japanese navy and supplied Japan with arms, fuel, and strategic commodities. The United States (which at the end of 19th century dropped its policy of isolationism and launched a proactive foreign policy) also strongly favored the Japanese side. In 1903, Japan completed its program of strengthening the military and was now transparently provocative. Japan's ultimatum demanded recognition of its exclusive rights in Korea, while granting Japan equal access rights in Manchuria (thus it sought in Korea what it wanted Russia to lose in Manchuria). Nicholas II wished to avoid the war and agreed to grant Japan the rights in Manchuria provided it promised not to use Korean territory "for strategic purposes". But on January 23, 1904, Japan severed diplomatic relations, and on January 27 Japanese destroyers attacked Russian ships in Port Arthur harbor and in Chemulpo Bay (near present-day

Incheon in South Korea) where the cruiser 'Varangian' and the gunboat 'Korean' were scuttled by their crews.

While Japan was no match to Russia militarily, the remoteness of the theater of operations from European Russia gave Japan a huge advantage in that particular region. The Japanese had about 200 thousand troops in the area, while the Russians had only 98 thousand spread thin from Vladivostok to Port Arthur. The Japanese navy was twice the size of Russia's Pacific squadron. The Trans-Siberian railway was not quite completed by then, and its easternmost section could handle only three pairs of trains per day. Since a railway journey from European Russia to Manchuria took a month and a half, monthly replenishment of the troops was capped at 20 thousand men. Losses inflicted on the Russian navy in the first weeks of the war made it unable to prevent Japanese landings in Korea and Liaodong Peninsula. On March 31, the flagship, armor-clad 'Petropavlovsk' blew up on the Japanese mine killing fleet commander Admiral S. Makarov. With only 3 out of 7 armor-clads left, the squadron was effectively locked in Port Arthur harbor.

In February, Japanese 1st army under Kuroki (60 thousand men) landed in Korea and advanced to Manchurian border, the Yalu River. On May 1, it swept aside the Russian force of 20 thousand at Tyurenchen. The 2nd Japanese army under Oku (50 thousand) landed in Liaodong Peninsula and advanced toward Port Arthur. By mid-May, Russian troops withdrew to Kwantung Peninsula (southern part of Liaodong peninsula) with their backs to Port Arthur. On July 28, the 3rd army under Nogi (45 thousand formed out of part of the 2nd army and troops landed at Dalny) began the siege of Port Arthur, while the 2nd army advanced north along the railway to Liaoyang (where the main Russian force was amassed). From the east, they were threatened by Kuroki's army, and the 4th army under Nodzu was soon landed between the 1st and the 2nd armies.

From early May, Port Arthur was cut off from the main Manchurian army under A. Kuropatkin. The attempt by the corps under Baron Stakelberg to break through and relieve Port Arthur was repulsed at the battle of Wafangou (June 1–2). On July 28, the Russian navy squadron in Port Arthur tried to break out and make a dash for Vladivostok, but after its commander, Admiral Witgeft was killed in the battle on the Yellow Sea, most ships returned to Port Arthur. Fighting in Liaoyang area started on August 17–22. On August 17, the Japanese attacked a bigger Russian force, were repulsed with 24 thousand casualties, and began to retreat (the Russians lost 18 thousand). Instead of exploiting this success, the commander, General Kuropatkin (who was fearful of being outflanked) himself retreated to the new positions at Shaho River (north of Liaoyang) on August 24. There, the Russian troops were brought up to 210 thousand and gave the Japanese (who had 170 thousand) another battle. It lasted from September 26 to October 5 and ended inconclusively after much bloodshed on both sides.

Port Arthur's garrison of 43 thousand faced first 50 thousand and then 100 thousand besieging Japanese. From August 6, it repulsed six assaults and lost more than half of its defenders (27 thousand), but also inflicted huge losses on the Japanese (110 thousand). On December 20, after the loss of Mount Vysokaya which dominated the city (its seizure enabled Japanese artillery to sink what was left of the fleet) and the loss of two forts on the right flank, the commander of Kwantung fortified area, General Staessel capitulated. The fall of Port Arthur became a turning point in the war, as it left a very bad taste both in the army and the country at large. On January 12, 1905, Russian 2nd army troops under O. Grippenberg went on the offensive at Sandepu in order to stop Nogi's army returning from the peninsula from joining the other Japanese forces. Yet, excessively cautious Kuropatkin (who by then was appointed commander of all forces in the Far East) ordered them to retreat even though they had an advantage over the enemy.

Kuropatkin now had 280 thousand men under his command and planned to go on the offensive in Mukden (today's Shenyang in China) area on February 12, 1905. But the Japanese troops under the overall command of Marshal Oyama (270 thousand) preempted him by attacking on February 5. The battle raged for three weeks across the 100-kilometer wide front. Kuropatkin had every chance to prevail but lost the battle and retreated after losing 59 thousand as casualties and 30 thousand as prisoners. The Japanese (who suffered 70 thousand casualties) were too worn out to continue the offensive. By March 9, Russian troops dug in at the new positions in Supingkai (now Siping in China). After that, there were no more large engagements on land. In early October, 1904, a new squadron commanded by Admiral Z. Rozhestvensky was dispatched from the Baltic to the theater of war. With the loss of Port Arthur, the squadron's epic journey lost its point, and its only option now was to sail on to Vladivostok. The squadron numbered 20 armor-clads and cruisers and 9 destroyers. On May 14, by Tsushima Island in the Sea of Japan, the squadron ran into the Japanese fleet with twice its number of guns (28 armor-clads and cruisers and 63 destroyers). After a 2-day battle, the squadron was wiped out with 19 ships lost and 5 surrendering.

Peace talks began on July 27, 1905 in Portsmouth (NH, USA) and were facilitated by President Theodore Roosevelt. The war did not bring Russia much economic or financial hardship: its golden reserves grew by 150 million rubles in the course of the war and exceeded the amount of paper money in circulation. Russia's credit rating was higher than Japan's (it borrowed at 5–6%, and Japan at 7–8%). By that time, Russian troops were just beginning a truly massive deployment. In the course of the war, the carrying capacity of the Trans-Siberian railway grew severalfold (to 14–20 daily pairs of trains compared to 3 at war's start). Fresh troops kept arriving from Russia, and in the trenches of Supingkai the Russians had 38 first-rate divisions against Japan's 20 (who were largely reservists by then). Japan's finances were in dire straits: tax burden grew by 85% (compared to 5% in Russia). With its larger human losses (86 thousand dead against Russia's 50 thousand), Japan hovered on the brink of utter exhaustion and depletion of human resources, whereas Russia was using for that war only a tenth of its military capabilities. Japan would have been unable to resist a new Russian land offensive. But what followed instead of an offensive was the signing of peace on August 23. It cost Russia the southern half of Sakhalin Island (Japan occupied it during the war), and gave Japan a free hand in Manchuria and Korea. The conclusion of peace was brought about by domestic developments in Russia, which by then was convulsed by a broad revolutionary movement.

From the early 1880s, in the circles hostile to Russia's government system (both inside Russia and in émigré communities) there emerged various Marxist groups and organizations which launched proselytizing efforts among factory workers. While the creation of 'Liberation of Labor' group led by G. Plekhanov (1883, in Geneva) was primarily an event belonging to the history of ideas, the 'Union for Liberation of the Working Class' founded by V. Ulyanov (Lenin) in 1895 from several Marxist groups meant real seditious business from the very start as it established contacts with the striking workers of St. Petersburg. In the 1880s, social democrat parties emerged in Finland, Poland, and Armenia. In 1898, in Minsk, there was launched Russian Social Democratic Workers Party. Its second congress in London (1903) gave it organizational shape. The activity of various *Narodnik* circles continued as well. In 1902, they united into a Socialist-

Revolutionary party (led by V. Chernov, N. Avksentiev, A. Gots, and others). Its ranks were 70% professional classes (or 'intelligentsia' to use the elusive Russian term), 26% factory workers, and 1.5% peasants. Nothing daunted, its objective was a socialist revolution with primary reliance on the peasants' support. From the late 1890s, liberal strand of the opposition, which was largely sustained by *zemstvo* milieu, revived as well. In 1902, its leader, P. Struve started publishing 'The Liberation' magazine in Stuttgart. In 1903–1904, there appeared 'The Union of Liberation' and 'The Union of Zemstvo Constitutionalists', which merged into the 'Union of Unions' in 1905.

With explosive growth of Russian industry, large cities concentrated vast masses of factory workers, many of whom were uprooted former peasants and were a receptive audience for subversive propaganda by the revolutionaries. Initially, the revolutionaries had little luck with weaving political demands into the purely economic agenda of worker strikes and protests. Only in the early years of the 20th century, when the revolutionary movement mastered organizational skills and gained the ability to influence striking workers, industrial action was quickly politicized. In 1900–1902, so-called 'political' strikes made up 20% of the total, but in 1903–1904 over 50% of strikes were 'political'. The biggest strikes were those at Obukhov mills in St. Petersburg in May 1901, November strike in Rostov-on-Don, and the general strike in southern Russia in the summer of 1903 (it spread to Odessa, Kerch, Batum, Tiflis, Nikolaev, Ekaterinoslav, Kiev, and Elizabethgrad with about 200 thousand striking workers). Those same years saw agrarian unrest as well (especially in Left Bank Ukraine).

Russo-Japanese war served as a potent catalyst for the revolutionary movement. All the strands of revolutionaries, especially the most radical ones (Lenin's faction of Social Democrats) argued for Russia's defeat in the war, and Russian defeats in Manchuria flushed them with enthusiasm. When news of the fall of Port Arthur came on January 3, 1905, it prompted the long-planned strike at Putilov works in St. Petersburg. The strike began with purely economic demands and quickly spread to involve 100 thousand workers. Social Democrat groups insisted that political demands be added and organized a march on the Winter Palace in order to present a petition to Nicholas II. That 'peaceful demonstration' was a transparent provocation by the socialists (especially the 'Society of Factory Workers' organized in 1903 by a suspected police informant, priest George Gapon). For one thing, it was known that the emperor is not in the capital, for another, barricades were coming up all over town even before the march reached the palace and was fired upon. Since blank shots had no effect, and agitators called for breaking through the cordon of troops, live ammunition was fired and killed and wounded several dozen. Clashes with the troops and police followed all over the city (with the loss of about 130 lives).

Those events of January 9 were both a trigger and a signal for pre-planned revolutionary turmoil all over the country, which got engulfed by both factory strikes and agrarian unrest. Several riots occurred in the army and navy (on June 14, sailors rioted at Black Sea fleet's armor-clad 'Prince Potyomkin', and on November 11–16 at the cruiser 'Ochakov'). Even though the army generally remained loyal, the supreme authorities of the country appeared befuddled and largely lost control over the situation as they lacked the nerve for decisive suppression of the revolutionaries. Nicholas II yielded to the wishes of liberal-minded circles. On February 18, he gave orders to prepare a law on the creation of elected representative body, and the manifesto on the 'Institution of State Duma' and 'Election Guidelines' were promulgated on August 6. That barely defused the situation though, because the real control over the movement belonged not to liberal-constitutional circles but to radical socialist revolutionaries. In autumn, all-Russian political strike was launched in Moscow.

On October 17, Nicholas II promulgated the manifesto that gave the State Duma legislative powers and granted the whole country guarantees of civil and political liberties (inviolability of person, freedom of conscience, freedom of speech, assembly, and unions). This was followed by a new wave of revolutionary demonstrations, but they backfired. October 18–22 saw spontaneous anti-revolutionary protests erupt in many cities, and large-scale clashes between the mobs followed. Overall though, the manifest was perceived as proof of the regime's weakness, and prospects for its violent removal from power were openly discussed in the revolutionary circles. On October 25–26, the naval base of Kronstadt was at the mercy of drunken mobs of sailors. On October 30, the same kind of riot occurred in Vladivostok where the reservists waited to be shipped home. The radicals decided to step up the pressure. In December of 1905, Moscow committee of Lenin's Social Democrats initiated an armed uprising in Moscow. It was spearheaded by about 8 thousand well-armed and trained fighters. Shooting from behind and from concealed positions, fighters killed soldiers and policemen and then melted into Moscow's maze of backyards and alleys exposing civilians to return fire. Networks of barricades were built in some neighborhoods, Presnya in particular (those maintained fire until December 19). These outrages finally prompted the government into decisive action. Semyonovsky guards' regiment was dispatched to assist Moscow garrison, and its commander, Colonel Min quickly imposed order and squeezed the fighters out of town.

Once the rebellion in Moscow was suppressed, the revolutionary activity ebbed (although unrest persisted into 1907). At this stage, the revolutionaries' main technique became terror. The number of terrorism victims exceeded the number of caught and executed terrorists. In 1906, the terrorists killed 768 officials and wounded 820. By contrast, over the whole period of 1905–1907, field court martials (which dealt only with armed persons caught in the act) issued 683 death warrants. Disturbance continued in the armed forces (July 17, 1906 riot in Sveaborg artillery regiment, July 19 riot in Kronstadt and on the cruiser 'Memory of Azov'). Nationalist protests in Finland, Poland, the Baltics, and Trans-Caucasia (where they were accompanied by mutual slaughter between the Armenians and Azeris) added to the overall destabilization. To a considerable degree, the flames were fanned by Russia's foreign enemies. American bankers (who were in sympathy with Japan) donated a million francs for the needs of the revolution with the proviso that money be split between all revolutionary parties and used to arm the people. Instances of direct funding of revolutionary parties by Japan were well known both to friends and foes of Russian government. In some cases, it was aid in kind (one gun-running steamship ran aground on the coast of Finland in August 1905 with 1780 rifles and 97 crates of explosives). It is telling that while the revolutionaries had to realize that the end of war will improve the government's ability to deal with them, they strongly advocated the speedy conclusion of peace at Japan's terms once peace talks began.

The events of 1905 ushered in something entirely new for Russia – the organization of legitimate political parties and the creation of legislative assembly (the Duma). After the manifesto of October 17, the main currents of political ideology in the country constituted themselves as parties. In November of 1905, the royalist circles created 'The Union of

Russian People' and in 1907 'The Union of Archangel Mikhail'.[20] The leaders of these two parties, V. Purishkevich, N. Markov, and A. Dubrovin, not only fully supported the existing regime, but also criticized it as insufficiently ruthless against the revolutionaries. In November, there appeared 'The Union of October 17', which primarily represented entrepreneurs, industrialists, and to a lesser degree landowners and professional classes (its leader was A. Guchkov). The '*Octobrists*' were loyal subjects who mostly advocated a number of economic reforms. In October, the former 'Union of Unions' reinvented itself as Constitutional Democrats (usually abbreviated as '*Kadets*' in Russian), the party representing liberal intelligentsia and urban middle class (its leader was P. Milyukov). They advocated for constitutional monarchy with a parliament and for the preservation of the empire's territorial integrity (with continuation of Finland's autonomy and its restoration for Poland). Their programmatic statements aside, the '*Kadets*' (unlike the '*Octobrists*') frequently supported the revolutionaries and even stooped to offering justifications to acts of terror. Nonetheless, the real divide in Russian political landscape was between all these parties and the revolutionaries: Socialist Revolutionary party, *Bolshevik* and *Menshevik* [21] wings of Social Democrats, and some nationalist groups, in Poland and Transcaucasia in particular.

The elections were held against the backdrop of continuing revolution, and proved a complete fiasco for the government. The first Duma elected in the spring of 1906 had 448 representatives of whom about 170 were '*Kadets*' and affiliated smaller groups, 15 were Social Democrats, a further 100 called themselves *Trudovik* (Labour) faction (deputies of populist leanings representing peasants), 70 were various nationalists from the empire's peripheries, 30 were moderates on the right, and 100 were independents. With such a leftist composition, this Duma immediately took up the agrarian issue and in such a radical vein that it provoked new unrest in the countryside. On July 9, the Duma was disbanded. '*Kadet*' deputies convened in Vyborg and appealed to the population not to pay taxes and evade military service until new elections are called. Yet, elections for the second Duma (held in February 1907) produced an even more leftist body. Out of its 542 deputies, 43% represented revolutionary parties (65 Social Democrats, 34 Social Revolutionaries, 101 *Trudoviks*, and 14 Popular Socialists), the '*Kadets*' won 19% (92 deputies, or half of what they had in the first Duma), nationalists, including Polish got 15% (78 seats.), '*Octobrists*' and moderates got 32, parties of the right had 22 seats, the Cossacks 17 seats, and 50 deputies were independents. This Duma gave a hostile reception to March 1907 speech by the chairman of the Council of Ministers, P. Stolypin in which he outlined his vision of comprehensive reforms. The majority preferred revolutionary change and an end to existing political and social order. On June 3, 1907, this radical Duma was disbanded as well, and a new law was adopted to change how elections were held. The third Duma (442 deputies) had a different complexion: the biggest faction (154 seats) were '*Octobrists*', who formed majority voting alliances on various issues with either parties of the extreme right, or with '*Kadets*'.

---

[20] In Russian, they came to be known as Black Hundreders. Ever since, the term stood for extreme reactionary chauvinist forces.

[21] During its second congress in London (1903), Russian Social Democratic Workers Party split into two factions: radical (led by Lenin), and more moderate one (which was closer to the mainstream of West European Social Democratic movement). The former became known as *Bolsheviks* (from the Russian word for 'majority') and the latter as *Mensheviks* (or those of the minority).

Internal upheavals reflected very badly on Russia's international position just as the alignment of forces in the world was changing again. That was becoming clear even during the Russo-Japanese war. In 1904, France entered into a military and political alliance with Britain ('Entente Cordiale') even though France was Russia's ally, while Britain strongly supported Japan. Conversely, Russo-German relations improved during the war. Wilhelm felt that he must support Russia in this struggle of the white race against the ascendant 'yellow threat'. In October 1904, when the ill-fated Russian squadron steamed through the North Sea, it mistakenly shot at and sunk some British fishing boats, and an Anglo-Russian war loomed, the Kaiser stated that Russia and Germany must stand together in this conflict. Nicholas II (who thought that Europe must be rid of British insolence) replied with the offer of draft alliance treaty between Russia, Germany, and France aimed against Britain. In those same days, the existing 1897 treaty with Austria was supplemented with a new agreement of neutrality in case of an attack by a 'third party' (meaning Britain on Russia, or Italy on Austria). In the event, Britain did not interfere with the passage of Russian squadron, and the idea became moot (especially as Wilhelm insisted that the treaty be prepared in secret from France, to which Nicholas objected). On July 10–11, 1905, emperor Nicholas received Wilhelm as his guest aboard the royal yacht at Bjorko (near Vyborg). The personal meeting resulted in the signing of secret agreement which bound the two countries to assist each other should they be attacked in Europe. Russia had to try making France join the agreement as well.

From the early 1890s and until 1906, the pillars of Russian foreign policy were the alliance with France, good relations with Germany, reluctant cooperation with Austria in the Balkans, and global opposition to Britain (and Japan in the Far East). But now that France and Britain drew closer together (having resolved their points of friction in the colonies), while antagonism grew between Britain and Germany (because of the German feeling that their country got too little in the race for colonies, and because of the British feeling that increasing strength of German navy threatens its maritime supremacy), the situation was different.

The new cabinet formed by the Liberals in Britain leaned toward defusing the standoff with Russia. In May 1906, it extended Russia the offer to start negotiations on points of friction in Asia. The agreement signed on August 18 in St. Petersburg gave Russia major concessions by recognizing Russia's interests alongside the length of its border in Asia. Britain dropped claims on Tibet and recognized China's sovereign rights to it (during Russo-Japanese war Lhasa was occupied by the British, and Tibet was forced to cede to Britain control of its foreign policy). Russia undertook to respect territorial integrity and independence of Afghanistan and recognized it as falling within the British sphere of influence (but with Britain's obligation to not undermine Russia's interests from its territory). Iran was carved into three zones. The north (with Tabriz, Tehran, the Caspian coast and the center down to Isfahan) became a Russian sphere of influence, the southeastern section adjacent to British India and Afghanistan became the British sphere, and everything in between, including the Gulf coast was declared neutral. The two countries established joint control over Iran's treasury revenues and undertook to maintain public order in case of turmoil. That agreement was very beneficial to Russia as it got significant advantages in exchange for dropping the pie-in-the-sky claims it could not hope to realize anyway.

In the spring of 1907, there was signed a Franco-Japanese agreement and in summer a Russo-Japanese one resolving the last points of friction left after the war. These agreements both drew the line under Russo-Japanese rivalry in Asia and pulled Japan closer to the Franco-Russian alliance. The secret protocols of Russo-Japanese agreement spelled out the spheres of influence in the Far East: Japan's included Korea and southern Manchuria and Russia's consisted of northern Manchuria and Outer Mongolia. Subsequent Russo-Japanese treaties of 1910 and 1912, gave both countries even more discretion within their spheres of influence. In 1910, Japan annexed Korea. In 1912, Russia wangled out of China the recognition of autonomy for Outer Mongolia with Russian protectorate over it. In 1913, Japan offered Russia a military and political alliance. At the time, Russia thought it premature, and it was delayed until World War I was on.

With all these shifts, relations with Germany cooled. When the two emperors met aboard a yacht again (July 21, 1907 at Swinemünde), the meeting brought no results. Soon, relations soured even more as 'the Bosnian crisis' unfolded. As Turkey was going through its 'Young Turk' revolution, Austria-Hungary saw the chance to annex Bosnia-Herzegovina, which it occupied ever since the Berlin Congress of 1878. Russia was ready to agree, but only if Austria-Hungary supported (in a new international conference) Russia's demand of free access to the straits (while they remain closed to warships of other nations) and also agreed on full independence for Bulgaria. Due to lack of interest from Britain, France, and Germany, such a conference was never convened, yet Austria annexed Bosnia-Herzegovina all the same (September 1908). Protests by Russia, Serbia, and Turkey were not joined by anyone else, and in 1909 Germany demanded that Russia recognize the annexation and drop the demand for a conference. Russia had to yield, all the more so because P. Stolypin was just embarking on his far-reaching reforms and was strongly opposed to a new war (which Russia was not ready for anyway). On October 22–23, 1910, when the emperors of Russia and Germany met in Potsdam, they agreed that Germany will not encourage Austrian expansion in the Balkans, while Russia will not support anti-German moves by Britain.

By the spring of 1912, there formed a Balkan Alliance consisting of Bulgaria, Greece, Serbia, and Montenegro. Its members saw it as being a defensive one against Austria-Hungary and an offensive one against Turkey. Using a massacre of Macedonians by the Turks as pretext, the allies went to war and quickly defeated Turkish troops driving the Turks out of almost all of European Turkey, even Adrianople. That created the threat of a general European war. Austria was adamant about not letting Serbia have access to the Adriatic Sea. Jointly with Italy, it patched up a new country of Albania out of territories intended for Serbia and Greece. Austria also started partial mobilizations and troop deployments closer to the Russian border. Russia responded by delaying demobilization of draftees who were due to go home that year. Yet, at the insistence of Britain and France, Russia decided not to press the issue of a Serbian Adriatic port, all the more so as it wished to avoid war. In 1913, the Tsar of Bulgaria unhappy with how territory seized from Turkey was divided by his allies of the year before (the Balkan Alliance), attacked them but was defeated with heavy territorial losses on all sides (Romania and Turkey joined this war too, and the latter won back Adrianople).

During their last face-to-face meeting in May of 1913, Nicholas tried to talk Wilhelm into improvement of relations by offering to drop his claims on the straits should Germany restrain Austria from the policy of annexations in the Balkans. Yet, the meeting did not lead anywhere. No matter the frequent mutual protestations of friendship, and the fact that the two had no major disputes with each other, the policy of both Germany and Russia essentially followed the outlines that emerged after the Berlin Congress of 1878 and

Triple Alliance of 1879, which brought about Franco-Russian rapprochement. Ever since, Germany never failed to put Austria's interest above that of drawing closer to Russia. At the same time, the differences between Austria-Hungary and Russia remained insurmountable. A conflict between the two (and by extension, a pan-European one) was a foregone matter, merely a question of time.

That time came on June 15, 1914 when G. Princip (a member of Serbian nationalist organization) assassinated Austria's heir to the throne, Archduke Frances-Ferdinand on a visit to Sarajevo. Austrian military establishment clamored for immediate declaration of war on Serbia. On July 10, Serbia was issued an ultimatum with a number of requirements any sovereign nation simply cannot swallow, including the entry of Austrian troops into Serbia and investigation of the assassination on Serbian territory by Austrian investigators. Since Nicholas II did not want war and was not yet prepared for one (Russia's military program was to be completed by 1917, while Germany and Austria-Hungary were done with theirs), he demanded that Austria extend the ultimatum's deadline, while he recommended that the Serbs accept the ultimatum (except for Austrian troops presence clause). At the same time, he asked Wilhelm II to restrain Austria from going to war. Yet, by that time Wilhelm was convinced that the war between the two alliances cannot be avoided, and that Germany will benefit should it start sooner rather than later. He refused, and on July 15 Austria-Hungary declared war on Serbia and started artillery shelling of Belgrade (separated from Austria-Hungary only by the river).

Nicholas II procrastinated till the last possible moment. For two days, he mulled the idea of a partial mobilization, but that would have made full mobilization more difficult if it became required to pressure Austria further. On July 18, the order for full mobilization was signed. Nicholas II immediately telegraphed Wilhelm with assurances that he would take no action while negotiations on the Serbian issue continued. In response, Germany required that mobilization be suspended by noon of the next day. On July 19, when Russia refused (because that was a matter of both national pride and a strategic impossibility), Germany declared war. On July 21, it declared war on France as well. The next day, when German troops crossed the border into Belgium, Britain declared war on Germany. Italy shirked its Triple Alliance responsibility to go to war on the technical grounds that Germany declared war first. On July 24, Austria declared war on Russia, and on August 11 Japan declared war on Germany.

System of government and military-economic potential

Other than the introduction of elected representative bodies in 1906, the machinery of state underwent no significant change till the last days of empire. As the country developed, the functions of some agencies were modified and some others were transformed. In accordance with the 'Organic Laws' adopted on April 23, 1906, the supreme elected legislative bodies were the State Duma and the State Council.

The State Duma was elected for the term of 5 years by three categories of voters: 1) landowners (qualifying requirement was real estate worth at least 15 thousand rubles or land ownership over anywhere from 100 to 650 hectares (that depended on local conditions)), 2) urban population, and 3) peasants. The latter did not have qualified voter requirement, and its representatives were elected through a pyramid of local assemblies: village assembly to borough assembly to *uezd* assembly. *Uezd* assemblies chose electors, who went to their governorate-level election conventions. Those conventions chose from the ranks of attending electors the number of Duma representatives (separately for each category of voters) assigned to this or that particular governorate. In 1907, urban electors were split into two constituencies based on property or business ownership. The Duma had its own administrative office, sections, and committees. Its chairmen were S. Muromtsev (the 1ˢᵗ Duma), F. Golovin (the 2ⁿᵈ Duma), N. Khomyakov (till March of 1910), A. Guchkov (till March 1911), M. Rodzyanko in the 3ʳᵈ Duma, and M. Rodzyanko in the 4ᵗʰ Duma.

In 1906, the State Council was reformed as well and became a legislative body. Half of its members were appointed by the emperor, and another half elected by *zemstvos*, governorate nobility assemblies, and non-government organizations. The members were elected for the term of nine years with a stacked rotation: one third of them had to be reelected every three years. The State Council consisted of a general assembly, 2 departments, 2 special assemblies and the State Chancellery. Its chairmen were Count D. Solsky, E. Frisch (1906–1907), and M. Akimov (1907–1914).

The Council of Ministers was reconvened in 1905 (it had not met since 1882). On April 23, 1906, the Committee of Ministers was abolished – its functions were inherited by the Council of Ministers (and in part by the departments of State Council). Its chairmen were Count D. Solsky (till October, 1905), Count S. Witte (till April, 1906), I. Goremykin (till July 1906), P. Stolypin (till September 1911), V. Kokovtsov (till January 1914), and I. Goremykin again (till January 1916).

The oversight of some major business of state continued to be entrusted to high-level ad hoc committees. In 1903–1905, the Special Committee on the Far East monitored developments in that region. The construction of Trans-Siberian railway in 1892–1905 was controlled by the Siberian Railway Committee. In 1905–1909, there existed the Committee on Defense tasked with coordination between army and navy ministries and other government bodies.

His Imperial Majesty's Personal Chancellery was revamped under Alexander III. In 1882, the scope of its responsibilities was sharply reduced. In fact, the emperor's chancellery as such was now reduced to what used to be its section 1. The special committee on civil service was added in 1894 (to handle such personnel management tasks as hiring, firing, and promotions for civil officials up to class 5). Section 2 was abolished, and its responsibility for the codification of laws was given first to Codification Department of State Council (1882–1894) and then to the code of laws section of the State Chancellery. Section 3 was abolished in 1880 with its portfolio inherited by the Ministry of Internal Affairs. That same year, former section 4 was spun off into a separate agency – His Emperor's Chancellery on the Charities of Empress Maria. In 1895, the Commission of Petitions was transformed into the Chancellery of Petitions.

In the Senate, the 2ⁿᵈ department of appeals was replaced with the department that handled complaints against governorate public reception offices (*prisutstviya*) on peasant matters (and all other peasant-related issues). In 1898, the 4ᵗʰ and 5ᵗʰ Department of Appeals and the Department of Metes and Bounds were rolled into a single Department of Courts. A Supreme Disciplinary Court was added to the Senate in 1885 to look into cases of improper behavior by judges.

The lineup of ministries was mostly unchanged, while their inner structure kept changing to adjust to evolving needs of the time. In 1883, the Separate Gendarme Corps was put under the Ministry of Internal Affairs but remained separate from that ministry's Department of Police. Governorates had their own gendarme directorates. The chief of police department and the commander of gendarme corps were now the same person – the first deputy minister. From 1880, city police departments had secret political police sections as well.

The Peasant Land Bank (1882) and Nobility Land Bank (1885) were established as parts of Ministry of Finance. In 1894, the Ministry of State Properties was converted into the Ministry of Farming and State Properties, which in 1905 morphed into The Main Authority on Farming and Land Management. It also incorporated the Resettlement Administration (which dealt with peasant colonization of Russia's remote borderlands launched as part of Stolypin's agrarian reform). In 1915, the Main Authority finally became simply the Ministry of Agriculture. A new Ministry of Commerce and Industry was created in 1905. It managed government-owned industry and was responsible for oversight of the private sector in industry. This small ministry was pieced together out of some elements from the Ministry of Finance (commerce and industry department, tariff-setting agencies, and factory inspectorate), the mining department of Ministry of Farming and State Properties, and the Directorate of Merchant Shipping and Seaports. The Main Directorate of Government Stud Farms was restored as a standalone agency in 1881.

Territorial administration of Russia remained unchanged till the empire's end. By the early 20th century, there were 78 governorates, 18 Oblasts, and 4 large cities with governorate status (Moscow, St. Petersburg, Odessa, and Baku). Under Alexander III, some changes were made in local government. In 1889, there was introduced the position of *zemstvo* warden. These had oversight of borough self-government, and were appointed from among the local nobility. In 1890, the statute on *zemstvo* bodies was modified. Out of three assemblies that elected *zemstvo* officials, the first one was now limited to landowning nobility (non-landowning nobility was assigned to other assemblies) and qualifying requirement was lowered to 125 hectares. Conversely, the qualification for voting in the second assembly (townsmen) was raised from 6 to 15 thousand rubles of annual turnover. The third assembly was altogether abolished, and its representatives in *uezd zemstvo* councils were now appointed by governors out of lists compiled by borough peasant meetings (the previous system was restored in 1906 though).

The city statute of 1892 changed the qualification for urban voters from one based on their tax obligation to one based on property ownership. In cities with population over 100 thousand the minimum plank of assessed real estate value was set at 3 thousand rubles, for governorate seats it was set at 1–1.5 thousand (depending on population size), and for *uezd* seats at 300 rubles. All owners of commercial and manufacturing establishments with guild licenses qualified too. In 1892, previously separate governorate public reception offices on *zemstvo* and city affairs were merged into one. In 1903, borough police chiefs received actual police departments. In 1906, Censorship Committees were transformed into Committees on Print Media.

In the justice system, in 1889, justices of the peace were replaced with town judges (except in the two capitals and Odessa), while in the countryside they were replaced with *uezd* members of circuit courts. But in 1912, the institution of justices of the peace elected by *uezd zemstvo* councils or city *dumas* was restored.

The Ministry of Finance part of state machinery added governorate and *uezd*-level public reception offices *(prisutstviya)* on taxation issues, and the ones dealing with regulation of drinking establishments. Factory inspection system made its debut in 1882. Chief factory inspector in the ministry presided over circuit inspectors (a circuit was made of several governorates). From 1886, there existed *prisutstviya* on factory matters in governorates. From 1899, their functions were inherited by district and local factory inspectors.

In the Baltic governorates, standard imperial system of police agencies replaced the old estate-based one. Separate estate courts were abolished as well (1889) and replaced with circuit courts (without jurors), appointed justices of peace and justices of peace assemblies. West Siberian governorate-general was abolished in 1882 (constituent governorates were given standard administrative structure). In 1887, East Siberian governorate-general was renamed into Irkutsk one (including Yenisey and Irkutsk governorates, Trans-Baikal and Yakutsk Oblasts). In 1894, part of it was made into a separate Amur governorate-general (Amur, Primorskaya (meaning "Maritime"), Kamchatka, and Sakhalin Oblasts).

After 1904, Siberian *okrugs* were replaced with standard *uezds*. In 1882, the governorate-general of the Steppes (drylands) was created (consisting of Akmolinsk, Semipalatinsk, and Semirechye oblasts). Governorate-general of Turkestan included Syrdarya, Fergana, and Samarkand oblasts (from 1899, Semirechye and Trans-Caspian oblasts were added to it). Viceroyalty of the Caucasus was abolished in 1883 and restored in 1905. It included Baku, Elizabethpol, Tiflis, Kutais, Erivan, and Black Sea governorates, Kuban, Terek, Dagestan, Kars, and Batum oblasts, and two *okrugs* – Sukhum and Zakataly. Warsaw governorate-general consisted of 9 governorates of the erstwhile Kingdom of Poland, governorate-general of Finland of 8 governorates of the Grand Duchy of Finland, and governorate-general of Kiev included Volhynia, Kiev, and Podolia governorates. Governorate of Moscow had the designation of governorate-general too. The remaining 49 governorates and 3 oblasts (of Don Cossack Host, Ural, and Turgay) were not part of any governorate-general.

In the 1880s, Russia's armed forces had essentially the same strength (850–880 thousand men) as before the war of 1877–1878. In the early 1890s, increasingly felt confrontation with the Triple Alliance and 1891 treaty of alliance with France engendered significant expansion of the army. Throughout this period, Russian army remained the world's largest. Its peacetime strength added up to 946 thousand (in 1892) and wartime mobilization called for 2729 thousand. For France, comparable numbers were 552 and 2605 thousand, for Germany – 521 and 2370 thousand, for Austria-Hungary – 317 and 1159 thousand, for Italy – 249 and 1164 thousand, and for Britain – 382 and 900 thousand.

All through the 1890s, the size of the armed forces grew steadily, and reached 1 million in 1897. That same year, it stood at 593 thousand in France, 585 thousand in Germany, 360 thousand in Austria-Hungary, 211 thousand in Italy, and 223 thousand in Britain. But viewed differently, over the preceding 40 years, the size of Russian army grew by 20.2%, while in Austria-Hungary it grew by 89.5%, in Germany by 53.9%, and in France by 46.7%. By 1904, the army had 1094 thousand men, by 1912 – 1385 thousand, and the military program adopted in 1913 called for adding a further 480 thousand by 1917.

In 1881, the term of military service was set at 6 years in the infantry and 7 years in the other branches. In 1888, it was reduced by one year, which was offset by a 3-year extension of the term of reserve duty. From 1906, the term of service was reduced to 3 years in the infantry and 4 years in the other branches. In the 1880s and 1890s, annual draft stood at 210 to 280 thousand men, in the early years of 20th century it grew to 300–320 thousand, and from 1908 to 450 thousand.

For the most part, the infantry retained its former organization, but riflemen and reserve units were restructured. In 1887, 20 riflemen battalions were rearranged into regiments of 2 battalions each. In 1898, 32 infantry reserve battalions were also rearranged into regiments of 2 battalions (so that in wartime they could be beefed up to 4 battalions). These regiments were further grouped into 8 reserve brigades of 4 regiments each.

In 1881, there were 192 infantry regiments, 9 riflemen brigades and 34 battalions of the line. In the second half of 1890s, those numbers were 193, 14, and 37. In the 1880s, infantry numbered 600–620 thousand, and in the 1890s – 630–740 thousand. In 1880, there were 19 army corps, and by 1898 there were 22 (due to the conversion of some reserve brigades), and the total number of battalions came up to 1138 (compared to 1034 in 1881). New brigades were added in 1900–1903: 5 Turkestan riflemen brigades and Siberian brigades numbered 4 through 7. In 1910, all infantry was given a uniform structure (infantry reserve and fortress infantry were transformed into regular infantry regiments, and Siberian riflemen regiments were given a 4-battalion organization). New army corps were formed: corps number 23 through 25, the 3rd Corps of the Caucasus, and the 5th Corps of Siberia.

From 1883, all cavalry regiments had 6 squadrons (previously, there were 4). By 1895, there were 22 cavalry divisions (91 regiment), 2 Cossack brigades, and 16 detached regiments, 11 *sotnias* and 4 squadrons. Cavalry reserve numbered 8 brigades. In the 1880s and 1890s, the cavalry numbered 70–80 thousand men.

The artillery retained its former organization. In 1888, artillery reserve was expanded and new mortar regiments came into being. In 1881, regular (not mounted) artillery brigades (they were 51) had 298 batteries (305 by 1891, and 317 by 1895). Additionally, by 1895, artillery had 1 detached regiment (4 batteries), 5 mortar regiments (16 batteries), 1 regiment of mountain artillery (3 batteries), 30 batteries of mounted artillery, and 20 Cossack batteries, as well as 6 brigades of reserve artillery (38 batteries) for the total of 428 batteries (compared to 383 in 1881). Artillerymen numbered 110–115 thousand in the 1880s, and 120–150 thousand in the 1890s.

Engineering troops went through many reorganizations. By 1895, their structure was settled at 25.5 sapper battalions grouped into 7 brigades plus 12 detached sapper battalions and companies, 8 pontoon battalions, 6 railway battalions, 6 field engineering depots, 2 siege depots, 9 companies of fortress mine-layers, 2 companies of river mine-layers, 6 military telegraph units, and 4 aircraft depots. In the 1880s and 1890s, engineering troops numbered from 23 to 35 thousand men.

By 1895, fortress troops had 53 artillery battalions and 10 companies, 2 infantry regiments and 29 battalions, 3 battalions of siege artillery, and 5 sortie batteries. The size of home guard troops shrank from 136.4 thousand in 1880 to 55.3 thousand in 1890, and only 23 thousand in 1900. Additionally, there were 6.5 penal battalions, 26 workmen and 26 warehousing details, and field gendarme details (mounted units serving as military police); the total strength of all those units fell from 93.2 thousand in 1881 to 20.3 thousand in 1895. The strength of Cossack units in 1895 was little changed from 1881: 51.5 regiment and 8.5 battalions (the total of 310 mounted and 51 infantry *sotnias* and 156 guns).

Militia organization was overhauled. In the 1870s, it consisted of individual detachments and mounted *sotnias* that could be attached to regular army units. From 1891, it was organized into brigades and divisions and integrated into the overall military system. Militiamen 1st class were those who had previously served in the army and served out their term in reserve. Militiamen 2nd class were those who never served on active duty. In wartime, the 1st class militia was expected to be called up first and supply 320 infantry detachments (20 divisions), 40 batteries (20 artillery regiments), 80 mounted *sotnias* (20 regiments), 20 companies of fortress artillery, and 20 companies of fortress sappers – the total of 400 thousand men. After 1900, mobilization plans called for the same number of units to be formed out of 2nd class militiamen.

By 1898, Russia ranked the third in Europe in the number of warships (Britain had 355, France 204, Russia 107, and Germany 77). That total (including ships under construction) was made up of 19 armor-clad battleships, 16 coastal defense armor-clads, 7 heavy cruisers, and 58 light cruisers. By 1896, Russia had 141 destroyers (France – 200, Germany – 182, Britain – 197, Italy – 107, and Austria-Hungary – 62).

The Baltic fleet consisted of 2 divisions, each made up of three squadrons (of 2 ship's companies each). The Black Sea fleet was one division (3 squadrons and 8 ship's companies). Since the Russo-Japanese war cost Russia a better half of its navy, it had to adopt a large-scale shipbuilding program (in 1908). By 1914, it was not completed yet. In 1909, the keels were laid for 7 Russian dreadnoughts with greater capabilities than their counterparts in other navies, but they were launched only in the autumn of 1914. Construction of 4 heavy cruisers (the world's largest) began in 1912 and was not completed in 1914. Speaking of truly modern ships only, by the summer of 1914 Russia had only 2 dreadnoughts, 1 heavy cruiser, 16 cruisers (and 4 under construction), 38 destroyers (and 45 under construction), and 14 submarines (13 under construction). At the time, Britain had 76 submarines, France 38, and Germany 28. By 1914, the navy had 59.5 thousand servicemen.

The Military (Army) Ministry included Military Council (its constituent committees were Coordination, Military Science, Military Hygiene, and Billets), the Main Headquarters (constituent directorates were Quartermasters, On-Duty General's, Military Communications, Military Topography, Mobilization, and Logistics and Troops Transport, plus the Main Court of Military Justice and a number of main directorates: artillery, engineering, quartermasters, military schools, military medicine, irregular troops, inspector-generals, committee of care for the wounded, and army chaplains office). The minister also presided over two special executive committees: on rearmaments and on fortifications. In 1914, the country was divided into 12 military districts: St. Petersburg, Vilna, Warsaw, Kiev, Odessa, Kazan, Moscow, Caucasus, Turkestan, Omsk, Irkutsk, and Amur.

The number of officers stood at 30–33 thousand in the 1880s, and at 34–39 thousand in the 1890s. By January 1, 1908, the army had 44.8 thousand serving officers (including 1300 generals and 7811 staff officers), for the ratio of one officer per 24 men (1:19 in France and 1:21 in Germany). On the eve of war in 1914, the army had 46 thousand officers, and the navy 2.5 thousand.

By the 1880s, *junker* colleges essentially satisfied the army's need for officer cadre. Now the emphasis was placed on educating as many officers as possible to a higher level – that of military colleges. In 1886, Riga and Warsaw *junker* colleges were closed. Some *junker* colleges added sections with military college-level courses (for graduates of civilian secondary schools), while all the rest switched to a 3-year course of study in 1901. Some were transformed into military colleges in 1902 (Moscow (named after Crown Prince Alexey in 1906) and Kiev Infantry Colleges and Elizabethgrad Cavalry College). In 1911, all the remaining *junker* colleges were revamped to become military colleges, and Russia's total of such colleges reached 17. In 1900–1914, they graduated the total of 21071 officers.[22]

In 1882, military gymnasiums were renamed cadet schools and kept that designation to the end. The Don Cadet School opened in 1883 in Novocherkassk, and the 2nd Orenburg Cadet School in 1887. Two prep schools with 3-years of study opened in 1888: in Irkutsk and Khabarovsk. Warsaw Cadet School (named after Suvorov) and Odessa Cadet School were added in 1899, Sumy and Khabarovsk cadet schools in 1900, Vladikavkaz school in 1902, Tashkent school in 1904, and Irkutsk school in 1913. Military progymnasiums were closed in 1882 except for the two in Yaroslavl and Volsk, which eventually became cadet schools (in 1896 and 1914). By 1914, there were 29 cadet schools with the total enrollment of 11.6 thousand[23]. In 1881–1900, cadet schools graduated 26.6 thousand men, and in 1901–1916 a further 20 thousand (throughout their history, Russia's cadet schools trained 64.5 thousand graduates).

By 1916, there were 7 specialized military colleges. In 1894, the 2nd Constantine College became an artillery college organized the same way as Mikhail's Artillery College. Two more artillery colleges were opened after World War I started: in Odessa (first graduating class in 1915) and Kiev (first graduating class in 1916). From 1881 to 1900, Mikhail's Artillery College graduated 2819 officers, and Nicholas Engineering College 1387 (and 1360 more in 1901–1914). A new engineering college was opened in Kiev in 1915. Military Topography College graduated more than 1000 officers through its existence. In 1901–1914, several thousand officers completed study in military academies (1076 in General Staff Academy, 550 in Artillery Academy, 484 in Engineering Academy, and 416 in Military Law Academy). In 1911, quartermasters' course in General Staff Academy was spun off into an academy in its own right (560 graduates in 1900–1914). In 1883, General Staff Academy added a course in Oriental Languages.

In 1882, there appeared branch of service schools for continued education of serving officers. They were formed on the foundation of army training units (model units that served for practical training of officers). The new schools trained battalion, squadron and battery commanders. These were the Officer Riflemen School (in Oranienbaum), the Officer Cavalry School (in St. Petersburg), and Officer Artillery School (in Tsarskoye Selo). More narrowly specialized officer schools appeared in later years: Officer Electrical Engineering School (1894), Officer Automobile School (1915), and Officer Railway School (from late 1890s to 1908). Officer aviation schools opened in Gatchina, Sebastopol, Kiev, and Baku.

Naval officers continued to be trained at Naval School (in the 19th and 20th centuries it graduated over 9.1 thousand officers). In 1915, it became a Naval College, while its junior grades were moved to Sebastopol as a Navy Cadet School. In 1913, midshipmen school was opened in St. Petersburg; in 1916, it enrolled 265 naval cadets.

---

[22] These were the School of Pages (the School of Finland was closed in 1902), Pavel's in St.Petersburg, Alexander's and Alexey's in Moscow, Kiev, Vladimir's in St.Petersburg, Kazan, Vilna, Odessa, Chuguev, Tiflis, and Irkutsk infantry colleges, Nikolayev, Elisabethgrad, and Tver cavalry colleges, Novocherkassk and Orenburg Cossack colleges. Nicholas (or Kiev's 2nd) and Tashkent colleges were added in 1914.

[23] St. Petersburg had 4 of them, Moscow had 3, and Orenburg 2. The others were in Orel, Voronezh, Nizhny Novgorod, Poltava, Polotsk, Pskov, Kiev, Simbirsk, Novocherkassk, Odessa, Omsk, Yaroslavl, Sumy, Warsaw, Khabarovsk, Tashkent, Vladikavkaz, Irkutsk, Volsk, and Tiflis plus the junior classes of School of Pages.

Naval Academy graduated over 300 officers in 1906–1914. The Navy also had a number of officer schools and what it called 'training classes': Naval School of Gymnastics, mine-laying classes, diver's classes, submariner classes, naval artillery classes, navigator classes, and Officer School of Naval Aviation.

In 1886, there was introduced a new officer rank – reserve ensign. Qualifying persons were civilians with college or secondary education who passed a special exam. They had to stay on reserve rolls for 12 years and go to training camps twice (for periods of up to 6 months). By the end of 1894, there were 2960 such reserve ensigns. The rank of brevet ensigns for servicemen on active duty was introduced in 1891. To qualify one had to be a college or secondary school graduate serving as a non-commissioned officer or a 'volunteer' warrant officer, or be a non-commissioned officer brevetted into a vacant officer position.

When World War I created the need for accelerated training of officers, there were set up a number of ensign schools with a 3 to 4 month course of training (5 in Kiev, 7 in Moscow, 4 in Peterhof, 2 in Oranienbaum, 4 temporary in Petrograd (St. Petersburg), 2 in Odessa, 2 in Omsk, 3 in Irkutsk, 2 in Kazan, 4 in Tiflis, 2 in Zhitomir, and one each in Dusheti, Gori, Telavi, Chistopol, Saratov, Orenburg, Tashkent, Gatchina, Pskov, also one in Ekaterinodar for the Cossacks), as well as one for engineering troops ensigns, one for topographers, and a navy ensign school.

Prior to mobilization in 1914, Russian army consisted of 37 army corps. The infantry had 13 regiments of guards (3 divisions), 16 of grenadiers (4 divisions), 208 infantry regiments (52 divisions), 6 border regiments in Trans-Amur region (3 brigades), and 44 Siberian riflemen regiments (11 divisions) of 4 battalions each. The regiments of 2-battalion structure were 4 regiments of guards (1 brigade), 20 army regiments (5 brigades), 16 Finnish regiments (4 brigades), 8 Caucasus regiments (2 brigades), 22 Turkestan riflemen regiments (6 brigades), and 6 scout battalions. All told, the infantry had 1294 battalions.

The cavalry was grouped into divisions: 3 divisions of the guards (and 1 brigade), 16 army divisions (and 3 brigades), and 6 Cossack divisions (and 4 brigades), plus some detached regiments, In total, there were 129 cavalry regiments: 13 guards', 21 dragoon, 17 lancers, 18 hussars, and 52 Cossack (17 of the Don Host, 11 of Kuban, 4 of Terek, 3 of Ural, 6 of Orenburg, 3 of Siberia, 4 of Trans-Baikal, and one each from Astrakhan, Semirechye, Amur, and Ussuri Hosts), 6 Trans-Amur border regiments and 2 native regiments (from Dagestan and Crimea), as well as some detached smaller units – the total of 772 squadrons and *sotnias*. There were also 6 field gendarme squadrons, 8 reserve cavalry regiments (and 1 reserve battalion) and 31 detachments of border guards.

The artillery was grouped into 70 artillery brigades (each infantry division had one), 18 artillery battalions (each riflemen brigade had one), 35 mortar battalions (attached to army corps), 7 heavy artillery battalions, the guards' mounted artillery, and 12 battalions of mounted artillery (attached to cavalry divisions) and 1 reserve battalion, plus 2 battalions of mountain artillery, 9 of Cossack artillery, Orenburg Cossack brigade, and 9 detached batteries – the total of 652 batteries and 4868 guns.

Engineering troops had 39 sapper battalions (attached to army corps), 9 pontoon battalions, 3 railway brigades (plus a detached regiment and 6 battalions), 7 signals companies, 3 aviation companies, 2 aircraft battalions, and 9 detached aircraft companies.

When mobilized, the army had to field 1830 thousand infantrymen (1816 battalions), 109 thousand cavalrymen (1110 squadrons), and 7976 guns. The tables of organization and equipment established that in wartime a corps must have 64 machine guns and 108 artillery pieces (a French one – 30 and 120, a German one – 48 and 160), and an infantry division must have 32 machine guns and 48 artillery pieces (a French division – 24 and 36, a German division 24 and 72). While Germany and France had completed their military programs, Russia's program (adopted only in 1913) had to be completed by 1917 (the objective was for a corps to have 156 artillery pieces and a division 54, for the total of 8538 guns). Russia had 263 airplanes (Britain had 258, Germany 232, France 156, and Austria-Hungary 65), 14 dirigibles (Germany – 15, France –5). Russian army was ahead of others in its supply of signals equipment: a corps had 16 telegraph stations, 40 telephones, 106 km of telegraph cable, and 110 km of telephone wires (compared to only 12 telephones and 77 km of field cable in a German corps). Mobilization target for the Russian army was 4037 automobiles (in Germany – 4 thousand, in France – 9.5 thousand, and in Britain 1.4 thousand).

When fully mobilized, the army fielded 273 infantry divisions, including 4 of the guards, 6 of grenadiers, 194 of infantry, 6 of border troops, 1 of marines, 2 special divisions, 8 of riflemen, 6 Finnish divisions, 7 of the Caucasus, 22 Siberian ones, 10 Turkestan ones, and 2 of Latvian riflemen. Newly formed units included 19 riflemen regiments attached to cavalry divisions, 42 Cossack scout battalions, and 133 cavalry regiments (87 of them Cossack) and 170 detached *sotnias.*

The Great War dramatically changed the number of officers as well. In July 1914, the army received its usual inflow of summertime graduates, and reserve ensigns called up that year were not demobilized due to the threat of war (about 5000). Thanks to all the reserve officers and retired officer reenlistment, once mobilized, the army had about 80 thousand officers (in prewar decade, each year added about 2000 reserve ensigns). After the outbreak of the war, accelerated training (3 to 4 months) in military colleges supplied the army with 92 thousand officers, ensign schools graduated about 140 thousand, and 25 thousand more were commissioned through promotion from the ranks or from non-commissioned officers for distinguished service, 2 more thousand were added through reclassification of some civilian ranks and the like. The number of naval officers grew by 5 thousand. All told, newly commissioned officers numbered at least 260 thousand.

War industry continued to meet all the needs of the armed forces. All the troops were rearmed with breech-loading arms by 1884. But in April of 1891, the army adopted a new rifle (designed by Mosin) which outperformed all its foreign competitors. Its production required retooling of all light arms arsenal mills. By 1903, almost 3 million such rifles were manufactured in Russia (and half a million ordered in France in 1893–1895). From 1904, the arsenal mill in Tula was producing Maxim machine guns. By the late 1890s, annual output of cartridges (at the mills in St. Petersburg, Tula, and Lugansk) stood at 250–270 million. In the 1880s, the artillery was rearmed with steel guns (only 2056 out of the total of 3988 guns were of steel in 1881). By the end of 19th century, field artillery was limited to just two gun types: a 3-inch field gun and a 6-inch caliber howitzer. Only in 1900–1903, Putilov, Obukhov, and Perm mills built 2650 advanced guns for the army and navy.

By the start of 20th century, artillery ordnance was produced at the government mills in the Urals (Zlatoust, Kusa, Satka, Kamensk, Baranchinsky, Verkhnyaya Tura, and Votkinsk), and at Olonets, at almost all artillery gun mills, and at some privately-owned plants (in Sormovo (now part of Nizhny Novgorod) and Nobel's plant in St. Petersburg).

All artillery shell cases were manufactured at the specialized plant in St. Petersburg (opened in 1895) and at Izhevsk mill. Warships were built at the New Admiralty and Baltic shipyards in St. Petersburg and at the shipyards in Nikolaev and Sebastopol. In the reign of Alexander III alone, there were launched 114 navy vessels, including 17 armor-clad battleships and 10 armor-plated cruisers. Absolute majority of the ships were built in Russia (only 10 heavy warships were being built for Russia abroad in 1898–1902). In 1913, Russo-Baltic plant built the world's first multi-engine heavy airplane '*Russky Vityaz*' ('Russian Knight'), followed in 1914 by the world's first 4-motor heavy bomber '*Ilya Murometz*'[24]. In 1912–1913, Russia built the world's first flying boats.

Enhanced capabilities of the war industry were based on a fairly advanced level of overall economic development achieved under the last two emperors. In that period, Russian industry grew faster than anyplace else in the world. Over the last 40 years of the 19th century, industrial output grew by 7 times (5 in Germany, 2 in Britain, and 2.5 in France). In Alexander's short reign alone (1881–1893), iron production grew by 160%, steel production by 217%, and coal mining by 129%. Over a longer period (1860–1895) output of iron grew by 4.5 times and coal production by 30 times. By 1895, annual oil output reached 5.5 million tons making Russia the world's largest oil producer.

In iron and steel industry, the Urals lost its lead to the south, which now produced 53% of all iron. Sormovo was the leading center for the construction of river steamers, and Kolomna led in the manufacturing of steam locomotives. Kharkov, Odessa, and Berdyansk were the leaders in agricultural machinery production. The fleet of river steamers grew from 400 in 1860 to over 1500 in the 1890s, and of sea-going steamers from 50 to 520. Railway network expanded from 22644 km in 1881 (without Finland) to 36131 km by 1894 (60% growth). From 1881, the government became more involved with funding railway construction by public money and bought out many previously privately built railways. From 1881–1887 to 1894 grain harvest rose by 26%. Foreign trade turnover grew from 430 million rubles in the 1880s to 1300 million rubles in the 1890s (75–80% was with Europe – 25% with Britain and 21% with Germany). Exports exceeded imports by about 20%, and foreign trade surplus was maintained throughout the period.

Economic expansion continued in the 1890s. A new spurt of growth began in 1893, and by 1899 heavy industry grew twofold, and consumer goods industry by 1.6 times. Russia continued to be the world's top oil producer, and advanced to the third place in the output of iron. The world's longest (835 km) pipeline (Baku–Batum) was built in 1897–1907. From 1890 to 1897, the output of textile industry grew from 519 million rubles worth of fabrics to 946 million, the output of mining and ore refining industries from 203 million to 394 million, and the output of metallurgical, metal processing and machine-building industries rose from 128 to 311 million rubles. By the end of 1890s, annual growth rate in leading industries reached 12% and higher. From 1890 to 1900, foreign investment grew from 200 to 900 million rubles (foreign investment total for 1893–1903 was 3 billion rubles). Domestic entrepreneurship expanded fast too. Russia's first joint stock company appeared as far back as 1799, and by 1866 there were 251 such companies, by 1893 they numbered 522, and in subsequent years that number grew by about a 100 a year to reach 1292 in 1903.

---

[24] Both were designed by the plant's Chief Engineer, Igor Sikorsky. After emigrating to America in 1919, he became famous for designing the first viable helicopters and transoceanic flying boats.

Financially, Russia was on a very firm footing. Gold standard was introduced in 1896, and banknotes were fully backed by gold. The monetary system was so stable that even in the most troubled years (of Russo-Japanese war and subsequent revolutionary turmoil) the exchange of banknotes for gold was never suspended, and the ruble's exchange rate stayed flat. Russia mined quite a quantity of gold (14–18% of world production in the 1890s), only the USA, Australia and South Africa produced more. Its golden reserves at the time were equivalent to 1315 million rubles. By the late 19th century, Russia had four principal taxes: land tax, real estate tax, tax on financial capital, and tax on commerce and business. Personal income tax became universal in 1904, but applied only to individuals making over 1000 rubles a year. Early in the 20th century, taxes accounted for only 7–8% of budget revenues.

In the early years of 20th century, the pace of economic expansion slowed somewhat (in 1900–1908 industrial output grew by 37%, and that of steel by 24%), but a new surge followed once the consequences of war with Japan and the troubles of 1905–1907 were overcome. That growth spurt much advanced Russia's economy. In fact, the five prewar years were so fat that Russia could afford its massive army and navy rearmament program adopted in 1913. The program was to be completed in 1917, but World War I made that impossible (the very unleashing of that war was in no little measure driven by the desire to prevent Russia from completing it).

In 1909–1913, the rate of economic growth was higher than in the USA, Germany, Britain, and France, and averaged 9% a year (13% a year in machine-building and 6% in consumption goods industries). New industrial plants were for the most part large. In 1887, Russia had 30888 industrial plants with the average employment of 43 workers, by 1908 that number grew to 39494 plants with the average of 69 workers. But the newly added 8606 plants employed the average of 157 workers.

In 1909–1912, average annual output of coal grew by 79.3% compared to 1898–1908, iron production by 53%, and steel production by 53%. From 1909 to 1913, coal production grew by 1.5 times, that of iron by 64%, and of steel by 82%. Overall, in 20 prewar years, iron output grew by 2.5 times, that of steel by 2.2 times, coal output by 3 times, oil production by 65%, copper production by 3.8 times, manganese production by 3.6 times, and machine building expanded by 4.1 times. In absolute numbers, Russia became the world's fifth largest industrial producer with 7% of the global manufacturing output.

Three quarters of all industry were concentrated in industrial hubs anchored by Moscow and St. Petersburg, in the Baltics, Poland, the Urals, and Donbass in the south. The length of railway network grew to 71 thousand km (without Poland and Finland). Russian-built steam locomotives of the time outperformed foreign ones. River fleet numbered 5.5 thousand steamships. By 1914, the railway network grew to 79 thousand km, 70% of which were owned and operated by the state (railway construction continued in wartime, and by 1917 the network grew to 81.1 thousand km with 15 thousand more under construction). From 1901 to 1913, merchant marine grew from 3038 to 3645 vessels, with summary tonnage growing by 25.8% and freight turnover of sea vessels by 64.3%. The turnover of domestic trade reached 18 billion rubles, the exports 1.5, and imports 1.1 billion rubles. Germany accounted for 30% of foreign trade, and Britain for 20%.

Following the agrarian reform of 1906, agriculture made significant strides as well. From 1901 to 1913, the acreage under crops increased by over 15%, crop yields by 10%, the harvest of grain crops went up from 57 to 82 million tons, i.e. by 40% (of which 88% was harvested on peasant-owned land and only 12% on estates of landowning nobility). Per capita production of grains went up from 450 to 550 kg. In 1913, the harvest of principal grain crops exceeded that of USA, Canada, and Argentina combined. While the population grew by 26.6% from 1900 to 1912, annual output of major crops (the average for 1908–1912 compared to the average for 1898–1902) outpaced it: 37.0% for wheat, 62.2% for barley, 31.6% for potatoes, 42.0% for sugar beets, and 44.8% for corn. Even with abundant supply of food commodities in domestic market, this left a major surplus, which was exported and served the prime driver of Russia's positive foreign trade balance.

As early as 1898–1902, exports of food commodities exceeded imports by 4 times, and the same is true for 1908–1912. Quickly mastered domestic cultivation of cotton in Turkestan ensured that the proportion of consumption met with domestically grown cotton went up from 31.7% in 1903 to over 50% in 1909. By the start of the war, Russia no longer needed imported cotton. From 1894 to 1914, the acreage planted with cotton expanded by 3.5 times, and harvests by almost 4 times. Also, by 1914, Russia accounted for about 80% of world production of flax fiber.

Throughout this period, Russia had a favorable foreign trade balance. In 1898–1902, Russian exports (739.6 million rubles) exceeded imports by 112.2 million rubles, and in 1908–1912, exports (1378.7 million rubles) exceeded imports by 358.8 million rubles.

Between the start of the century and the outbreak of the war, material wellbeing of the population grew noticeably, including that of factory workers. The average workday got shorter (from 11–12 hours to 9.5–10 hours). From 1904 to 1913, average annual wages in manufacturing industries went up from 205 to 264 rubles (by a third). In the two capital cities, those wages in metalworking industry exceeded 500 rubles, while family subsistence income there stood at 300–360 rubles. Per capita tax burden in Russia (both direct and indirect taxes) was several times lower than in other European countries.

This improved wellbeing found expression in the growth of bank deposits by private individuals. Russia had a large number of small banking institutions of various types: by 1913, there were 7974 credit associations, 4809 peasant savings and loans agencies, 3019 savings and loans societies, and 104 *zemstvo* banks. Deposits in government-owned savings banks grew especially fast: in 20 years from 1894 to 1914, they went from 330.3 million rubles to 2236 million. Over the same period, small savings and loans agencies grew their deposits from 70 to 620 million rubles and by 1917 accumulated 1.2 billion rubles.

By 1912, 28.6% of all deposits in savings banks belonged to peasants, 21.3% to factory workers and domestic servants, 32.9% to clerical workers, civil servants, and the clergy, 9.3% to tradesmen, and 7.8% to other professional classes. In a mere 4 years, deposits in savings banks grew by almost a third (30.8%). It is worth noting that deposits of factory workers grew the fastest (by 38.9%), those of rural population by 32.8%, of professional classes by 31.3%, of civil servants, clerical classes and the clergy by 26.8%, and of tradesmen by 22%. By 1914, Russia lagged behind only 4 big nations in terms of overall development and stood on par with Japan (and somewhat ahead of it) in that respect.

Russia's finances were quite stable by the war's outbreak: in 1908–1912 it had either balanced budgets or (in the last three years of that period) significant budget surpluses. The government never resorted to issuing banknotes not backed by gold. Moreover, gold reserves (1745 million rubles by the war's start in 1914) were larger than the paper money supply in circulation (1633 million rubles).

Chapter 12

Russian society in the second half of the 19th and early 20th century

All through this last period of Russia's imperial history, the population continued its rapid growth. By the early 1880s, it stood at 84 million, by 1897 at 128.9, and by 1914 at 178.4 million. In this period, the greater half of the population (about 60%) lived on lands that were incorporated into Russia at Peter's time or later. Those territories had significantly higher population densities as well (10 per km^2 in 1897 and 13.7 by 1914, compared to all-Russian averages of 5.9 and 8.2 per km^2 for the same dates). Population densities of European countries were incomparably higher: in the 1880s, they ranged from 60 to 100, and by 1913 from 70 to 180 per km^2. Russia's proportion of urban population stayed low too – only 12.5% in 1890 (32.5% in Austria, 37.4% in France, 47% in Germany, and 72.1% in Britain).

By 1914, the proportion of ethnic Russians (Great Russians, Little Russians, and White Russians) in the empire's population stood at 66.7%, just a tad lower than in mid-19th century. Like before, the biggest ethnic minority were the Poles (6.5%). The proportion of Jewish population grew sharply to 4.2%. The Germans accounted for 1.4%, the Finns for 1%, Lithuanians 1 %, Estonians and Latvians 1.7%, and Moldovans 0.7%. The biggest baptized minorities in the Volga River basin were the Mordvins (0.7%) and the Chuvash (0.6%). The big Christian minorities in the Trans-Caucasia were Armenians (1.2%) and Georgians (1%). Of all the Muslim minorities, the biggest lived in the Volga River basin – the Tatars and Bashkirs (2.8%), followed by the Kazakhs (2.7%), Caucasian Tatars, or present-day Azerbaijanians (1.2%), and the Uzbeks (1.2%). All the other, smaller minorities collectively accounted for 5.3%.

Over the second half of 19th century, Russia's social structure underwent profound change. The overall pattern can be summed up as gradual dismantlement and dissolution of differences between estates, even though in formal terms the estates continued to exist and be legally recognized until November of 1917. With the growth of both social and territorial mobility, a person's social and occupational position was increasingly often at odds with the formal belonging to an estate and became more important for one's self-identification.

In 1856, there occurred an upward revision of ranks that conferred hereditary nobility: for military officers, it was now class 6 (colonel) and for civil servants – class 4 (senior state councilor). The qualifications for personal nobility did not change – it was conveyed by all officer ranks and by civil ranks starting with class 9. That system of ennoblement for service to the state survived until 1917. In 1900, the granting of hereditary nobility to recepients of order of St. Vladimir 4th class was abolished. Since the 3rd class of that order (as well as the orders of Anna and Stanislaus 1st class) could be awarded only to persons with high ranks (who belonged to nobility anyway), the only remaining path to nobility through decoration by an order was to become the Knight of the Order of St.

George. The award of hereditary nobility to the heirs of two generations of personal nobility was also abolished.

On the other hand, from 1874, hereditary nobility was granted to all children of a qualifying person regardless of when they were born. Since after 1856 the children of lieutenant colonels and majors did not receive hereditary nobility, they were recognized as a special estate dubbed 'staff officers' children' (until 1874, children of colonels born before their fathers won that rank were part of this special estate as well). Even though the plank for gaining nobility was raised, the inflow from below remained massive since the machinery of civil administration and the system of higher education were fast expanding. In 1875–1896, those two tracks (a senior service rank or award of an order) gave hereditary nobility to 39.5 thousand persons (and by no means all who qualified filed the paperwork to get it).

That said, the proportion of nobility in Russia was amongst Europe's lowest. Throughout the 19th century, it stood at 1.5% of the total population (one third of that were non-hereditary). But even so, most of its members were former 'men of miscellaneous ranks' and their descendants. That was due to the fact that the path to nobility lay through service, and both the civil service and the officer corps steadily expanded. By 1857, civil service counted 118.1 thousand men (of whom 86 thousand were bureaucrats with ranks). By 1880, that number grew to 129 thousand, by 1897 to 144.5 thousand (with 101.5 thousand bureaucrats with ranks), and by 1913 to 252.9 thousand.

The number of military officers in the latter half of 19th century ranged from 30 to 40 thousand, and stood at about 50 thousand by 1914. In the 1860s, about 44% of all officers were not of gentle birth (about 50% by century's end). According to 1912 data, 53.6% of all officers (44.3 % in infantry) came from the nobility (including children of non-hereditary nobility), 25.7% from townsmen and peasants, 13.6% from citizens of honor, 3.6% from the clergy, and 3.5% from merchants. World War I profoundly affected the social composition of the officer corps. Of 260 thousand officers who were commissioned in 1914–1917, up to 70% had peasant backgrounds, and only 4–5% came from the nobility. Among civil servants, those of common origins accounted for 70% at the end of the 19th century and for 80% in the early 20th century.

By the start of 20th century, noble families that could prove their noble lineage from before 1685 accounted for about a quarter of all the families recorded in nobility registry books. If one further takes into account that a great many who gained hereditary nobility through service and were not landowners failed to register their names in those books at all (in itself, it conferred no privileges), one can argue that 90% or more of nobility families existing circa 1900 received their nobility through service at some time in the previous two centuries. Generally speaking, one gained nobility through two or three generations of his family's service. It could be longer but often (in the military) sooner.

It was at this time, that we can take the full measure of what the principles of replenishment of the noble estate adopted early in the 18th century wrought. The estate was based on two pillars: hereditary privilege and admission of new members based on their abilities and personal accomplishment. Pretty much every educated person regardless of his origins gained first the personal nobility and eventually the hereditary one. As one contemporary justly noted, "the rights that nobility enjoyed as an estate, in effect belonged to the whole demographic of Russia's educated men". Russia was the only country where ennoblement through service upon reaching a certain rank was happening by default. While claims to nobility based 'on the deeds of forefathers' had to be confirmed by the Senate (which looked quite carefully into documentary proof of noble origins), people who gained nobility by reaching a certain rank in the service of the state were recognized as such "from the rank itself and without special confirmation". Unlike in some other countries, neither ranks, nor the nobility itself were ever sold in Russia (other than for state service, they could be awarded only for a special contribution to art or industry).

The nobility was gradually losing its connection with the land and with ancestral homes of their forefathers (the first to whom it happened were personal nobility who lost the right to be elected to local nobility assemblies and local administration in the 1860s). By 1858 (that is to say even before the emancipation of serfs in 1861), the number of landowning nobility shrank to 65.5 thousand from 72 thousand in 1833 (on the same territory) and stood at the same level as in the 1720s. By that year, the whole noble estate with children of both sexes (omitting Poland and Finland) numbered 888.8 thousand, of whom 31.1% were personal nobility families, 16.6% were hereditary but with no land or serfs, 21.4% had less than 20 'souls' (serf peasants), 18.5% had 20 to 100 'souls', and only 12.4% had over 100 'souls'. In 1867, the noble estate of the whole country (with family members) consisted of 1012 thousand individuals (654 thousand of them hereditary and 358 thousand personal), and in 1897 the number was 1853 thousand (1222 hereditary and 631 personal).

Following the reform of 1861, even those in the nobility who still owned land started losing it fast. Landed estates were sold to people of other social backgrounds on a massive scale. Prior to 1861, somewhat more than 80% of hereditary nobility were landowners, but by 1877 that proportion fell to 56%, by 1895 to 40%, and by 1905 to 30%. By 1897, landowners accounted for only 29% of all nobility (compared to 63% before 1861) and by 1905 for 22%. Also, by the end of the century, about 60% of nobility landowners were petty landowners (with less than 100 hectares), a quarter had 100 to 500 hectares, and only 15% belonged to the top stratum (over 500 hectares). By 1917, more than a half of all acreage that belonged to the nobility prior to 1861 was already owned by people of other estates.

At the same time, the noble estate was fast losing its special rights and privileges. Their exclusive right to own land (as private individuals) was lost as early as in 1801, and the reform of 1861 took away their right to own serf peasants. In 1862, they lost the right to appoint *uezd* police officials, and in 1864 their monopoly on forming local governments. In 1863, what used to be the nobility's privilege – exemption from corporal punishment – was extended to all estates, and the reform of justice system in 1864 took away their privileges in courts of justice. Introduction of universal military duty in 1874 dealt away with the nobility's privilege of accelerated commissioning as officers. Tax immunity was lost in the 1860s with the introduction of universal income tax. To sum up, by the last quarter of 19th century, the nobility lost all its special privileges as an estate. For the last 40 years of empire, it was the topmost estate only in the sense of formal status and public prestige.

The clergy's position as an estate was much eroded too. The reforms of 1860s included major changes in the legislation regulating the clergy. The main thrust was to overcome its insularity as an estate and make the clergy a relatively open socio-occupational group. In 1860, family origins of the priests were as follows: 49% were sons of priests, 17% sons of deacons, and 34% sons of sextons (for deacons, these proportions were 9%, 17% and 74%). In 1867, hereditary transfer of clerical positions was strictly forbidden, as well as the whole traditional right of 'family ownership' of the parish. The rule stipulating that men of cloth may marry only within their own estate was abolished too.

In filling church vacancies, bishops were now expected to take into account only the applicants' professional qualifications.

The principle that children born in clergy families belonged to that estate by default was abolished in 1869. In fact, they were now automatically excluded from that estate at birth, and could return only when they personally embarked on church careers. Under the new system, children of priests and deacons became hereditary citizens of honor at birth (non-hereditary in case of children of sextons), which encouraged them to get a secular education and enter civil service or become a member of professional classes. Schools of divinity became open to all estates. There was a mass exodus of clergy children educated in seminaries into colleges and universities. University of Novorossiya (in Odessa) proves the case in point – in the 1870s and 1880s, children of the clergy predominated in the student body (up to 65% in 1877–1882, and almost a 100% in the school of history and philology). In St. Petersburg Institute of History and Philology 57% of graduates were born to clergy families.

Steps were taken to emancipate the clergy. Previous limitations that censored what they could say or write were removed. Dependency on the bishops' goodwill was much weakened (the latter no longer could punish priests by transferring them to remote parishes, nor forbid priests to retire with pension after less than 35 years at the altar, nor stop the priests from defrocking themselves). All the bishops were left with as punishment was to impose penance. Cases of serious clerical misconduct could be taken up only by consistory courts, while crimes by clergymen were judged at the courts of general jurisdiction. By the 1860s, 79% of diocesan consistory members were parish priests (rather than monks as before). Monks were also allowed to freely disown their vows and return to the estate they belonged to before (but the ranks and orders they received before taking the vows would not be restored, and they would be barred from civil service and from living in the same governorate where they were monks).

Yet, in practical terms, the overwhelming majority of the clergy still came from within the estate (in 1904, only 3% of 47.7 thousand priests were from secular estates). While from 1880 to 1914, the proportion of non-clergy children among students in seminaries grew from 8% to 16.4% (and to 25% in preparatory schools for future seminarians), most of them never became professional churchmen. Moreover, the majority of seminarians hailing from clergy families chose to pursue secular careers as well (in 1914, out of 2187 graduates of seminaries only 47.1% chose church service). This erosion of clerical estate explains a significant presence of its ex-members in the revolutionary circles (with the clergy accounting for only 1% of the population, it supplied 22% of the members of populist *Narodnik* groups).

The total number of the clergy stayed static: 114.5 thousand in 1860 (without family members), 92.7 in 1880, 106.6 thousand in 1904, and 111 thousand in 1913 (the number of priests for the same dates was 37.8 thousand, 37 thousand, 47.7 thousand, and 50.4 thousand). The clergy remained a well-educated estate. It that regard, they were not different from the nobility. In 1897, 58.5% of all clergy had secondary education or better.

Due to the expansion of seminary education, 82.6% of all priests were seminary-educated by 1860 (87.4% in 1880 and 63.8% in 1904). For the deacons, these numbers were 15.6%, 12.7%, and 2.2%). In 1897, the whole estate (celibate clergy and marrying clergy with their male children) numbered 240 thousand (as before, about 10% were monks and nuns). If all female family members are included, in 1858 the clergy numbered 567 thousand, in 1870 – 609 thousand, in 1897 – 501 thousand, and in 1913 – 607 thousand. In the 1860s, it accounted for 1% of the population, and in the last 15–20 years before the war for 0.5%.

From the mid-century to its end, the numerical strength of what was considered a combined townsmen estate grew by 2.5 times. In 1858, it numbered (without Poland and Finland) 2067 thousand, in 1863 – 2342 thousand, in 1870 – 2979 thousand, and in 1897 – 5101 thousand. Over this period, the predominance of lower strata (*meschane,* or petty townsmen, and guild members) only grew. In the years used above, they accounted for 90%, 89.5%, 92%, and 95% of the total. Accordingly, the proportion of high strata declined. Merchants went from 9.7% of the total in 1858 (only 0.7% in the top two classes) to 10% in 1863, 7% in 1870 and 2% in 1897, the percentage of citizens of honor for those dates was 0.5%, 0.8%, 1%, and 3%.

In 1866, poll tax and collective responsibility of the townsmen for paying it were replaced with personal income tax. Wealth disparity of urban population was glaring. The statute of 1870 on elections to city self-government bodies established the division of all townsmen into three vertical categories by tax paid, so that each category corresponded to a third of all tax collected (to be included in the lowest category it was enough to have real estate or proof of business ownership). The upper strata of electors included only 0.4% of all urban population, the middle one – 1.8%, and the lower one – 19.2%. The remaining 78.6% of urban residents were too poor to pay taxes and, accordingly, did not qualify to vote.

The fastest growing category of townsmen in the second half of 19th century was citizens of honor. That was because children of the clergy were now listed in that estate at birth. In 1858, that estate numbered 10.9 thousand, in 1863 – 17.8 thousand, but by 1870 it grew to 29 thousand, and by 1897 to 156.6 thousand. As to the merchants, the 3rd class was abolished in 1863, and the threshold of capital ownership for entry into the remaining two classes was raised. Besides, people of every estate were allowed to enter the merchant class. Yet, those steps did not bring about the growth of merchant estate. In fact, it shrank. The reason for that is twofold. Firstly, some of the merchants were also citizens of honor and preferred to be listed under that more prestigious estate. Secondly, it was much easier for people in lower estates to gain social standing by getting a good education (and therefore a citizen of honor status), than to amass the capital needed for entry into the merchant guild. While in 1858 there were 204.8 thousand merchants, and 235.7 thousand in 1863, by 1870 their number fell to 208.4 thousand, and then shrank to 116.4 thousand by 1897. From 1898, membership of merchant guilds became a matter of prestige alone, since the law on business taxation gave all estates equal access to becoming an entrepreneur.

The milestone in the evolution of peasant estate was the manifesto on abolition of serfdom (February 19, 1861). Less than 40% of all peasants were serfs by that time. The manifesto declared former landowners' serfs to be free rural residents with full civil rights (freedom of entering into contracts, of acquisition of real estate, of litigating in courts, etc.). Since the serfs were emancipated without land, they had to buy out their allotments, and had to bear certain obligations to the landowners in lieu of part of buy-out price. The size of allotments and obligations in each individual case was fixed once and forever in the agreement between the landowner and the peasant and recorded in a special deed (that process was mediated by lay arbitrators – an institution created just for that purpose). About a fifth of the buy-out price was to come as down payment from the peasant, while the rest was paid by the government. The peasants then had 49 years to repay the government in installments. The law of December 1881 declared that all temporary obligations of peasants to landowners would be considered fulfilled from January 1, 1883, and that peasant allotment buy-out was now mandatory. Peasant repayments of compensation the government paid to landowners on their behalf were first reduced in 1883, and then fully forgiven from January 1, 1907.

With the emancipation, all the different categories of peasants were put on the same legal footing, but social realities and geography explained significant disparities in their material well-being. The size of allotment and the number of horses and livestock could vary most widely between governorates. In densely populated western governorates, an average allotment was 4–5 hectares, while in northern and eastern governorates it could be as high as 50 hectares. The number of horses in a peasant household in steppe governorates beyond the Volga River was 3 to 4 times greater than in Ukrainian governorates. Rapid population growth meant that peasant family holdings fragmented and got smaller. In the 1860s, average land allotment in the governorates of European Russia was 17.8 hectares, but by 1880s it shrank to 13.3, and by the 1890s to 9.4 hectares.

Prior to 1861, social stratification of the peasantry was blurred and held back by serfdom itself. It was not sharply manifested and rather fluid due to the vicissitudes of farming life (depending on the number of dependent children and other factors, the same household could be considered poor, middling, or well-off through various stages of a person's life). But the reform gave a major push to stratification. Now that accumulated property was passed down as inheritance, well-off households tended to remain so in the next generation. Conversely, descendants of those who got destitute through sloth, drink, or any other reason, found it increasingly difficult to get on an even keel again. But overall, even with social stratification underway, by 1914 the peasantry remained a relatively homogenous class with no glaring income disparities.

A significant proportion of peasants abandoned the countryside for cities to become industrial workers or domestic servants. Even before the emancipation, some peasants (serfs included) amassed enough wealth to buy their freedom, become entrepreneurs, and enter the merchant estate. Such instances became more common after the emancipation, but still applied to only a few percentage points of all peasantry. The absolute majority of peasants remained part of their village communes. The communes combined the principle of collective land use management with that of individual tilling of land allotted to each family. Every village household received as its allotment a certain number of strips of both fertile and lean land in order to level out everyone's chances of getting an average harvest. Those strips had to be periodically redistributed at commune meetings to allow for changing household size, etc.

In 1868, the commune's collective responsibility for the payment of taxes was abolished for small communes (less than 21 male souls). Their members now could pay individually. By 1903, collective tax responsibility was abolished for good. In 1876, the communes were allowed to redistribute farmed strips whenever they chose to, and not at stipulated time intervals. Nevertheless, in later years and until early in the 20th century, the authorities did not encourage peasants to detach themselves from the communes. The law of 1886 stipulated that redistribution of land between family members could be done only with the commune's permission. In 1889 peasant allotments were made inalienable, non-peasant ownership of allotted lands was banned, and separation from the commune now required a two thirds majority vote of the commune. In 1893, the commune's ability to reallocate land strips was constrained by the requirement that at least 12 years must pass between reallocations. In 1894, leaving the commune was made conditional on full repayment of money owed the government for land buyout of 1861 and on approval by the commune.

Even by the end of 19th century, some peasants already left their village communes choosing instead to own their plots as freehold private property. In fact, peasants made up 56.7% of all private landowners (23.8% were nobility, 12% petty townsmen, and 2.6% were merchants and citizens of honor), but they owned only 5.5% of all such privately held land. The overwhelming majority of peasant land remained a collective property of peasant communes. In 1900, the acreage of land belonging to peasant communes was still a third larger than the acreage belonging to all categories of individual owners.

Early in the 20th century, government policy regarding the preservation of peasant communes took a sharp turn (largely due to the position taken by chairman of Council of Ministers, P. Stolypin). The law of November 9, 1906 gave peasants the right to leave their communes any time with the right of full private property to the land they tilled. The laws of June, 1910 and May, 1911 made detaching oneself from a commune even easier. About 2.5 million peasants immediately wished to take advantage of the opportunity and get their share of communal land as private holdings, but their desire to leave was taken ill-naturedly by many commune members and in any case called for much land survey and parceling work. The process proceeded slowly, and by 1914 only 13% of communal land was unbundled to become private property of farmers.

Along with the laws on freedom to leave the communes, the government undertook a vigorous policy of voluntary peasant resettlement to imperial peripheries in Siberia and Central Asia. As early as 1889, there was passed a resettlement law which limited the peasants' ability to resettle on empty lands at their own discretion, yet encouraged organized peasant colonization of Siberia (a special Resettlement Directorate was created in the Ministry of Internal Affairs to facilitate such migration). Stolypin's reform created additional incentives. The settlers were freed of taxes for a number of years and received 15 hectares of land per person or 45 per family. They were given 200 rubles as relocation allowance and the government paid all transportation costs for the families and all their movable property. State Peasant Land Bank was empowered to buy up nobility landowners' lands and resell them to peasants at favorable terms. It issued long-term loans worth up to 90% of land purchased at the annual interest rate of 4.5% (from 1901 to 1912, the total of such loans went up from 222 million rubles to 1168 million rubles). All of these measures helped expand peasant land ownership: while in 1894 there were 2 hectares of peasant land per each hectare belonging to nobility landowners, by 1917 that proportion changed to 5.5:1.

As part of political reforms of 1905–1906, peasant population received full equality of rights with other estates. Earlier, in 1895, new passport rules made it much easier for peasants to move around the country. The last remaining limitations on their entry into civil service, admission to colleges, becoming a priest or taking monastic vows were lifted.

The reforms of the 1860s turned every physical person in the country into the subject of law. They also gave final shape to the definition of a legal entity. Legal entities could be public or private, an association or an agency. Since all the limitations on incorporating as a legal entity were lifted, this period witnessed an explosive growth of all kind of societies, associations, and the like (both in commercial and cultural fields). Both physical persons and legal entities were allowed to enter into any agreements and contracts then known and practiced in the world (as long as they were not in contravention of laws or undermined public order). A number of provisions adopted in 1870 detailed the legal status of joint stock companies, and also the hiring and insurance rules. Not every deal had to be notarized, but for some important categories it was mandatory. The population quickly learned to use the new tools offered by civil law. From 1884 to 1913, the number of notarized documents grew by 5.5 times.

The last remaining limitations on ownership of private property were lifted for all social groups (as long as they did not impinge on property rights of others). The government also held on to the right of eminent domain if land was required for the needs of the state. Bequest of property to descendants in this period primarily relied on written wills, and in cases of intestate death parents no longer could inherit. In the area of family law, women's rights to separate ownership of property were strengthened, although some other limitations remained: for instance, women were not allowed to work for hire without a husband's consent or to issue promissory notes. Parental consent to marriage was no longer required. Legal grounds for dissolution of marriage were somewhat expanded as well. From 1902, illegitimate children acknowledged by their fathers were legitimized with the right to their father's family name and inheritance.

In 1864, the age of full discretion (i.e. responsibility for a crime) was lowered to 17, while being 14 to 16 years of age was grounds for mitigation of sentence, and those 10 to 13 years old were considered conditionally competent. Yet, the Criminal Statute of 1903 raised the age of discretion to 21 again, and age brackets for sentence mitigation or competence set by the Statute of 1845 were restored. While the Statute of 1845 treated intoxication as a mitigating circumstance (the crime was considered unpremeditated), the Statute of 1903 recognized as such only complete inebriation where a person loses all control of his behavior. The Statute of 1903 was streamlined compared to its predecessors – only 687 articles, which was 2.5 times fewer than in 1866 and 3.4 times fewer than in 1857.

The number of articles devoted to protection of individual rights grew twofold, and now they were about a third of the total (25 articles dealt with crimes against the faith, 52 with crimes against the state, 51 with abuse of office, 329 with crimes against the state's material interest and property, and 201 with crimes against individuals). The types of punishment were reduced to eight: 1) capital punishment, 2) hard penal labor, 3) exile to remote areas, 4) incarceration in a house of corrections, 5) imprisonment in a brig (military custody), 6) incarceration in jail, 7) short-term detention, and 8) a fine from 50 kopecks to 100 rubles. In case of the privileged estates (nobility, clergy, merchants, and citizens of honor), all sentences (except military custody, detention, and fines) carried additional penalty of attainder (stripping of estate rights). Contrary to popular belief about prevalence of court corruption at that time, the percentage of convicted defendants was pretty much the same no matter their estate (20% for nobility, 17% for the clergy and merchants, 19% for petty townsmen, and 25% for peasants). The percentage of those sentenced to more serious punishments was almost twice higher for defendants from the privileged estates (who had greater opportunity for graft or abuse of office). In the 1860s, exile and hard penal labor were meted out to 4.4% of convicted noblemen, 3.9% of clergymen, and 3% of citizens of honor, but only to 1.4% of convicted petty townsmen, less than 2% of peasants and 1.6% of *inorodtsy*.

Capital punishment was used very seldom and only for crimes against the state and military crimes (from 1881, executions were no longer public). Most such sentences were never carried out. Over a long period from 1826 to 1905, less than 900 persons were executed, and in 1905–1913, less than 3 thousand (notwithstanding the orgy of terrorist violence in 1905–1907). Corporal punishments were mostly abolished as early as 1863.

Afterwards, that sentence was kept only for male peasants if sentencing was done by the peasants themselves in borough courts. The number of lashes was capped at 20, and up to 40% of villagers were exempt anyway (the old, the sick, ex-soldiers, etc.). Those in detention and penal colonies could get the lash too, but only for disciplinary violations and with the governor's sanction. In 1903–1904, even that group was made exempt. By the 1880s, a prison term could be served in a house of corrections, a military brig, or in jail. By 1861, the country had 31 thousand prisoners, in 1885 – 95 thousand, and by 1913 – 169 thousand. In the 1880s, less than a third of them did penal labor, and about 60% in the 1900s. By 1897, almost 300 thousand residents of Siberia were exiles. Prior to 1903, penal colony term could be anywhere from 4 to 20 years, but in later years it was limited to 4 years or less (from 1875, almost all penal labor camps were in Sakhalin Island).

Social shifts that followed the emancipation of 1861 and the growth of cities, where factory workers and marginal underclasses were concentrated, led to a sharp growth in crime. Factory workers had the highest incidence of crime: even though they numbered only 3.2 million in 1897, they accounted for 30% of all convicts. Most of them came from the countryside (and were still formally considered part of peasant estate), but they committed 19 times more crimes than those peasants who actually stayed on the land. Already in the first post-reform decade, the incidence of crime per 100 thousand of population almost doubled to 868, and in later years the trend escalated (1397 in the 1880s, 1332 in the 1900s, and 1719 in 1911–1913). While previously almost 70% of all crimes were those against the system of government or public property and funds, now over 85% of the total were crimes against persons and private property. Average annual number of robberies and cases of banditry in 1909–1913 was 50 times that of pre-reform years, of cases of infliction of bodily harm 26 times, of sex crimes 24 times, of theft 8 times (151 thousand cases), and of murder 8 times (32.6 thousand cases). For murders and cases of bodily harm, figures were even worse in 1899–1908.

That upsurge in crime was helped by lenient sentencing practices. In 1910–1913, 54.3% of all convictions called for correctional punishment without stripping of rights (in only 6.7% of all sentences prison term was a year or more). In 37.3% of cases, the sentence involved stripping of rights (but in only 14% of the sentences the prison term was 2.5 years or more), and only 8% of convicts were sentenced to hard penal labor (over a half for terms under 6 years, and only 1.4% of all convicts for the terms over 10 years). Verdicts of acquittal were very frequent, especially in the trials by jury. In 1873–1883, the latter acquitted 38% of all defendants (even 43 % in 1883), and in 1887–1891 – 36% (in Europe, juries acquitted only 15–25% of defendants).

Crown courts (without a jury) passed fewer, but still many verdicts of acquittal: 23% in 1873–1883, and 30% in 1894–1897. As a result, incidence of crime in Russia got much closer to that in other European countries (only 1.2 times less than in Britain, 1.9 times less than in France, and 2.4 times less than in Germany, while earlier the difference was several-fold). Suicides remained few (5 to 10 times less than in other European countries). Their incidence even declined somewhat (from 2.7 per 100 thousand population in the 1870s to 2.3 in 1901–1905). By contrast, it steadily grew in all European countries through this period and by the turn of the century reached 17.6 in Austria-Hungary, 10.3 in Britain, 21.2 in Germany, 20.4 in France, and 10.2 in the USA.

The educational system expanded at a fairly fast pace in this period, with a major acceleration after the year 1900. In 1858, there first appeared girls' schools open to all estates. All-encompassing reforms of the early 1860s did not bypass public education. The

172

law of July 14, 1864 decreed that coordination of all issues of elementary and secondary education will be entrusted to newly established governorate, *uezd*, and city-level school councils made up of representatives from the administration, clergy, and *zemstvo*. The position of public schools' inspector (who reported to governorate school council) was created in 1869, and in 1874 he was made deputy to another newly created official – public schools' director of studies. School councils were responsible for providing elementary education.

According to the regulations of 1864, the hierarchy of schools coming under the Ministry of Public Education was as follows: elementary schools (former parish schools), 6-grade *uezd* schools, progymnasiums (4 to 6 grades)[25], and 7-grade gymnasiums of two types: classical (i.e. humanities) gymnasiums and what was known as 'real' (applied science and trades) gymnasiums. In 1872, classical gymnasiums switched to an 8-year course of study, and 'real' gymnasiums were renamed 'real' schools and kept a 7-year course of study. That same year, *uezd* schools were rebranded city schools. New regulations of 1874 essentially designated elementary schools as peasant schools.

A large number of educational institutions were not part of the Ministry of Education system. There were numerous church parish schools, which from 1884 fell under the general jurisdiction of the Synod, while their administration on diocese level belonged to the councils including representatives from the clergy, the faculty of a local seminary, and the director and inspector of public elementary schools of that governorate. In 1881–1894, the number of such schools grew by 8 times, and enrollment by 10 times. By the mid-1890s, Russia had 52 colleges and universities (not counting the military ones) with over 25 thousand students, 177 classical gymnasiums for boys, 58 progymnasiums, 104 'real' schools for boys, 55 seminaries, 105 seminary prep schools, 163 gymnasiums for girls, 30 gymnasiums for girls run by Empress Maria's charities, 61 diocesan high schools for girls, and 78.7 thousand elementary schools (with the total enrollment of about 3.8 million).

A new university charter adopted in 1863 confirmed the autonomy of universities (all decisions were taken by the faculty at academic councils). The charter of 1884 dealt away with elections of university presidents, and all presidents, deans, and professors became the ministry appointees, but in 1905 university autonomy was restored. Most universities had three departments: physics and mathematics, history and philology, and medicine. Several more universities were launched in this period. In 1865, Richelieu Lyceum in Odessa (in existence from 1817) was restructured into the University of Novorossiya. Siberia's first university in Tomsk was founded in 1888. Saratov University opened in 1909, and Perm University in 1916 (based on the local branch of University of St. Petersburg). At war's start, Warsaw University was evacuated to Rostov-on-Don, and in 1915 it was renamed Rostov University. A private university (named after Shanyavsky) was launched in 1908 in Moscow. In 1868, one new lyceum (named in memory of Crown Prince Nicholas) opened in Moscow.

---

[25] The term 'gymnasium' is understandably confusing to English-speaking readers. Loosely speaking, they are comprehensive schools. Progymnasium can be loosely equated with present-day junior high school, and a 'full' gymnasium with a high school. Classical gymnasiums were in many ways what would today be called a prep school (with graduates pursuing college education), while 'real' gymnasiums laid emphasis on applied sciences and trades, had many traits of present-day vocational schools, and their graduates were admitted to technical colleges (without exam) but not to universities.

Since all levels of the educational system separated the sexes, and women were not admitted to universities, there came into existence women's colleges (known as 'higher courses'). St. Petersburg' and Moscow's Women's Medical Colleges opened in 1872, Kazan Women's College in 1876, Bestuzhev Women's College in St. Petersburg in 1878, Kiev Women's College in 1878, and the one in Odessa next year. St. Petersburg Women's Medical Institute appeared in 1897, Stebutov Women's Agricultural College (in St. Petersburg) in 1904, and Women's Polytechnic College in St. Petersburg in 1906. In 1907, school teacher colleges for women opened in St. Petersburg and Kiev. Women's medical institutes opened up in Moscow (1909), Odessa (1910), and Kharkov (1910), Novocherkassk Women's College in 1910, and Shelaputin Pedagogical Institute in Moscow in 1911.

Specialized institutions of higher learning (in engineering, earth sciences, and humanities) underwent the most vigorous expansion of all. A whole network of polytechnics and institutes of technology was added to existing applied science colleges: in Riga in 1862, in Kiev in 1898, in St. Petersburg and Warsaw in 1902, in Novocherkassk in 1907. In 1886, the Institute of Electrical Engineering opened in St. Petersburg. One technology Institute opened in Kharkov (1885) and another in Tomsk (1900). Moscow Institute of Railway and Road Engineers opened in 1896, and Ekaterinoslav Mining Institute in 1899. In 1865, Agriculture and Forestry Academy was founded in Moscow (later known as Moscow Agricultural Institute), New Alexandria Agricultural Institute in 1869 (in Pulawy, Poland), Dairy Farming Institute in Vologda in 1911, Voronezh Agricultural Institute in 1912. Veterinary medicine institutes opened up in Kharkov in 1862 and in Kazan in 1874. In 1885, Grand Duchess Elena Pavlovna Institute of Clinical Medicine opened in St. Petersburg.

St. Petersburg Institute of History and Philology (1867) became the primary supplier of teachers for public schools. One Institute of Archeology opened in Petersburg in 1877 and another in Moscow in 1907. Vladivostok Oriental Studies Institute opened in 1899, and Oriental Studies Academy in St. Petersburg in 1908. Colleges of economics came into being as well: Pobedinsky College of Economics in St. Petersburg in 1897, Moscow (1903) and Kiev (1908) Institutes of Commerce, and private Petersburg Higher Institute of Commerce (what would be called an MBA school today) in 1910. Two music conservatories were launched: in St. Petersburg (1862) and Moscow (1866). Music and Drama College of Moscow's Philharmonic Society opened in 1878. While the universities were administered by the Ministry of Public Education, all the specialized colleges came under other government agencies. From the 1860s to 1900, various engineering colleges had 11.8 thousand graduates, and 18.4 thousand more in 1901–1917.

In 1908, elementary school education was made mandatory, and with vigorous addition of 10 thousand new elementary schools every year, their number reached about 130 thousand by 1913. In 30 years from 1884 to 1914, the budget of Ministry of Public Education increased by more than 6 times (from 25 to 161 million rubles), enrollment in public elementary schools it supervised almost doubled (from 3.3 to 6.4 million), and in secondary schools more than tripled (224 thousand to 733 thousand). By 1914, all students in elementary and secondary schools numbered 9.7 million. In a quarter century (from 1890) it nearly quadrupled, and in relative terms stood at 60 schoolchildren per 1000 population. In that regard Russia still lagged behind leading European nations (140–150), but from mid-19th century the gap quickly narrowed.

In the early 20th century, the system of secondary education embraced gymnasiums, 'real' schools, schools of commerce, and seminaries. Graduates of classical gymnasiums were admitted to universities without entrance exams, and the graduates of 'real' schools were freely admitted to specialized engineering colleges and the like, but had to take an entrance exam for universities. Schools of commerce first appeared in the last years of the 19th century. They had an 8-year course of study and most of them were either private or funded by the societies for the spread of knowledge of commerce (many gymnasiums and 'real' schools were private as well). Their graduates had the same rights as graduates of 'real' schools. Graduates of seminaries were on the same footing as graduates of gymnasiums. By 1914, there existed 508 gymnasiums for boys, 319 'real' schools, over 200 schools of commerce, as well as 450 specialized secondary schools with professional career tracks (farming, forestry, land survey, engineering, railways, fine arts, etc.). Gymnasiums for girls numbered 991 (44% of them private) plus over 80 diocesan high schools for girls. Girls completing all 8 years of gymnasium were admitted to women's colleges without entry exams. Additionally, there existed various specialized secondary schools: teacher training schools and seminaries, schools with emphasis on engineering, medicine, and fine arts (such as the famous Stroganov school, or Baron Stieglitz school of technical drawing).

By 1914, Russia had 105 institutions of higher education with the enrollment of 127 thousand. That was considerably more than in European countries (79.6 thousand students in Germany, 42.4 in Austria-Hungary, 42 in France), while even in 1890 Russia lagged behind them a bit (12.5 thousand students versus 13 in Britain, 20 in France, and 17.5 in Austria-Hungary). In terms of the number of college students per 10000 population, Russia was on par with other European nations. By 1916, enrollment in colleges and universities grew to 136 thousand.

Rapid expansion of educational system was accompanied by an explosive proliferation of periodicals. While previously the publishing scene was dominated by magazines, now newspapers became increasingly prominent. In the first 5 years of the reign of Alexander II, there appeared 142 new periodicals (59 in 1858 alone), which was twice more than in 15 preceding years. 247 new periodicals were added in the 1860s, 196 in the 1870s, 214 in the 1880s, and 92 in 1891–1894 (by the end of Alexander III reign) – a total of 695 new periodicals in Russian language alone. At the end of 19th – early 20th century there appeared several thousand more periodicals. Most of them were short-lived and came out for only a few years. Nonetheless, in 1913, Russia had 1055 newspapers in print (with combined circulation of 3.3 million copies (compared to 667 with 0.9 million copies in 1890) and 1472 magazines. These numbers were behind those in major European countries because of Russia's lower literacy level (it amounted to about 57% of that in France, Germany, and Britain). Conversely, Russia was well ahead of any other country in the number of book titles published. In 1913, 30.1 thousand titles of books and brochures were published in Russia compared to 23.2 thousand in Germany, 12.4 in Britain, 12.2 in the USA, and 9.8 in Japan. In fact, even earlier, in 1888–1889, Russia was behind only Germany and France on that count. By 1913, the number of public libraries in Russia exceeded 14 thousand, compared to only 145 in 1880 (when Britain had 202, the USA 59, France 505, and Germany 594).

As a matter of fact, educational attainment was the key driver of upward social mobility in the country. Nowhere else, civil service awarded so many perks and benefits for educational achievement, and nowhere else such a large proportion of educated individuals chose civil service. In Russia, it was educational attainment that best ensured rapid career growth for a bureaucrat. While everybody else regardless of origins (the nobility included) had to start in civil service as humble clerks, graduates of classical gymnasiums received class 14 rank right out of the gate, and university and college graduates received class 12 rank (or even 10 if they graduated with a candidate degree). Those with a master's degree (and medical doctors) started service with class 9 rank, and those who earned a doctorate started with class 8. The advantages enjoyed by well-educated people in the service of the state were so significant (the law of 1834 stipulated that they be promoted to every next rank at half the customary length of service), that there was concern about educated people being lured away from all other pursuits a society needs. In 1856, the department of laws lamented that this state of affairs "has sucked into the civil service all educated people, and such persons would always choose service over becoming an industrialist, a merchant, or a landowner" meaning that "Russia will not advance in commerce, industry, or agricultural improvements". Therefore, accelerated promotion was abolished, but the privilege of getting a higher initial rank remained. Even before the military reform of 1874, privileges associated with education were heftier than those conferred by belonging to a privileged estate. Everyone joining the army to become an officer had to serve a while in lower ranks before being commissioned an officer. For those who joined on the strength of their birthright alone, that 'wait period' was 2 years for hereditary nobility, 4 years for children of personal nobility, citizens of honor, merchants, and professionals, and 6 years for everyone else. By contrast, those (of any origin) who joined on the basis of educational privilege were commissioned within 2 months (if college education) or 1 year (if secondary education).

Overwhelming majority of college graduates chose civil service. For instance, 70% of Nezhin lyceum graduates were government bureaucrats, 10% officers, and only 6.8% did not serve at all. Only 1.9% of the graduates of Yur'ev (today's Tartu, Estonia) veterinary institute never served. Pretty much a 100% of the graduates of History and Philology Institute in St. Petersburg served, and a quarter of them reached the rank of senior state councilor (civil equivalent of a general). That is why the bureaucracy was the most educated segment of Russia's population. Of those serving in the State Chancellery, 69% had college education, 17% secondary and 14% elementary. The same breakdown is seen among those serving in the Agency for Management of Empress Maria Charities. In those humanities colleges that did not graduate civil service entrants but rather served as institutes of continuing education, the overwhelming majority of students were bureaucrats or even military officers (who accounted for about a quarter of graduates of St. Petersburg Institute of Archeology, and about a half of the graduates of Institute of Oriental Studies).

Yet, by the end of 19th century, rapid expansion of secondary and higher education ensured that quite a few educated people chose careers outside government. It should be mentioned that Russia always had a far leaner bureaucracy than any other European country, less than 2 bureaucrats with a rank per 1000 population. If clerks without ranks are added, by mid-19th century Russia had 2 bureaucrats per 1000 population compared to 4.1 in Britain and 4.8 in France. In the latter half of 19th century, far more people worked in various bodies of local self-government than in civil service. By 1880, *zemstvos* employed 52 thousand, and *zemstvos* and city *dumas* combined – 140 thousand (that alone was more than in all the crown administration). Another 180 thousand worked in borough and village-level rural administration. But even if all those groups are added together as administrative machinery of the state, Russia still had far fewer bureaucracy than other countries – 6.2 per

1000 population in 1910, whereas Britain had 7.2, France 17.6, Germany 12.6, and the USA 11.3.

By the early 20th century, the spread of education and vertical social mobility created in Russia what can be dubbed a cultured, or educated class, which took over the role historically played by the nobility. Before the mid-19th century, the 'cultured class' consisted exclusively of the nobility (by current status, not necessarily by birth). By 1900, the 'cultured class' included (other than bureaucracy and the officer class) what can be called urban professional classes (medical doctors with a private practice, engineers, teachers, clerks, etc.) and accounted for something like 3–3.5% of national population. By comparison, the nobility accounted for 1.5%, so not the whole cultured class reached nobility ranks. What was more important though, is that 80% of the 'cultured class' were not born as nobility, yet at least half of them (73% in case of those serving the state) had nobility status (thanks to civil service and educational vehicles of social uplift).

The cultured class largely self-reproduced, which helped perpetuate its cultural traditions (while most of its members joined this class through personal achievement, their children almost invariably got the proper education and remained part of it). Yet, it was steadily and increasingly replenished by people of lower social status. Prior to 1863, it was difficult to find anyone from the lower estates in a gymnasium (3/4 of students were children of nobility or civil servants), but later they gradually became accessible to all estates. In 1880–1898, the proportion of children of nobility and bureaucracy in enrollment fell to 52% (to 25.6% for children of hereditary nobility), and by 1914 it fell to 32.5%. In the mid-1850s and early 1860s, children of nobility and civil servants made up 65% of university students (with another 8% from the clergy), but by 1880 those proportions stood at 46.6% and 23.4%, by 1895 at 45.4% and 4.9%, and by 1914 at 35.9% and 10.3%. The proportion of hereditary nobility in university enrollment fell from 22.8% in 1897 to only 7.6% in 1914 (compared to 14.5% of peasant and 24.4% of petty townsmen origins). In colleges of less exalted kind, the proportion of those from privileged estates was even lower. By 1914, hereditary nobility made up 9.7% of enrollment in engineering and polytechnic colleges, and 5.8% in veterinary colleges (54.1% and 23.7% respectively for children of peasants and petty townsmen). In five engineering colleges under the Ministry of Public Education, 26.5% of the student body were children of nobility and civil servants, 2% came from the clergy, 14% from merchants and citizens of honor, 31.5% from petty townsmen, and 22% from the peasantry.

Since the nobility gradually lost its land holdings, and the great majority of those who came into civil service from other estates never had any in the first place and relied on the salaries alone, by the 20th century, the whole class of those serving the state had very little connection with land ownership, and surprisingly few owned any real estate at all.[26] Even in the late 19th century, only a third of all hereditary nobility had landed estates (and very few of those who served did). That is true even for the highest strata in the military and civil service. In 1903, only 15% of lieutenant-generals had landed estates, while among even the full generals 58.7% owned no real property. Even in the army's elite, officers of the General Staff, 95% owned no real property. In the topmost bureaucracy (the first 4 classes) the percentage of those who had no real property and relied on salaries alone stood at 50% in 1878 (75.9% for class 4 officials). In 1915, only 12% of the bureaucrats in the top

---

[26] The majority of civil servants and officers either rented their city apartments (housing allowance was a standard part of remuneration), or qualified to have free living quarters from the government.

4 ranks had some ancestral land, and only 29.5% had any real estate at all, be that land, a house, or a summer cottage (including property of family members).

Average income of professionals was then 1000–1100 rubles a year, even though some (elementary school teachers for instance) received about the same salary as factory worker wages (250–300 rubles). Top bureaucrats were paid 2 to 6 thousand rubles a year, generals 7 to 8 thousand, senior officers 2 to 4.5 thousand, and junior officers 0.7 to 1.5 thousand. The ministers' salaries were about 22 thousand rubles, their departmental directors received 8 thousand, and deputy directors 5 thousand. Members of the State Council were paid 18 thousand, senators 8 thousand, railroad directors 12–15 thousand, governors 10 thousand, deputy governors 4.5 thousand, gymnasium principals 3 to 4 thousand, 'real' school principals 5.2 thousand, university professors 3 thousand (5 thousand and more in technical colleges). *Zemstvo* medical doctors were paid 1.2–1.5 thousand, engineers in the private sector earned 2 to 4 thousand, secondary school teachers 0.9 to 2.5 thousand. Lawyers made from 2 to 10 thousand, provincial journalists 0.6–1.2 thousand, painters 0.5 to 2 thousand, actors 0.6–1.8 thousand (the stars of the time earned times more, of course). That kind of income allowed members of the 'cultured class' to lead comfortable lives, rent large apartments and have domestic servants. But while in earlier times the whole 'cultured class' or its absolute majority were somehow involved with the machinery of state (in most cases quite directly through civil or military service), the explosive expansion of this class at the turn of the 20th century placed much of it outside the sphere of government service, where it proved receptive to subversive propaganda by the revolutionary parties and spread it further.

Chapter 13

World War I and the collapse of the Russian Empire

The declaration of war in 1914 was welcomed in Russia with a tidal wave of patriotic fervor. The mobilization went through flawlessly. Even the leftist circles expressed their full support of the government. The Duma passed all the necessary legislation and approved all the funding the government requested for the war effort. Even the *Trudovik* faction voted for allocating funds for the war, and only Social Democrats abstained during the vote. Lenin spoke out in favor of Russia's defeat, but he and his followers were voices in the desert: even the faction of Social Democrats aligned with G. Plekhanov voiced ardent support for war against Germany. The sales of spirits were banned for the duration of the war. Grand Duke Nicholas Nikolaevich was appointed the supreme commander-in-chief, his staff commander was General N. Yanushkevich, and his quartermaster-general was General Yu. Danilov. General N. Ivanov was appointed commander of the South-Western Front and general Ya. Zhilinsky commanded the North-Western Front. On July 24, 1914, the Council of Ministers was given the extraordinary powers to deal with most issues independently ('in the emperor's name' as the formula went).

At war's start, there were founded a number of non-governmental organizations seeking to help the state in its war effort. The congress of *zemstvo* representatives from 41 governorates on July 30 announced the founding of all-Russian Zemstvo Union. Its governing body was to be the convention of commissioners (two from each governorate: one from *zemstvo* council and another from *zemstvo* executive board). The Main Committee of 10 members chaired by the Chief Commissioner (Prince G. Lvov) was to direct work between conferences, while *zemstvo* executive boards and so-called frontline committees were to serve as local chapters. On August 8–9, the congress of city mayors established the all-Russian City Union with identical structure (its chief commissioner was Moscow's mayor, M. Chelnokov, and the deputies were A. Guchkov and M. Tereschenko). The two unions had departments devoted to specific wartime needs: procurement, food supply, evacuation, hygiene, meals and medical aid stations, etc.

Germany's plan was to direct its principal effort against France with the hope of getting it out of the war. Then, Germany would turn around and strike Russia with its might. Therefore, Germany initially stuck to defensive tactics on its eastern front (it only took a handful of Polish cities close to the border). Austria-Hungary was preparing an offensive from Galicia toward Lublin and Kholm and counted on instigating an anti-Russian uprising in Poland. But on August 1, 1914, Russia took a preemptive step with the promulgation of the appeal to the Polish people in which Poland was promised not only the autonomy even broader than that of Kingdom of Poland before the rebellions, but also the reintegration into the new Poland of historically Polish lands that the partitions gave to Germany and Austria-Hungary ("Let the boundaries slicing the Polish people into parts be

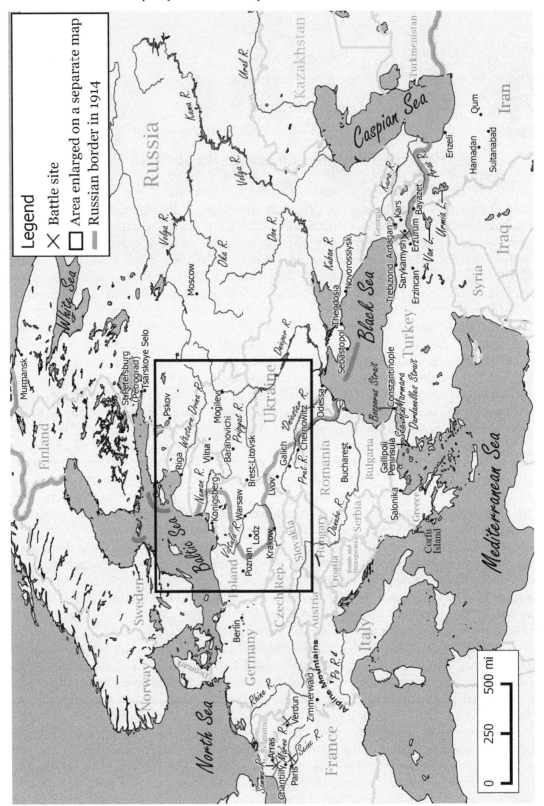

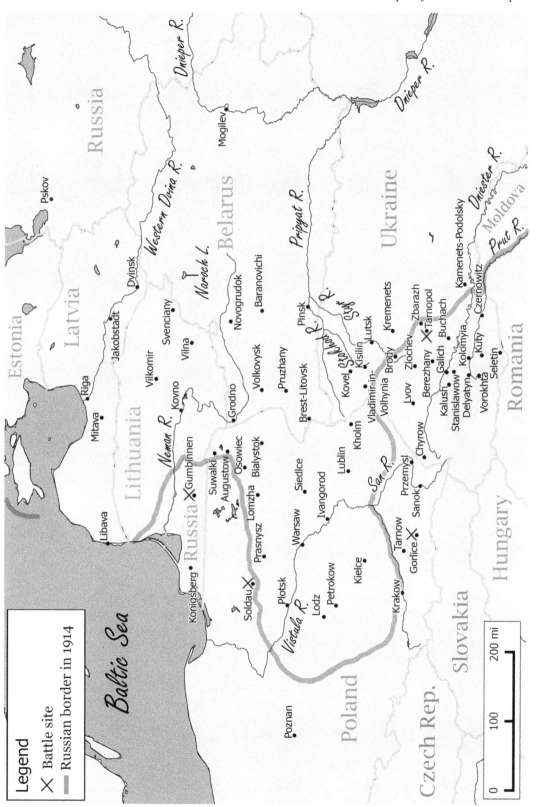

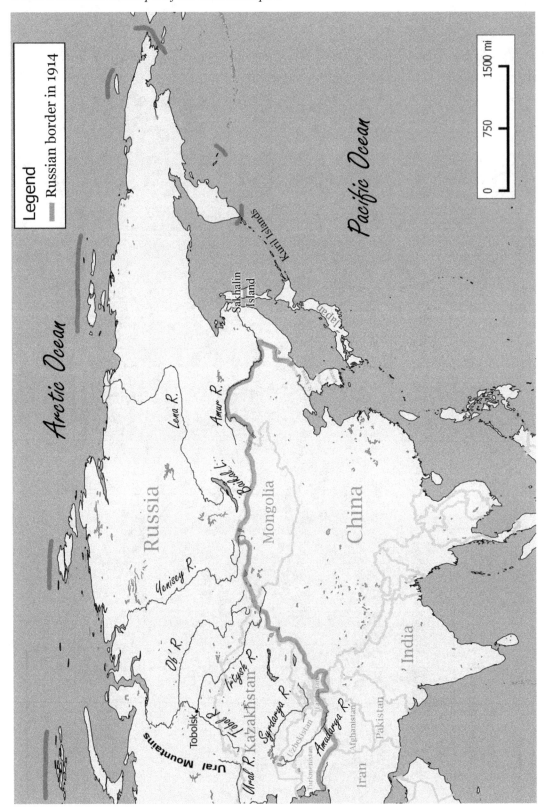

obliterated. Let it reunite under the scepter of the Russian Tsar, where Poland will revive, free in its faith, language, and self-government"). After the appeal, all prominent public figures in Poland declared their loyalty to Russia, and the Polish battalions under Pilsudski recruited in Austrian Galicia found very few volunteers in Russian Poland.

In the immediate wake of mobilization, army strength was brought up to about 3.5 million men, but its full deployment in the theater of operations would require another two months. Yet, the dire situation of its western allies (French attempt to advance in Alsace failed, while German troops advanced into northern France via Belgium and were already threatening Paris) prompted Russia to make haste. On August 4, Russian troops entered Eastern Prussia. The 1st army under P. von Rennekampf defeated the Germans by Gumbinnen (August 7) and advanced on Königsberg. German commander, M. von Prittwitz decided to withdraw the army from East Prussia. That decision sent shockwaves through Berlin, and an immediate order was issued to redeploy two army corps from the French front, and reroute to the east 4 more corps that were in transit to the western front. That saved the French who were now able to stop the Germans in the battle of Marne River, and essentially derailed the German plan of a lightning-fast victory in the west. In East Prussia, Russia suffered the consequences of its generosity though. Leaving only a defensive screen against the 1st army, the Germans used dense railway network of the region to throw all their forces against the 2nd army (under A. Samsonov), which was advancing from the south. It was surrounded in the area of Soldau, and the fighting of August 10–18 completely wiped out 2 of its corps. Then the Germans wheeled around to throw their full force against the 1st army and forced it to retreat. While the defeat was by no means a strategic disaster, the country perceived it as a catastrophe, and the morale of the army and the whole country was much affected.

On August 23, 1914, Russia, Britain, and France signed the mutual obligation not to enter into separate peace with Germany or advance peace offers without prior agreement with both allies. Strictly speaking, it was only from this moment that the Entente became a formal alliance. The allies also had a preliminary discussion on their objectives for when the war ends (something not raised before). The allies agreed to guarantee Turkey's territorial integrity as long as it stayed neutral. In fulfilment of the promise given to the Poles, Russia claimed Austrian Galicia and Poznan (the German slice of Poland), while the allies preferred to show lenience to Austria so as to drive it away from Germany.

Failures in Eastern Prussia were more than offset by victories on the South-Western Front. Having repelled the Austrians' advance on Lublin, five Russian armies (the 3rd under N. Ruzsky, the 4th under A. Evert, the 5th under P. Pleve, the 8th under A. Brusilov, and the 9th under P. Lechitsky) went on the offensive. By August 29, after 3 weeks of fighting, they thoroughly trounced Austrian armies, and took 120 thousand prisoners. Russian troops penetrated 300 km deep into Austria-Hungary, seized Galich and Lvov, crossed San River and besieged Przemysl. On September 15, the 1st and 10th (commander F. Sievers) Russian armies began the offensive in Suwalki and Augustow area on the Prussian border, and by early October seized some German territory.

In late September of 1914, the Germans and Austrians built up an offensive into the heart of Poland and advanced to within a few kilometers of Warsaw. But in the Warsaw–Ivangorod operation of October 1–7, that offensive was beaten back, and Russian troops reached the western border of Poland and threatened Krakow. At the same time, to the south, there was bitter fighting between the Austrians and Russian 3rd and 8th armies at the San River, Przemysl and Chyrow. On October 22, the Austrians began to retreat along the whole length of the front. In early November, the Germans undertook a new offensive in Poland and forced the Russians to retreat in Lodz area, but were themselves enveloped and barely managed to fight their way out of encirclement. German advance faltered, and by November 15 Russian troops approached Krakow but soon stopped the offensive. Both sides were seriously exhausted. By late December, the eastern front settled into a trench warfare along its whole length from the Baltic to Romania. At the same time, the western front went quiet from the North Sea to Switzerland.

On the Baltic Sea, fighting was limited to skirmishes. German cruiser 'Magdeburg' and Russian cruiser 'Pallada' blew up on the mines. While German navy was stronger than Russian (but much weaker than British) it did not dare attack Russia's strong coastal defenses. After concluding a secret military alliance with Germany in summer, Turkey entered the war on the Central Powers side. Since Russia's three modern dreadnoughts in the Black Sea were still under construction, while the available armor-clads were slow, two German cruisers ('Goeben' and 'Breslau') entered the Black Sea (October 16) and shelled Odessa, Sebastopol, Theodosia, and Novorossiysk. Turkey's entry into the war created the Caucasus front. It was commanded by the viceroy in the Caucasus, Count I. Vorontsov-Dashkov. His deputy was A. Myshlayevsky, and the staff commander was N. Yudenich. Russian troops took Bayazet, but soon the Turks went on the offensive and by mid-December reached Ardagan and Kars. Yet, in the course of Sarykamysh operation (December 8 to January 5, 1915) they were completely defeated (of 90 thousand troops only 12.5 remained) and retreated back into Turkey (N. Yudenich became the Army of the Caucasus commander on December 25).

Overall, the fighting in 1914 favored Russia. In the north, the frontline bit into Eastern Prussia, in Poland it followed the line Plotsk – east of Lodz and Petrokow – Kielce, and in the south Russia held a major chunk of Austrian Galicia (along the line Tarnow – Gorlice – to the west of Sanok, Kolomyia and Czernowitz). In the Caucasus, the front line was all inside Turkish territory and extended into Persia to Lake Urmia. But the shortage of arms and ammunition (especially artillery ordnance) began to be felt by the end of the year. All the sides to this war deluded themselves that it would be a short one, and expended much more materiel within the half-year of fighting than they expected. Their ability to make good the shortage was not the same though. Russia produced about 100 thousand artillery shells per month but was using over a million a month. Another mistake caused by miscalculating the duration of the war was that excellent NCO cadre called up from reserve was quickly wasted at the front. Called-up NCOs were often not needed at the front yet and were put to fight as common soldiers only to become the casualties of the early months of the war. They would have been much better used to train raw recruits.

The campaign of 1915 began well for Russia. In January, German offence in the areas of Grodno and Prasnysz was repulsed. Joint Austrian-German offensive in the Carpathians was repulsed as well. Besieged Przemysl fell on March 9 with the surrender of 117 thousand troops. Russian troops crossed the Carpathians and entered Hungary. Yet, at this time German-Austrian alliance decided to concentrate efforts on the eastern front in order to defeat Russia decisively and take it out of the war (they amassed 140 divisions in the east and left only 90 on the western front). On April 18, 1915, German and Austrian troops under General A. von Machensen went on the offensive in Galicia. With a huge superiority in troops (twofold) and artillery (fourfold) they broke through the Russian front near Gorlice by wiping out Russian trenches with enormous barrage from heavy guns (700 thousand shells were fired within a few hours). By early May, Russian troops withdrew from the Carpathians to the line on San River, but held out for only 2–3 weeks there. Przemysl was abandoned on May 21 and Lvov on June 9. At the same time, Germany mounted an offensive in the north along the Neman River. By mid-July, the Germans took Libava and approached Mitava. On July 22, Russian troops withdrew from Warsaw, and by August 10 the cities of Mitava, Lomzha, Siedlce, Lublin, and Kholm were lost. By August 20, Russia lost Kovno (Kaunas), Augustow, Osowiec, Bialystok, Brest-Litovsk, Kovel, Vladimir-in-Volhynia, Lutsk, and Brody.

The shortages of ammunition and arms, which were at their worst at this phase in war, had the most grievous effect. They undermined the morale in the army, while the country at large talked about treason, and a swell of critical attacks on the government came from liberal and left-leaning circles. Since both the military and civilian circles pinned blame on the Army Ministry, the minister, V. Sukhomlinov was fired, even though staving off that hunger for ammunition was not within his powers. Mindful of the importance of being on the right side of public opinion in wartime, Nicholas II fired some more ministers who were especially unpopular and convened the Duma in July. Yet, these steps backfired: irresponsible elements in the Duma and outside it decided that the time was propitious for wangling out of the authorities the concessions they previously refused to make. The Duma turned into the venue for sharp attacks against the government and supreme command, which only helped to build up the public's mistrust of the regime. Against that background, Nicholas II decided to make himself the supreme commander-in-chief, and on August 23 he arrived at the general headquarters (which shortly before was moved from Baranovichi to Mogilev). He appointed M. Alexeyev as his chief of staff, while the Grand Duke Nicholas was made viceroy in the Caucasus. The North-Western Front was split into the Northern (commander N. Ruzsky) and Western (A. Evert).

By late August, 1915, a 'progressive bloc' with the majority of votes emerged in the Duma (300 deputies out of 420). In encompassed the moderates and left-leaning circles (its leaders included Baron V. Meller-Zakomelsky, P. Milyukov, P. Krupensky, V. Shulgin, D. Grimm, A. Shingarev, N. Nekrasov, and others) and began to promote the idea of the 'cabinet of trust', meaning the government answerable to the Duma. The emperor strongly opposed the idea, and on September 15 he fired several ministers who argued for making concessions to the 'progressive bloc' (A. Samarin, Prince N. Scherbatov, A. Krivoshein, and P. Kharitonov). In those same months, the revolutionary circles stepped up their activity. At August 23 conference of socialists in Zimmerwald (Switzerland) Lenin demanded that "imperialist war be turned into a civil one". Resolution of the conference declared that the objective of "the proletarians of the world" should be to fight for immediate peace – the slogan widely used in revolutionary propaganda inside Russia and a shot in the arm for the revolutionary movement that seemed to wilt at the war's outbreak.

After August 20, 1915, Russian troops had to abandon Grodno, Vilna, Vilkomir, Svenciany, Volkovysk, and Pruzhany. In September, German cavalry units pierced the front south of Svenciany and reached Moscow–Brest railway, but by September 19 those units were destroyed or pushed back. In the south, Russian troops had a major success by Tarnopol and won back part of Galicia. In September, the allies finally attempted an offensive at Arras and in Champagne, which gave Russia some relief at the eastern front. By the end of September, the front line stabilized again and ran from Riga to Jacobstadt to Dvinsk to Lake Naroch to Novogrudok to Baranovichi to Pinsk to Kremenets to Tarnopol and the Dniester River. By the autumn of 1915, the Central Powers had 137 infantry and 24 cavalry divisions on the eastern front compared to 85 infantry and 1 cavalry division on the western front. Russian defeats of 1915 had repercussions in the Balkans, where Bulgaria entered war on the Central Powers side on September 23. That put Serbia into an impossible position, and in December remnants of its army had to abandon the country and evacuate to the island of Corfu. The Balkans were almost completely controlled by the Central Powers. The British sustained heavy losses in their attempt to take Gallipoli, but never seized the Turkish positions and evacuated by the end of December. In the Caucasus, the Turks put together an army of 150 thousand against 133 thousand Russians and briefly went on the offensive in summer, but on June 26–July 21 they were stopped. Since the activities of Turkish and German agents (and of the armed bands they created) led to deteriorating situation in Persia, an additional corps under General Baratov was landed in Enzeli and unleashed an offensive towards Qum and Hamadan. Following the Hamadan operation of October 17–December 3, the front line stretched from Lake Van to Sultanabad, which provided an effective shield for Iran itself and also thwarted Turkish attempts to incite the Muslims of Central Asia to rise against Russia.

Once the front was stabilized and the refugees accommodated, the events of 1915 did not significantly affect the prevailing calm in Russia, especially since the economy was as yet little hurt by the war: increases in the price of staple foods did not exceed 25–40% (even though meat and sugar consumption grew) and did not inflict pain since the salaries and wages rose too. Military industry was going through a boom with large new plants under construction and older ones retooled. Big orders for military supplies were placed in the USA and Britain. On August 17, 1915, there were instituted a number of Special Councils. Those were the highest government bodies chaired by specially appointed ministers and answerable to the emperor alone: the council on defense of the state, the council on fuel supply, the council on provision of food, and the council on transportation and refugee accommodation. On June 28, 1916, this newly added governmental superstructure was topped with the Special Ministerial Council for coordination of army and navy supply and logistics.

By this time, nongovernmental Zemstvo Union and City Union had built up a major operation to help the army. They took over some quartermaster supply functions and did particularly much with the setting up of meal stations and the system for moving the wounded from the frontline to hospitals in the rear. On July 10, 1915, the two unions set up *Zemgor* (joint *zemstvo* and city committee on victualling the army) and the Central Military-Industrial Committee dealing primarily with the placement of army procurement contracts. The Committee had a ramified network of local offices, and by the late 1916 it received 16.7% of all procurement orders, and fulfilled 11% of such orders. Zemstvo Union numbered about 8 thousand various local offices and hundreds of thousands of employees, but its main source of funding was the treasury. But as the Duma was engaged in shrill polemical fight with the government, the role of *zemstvo*-like nongovernmental organizations was grossly exaggerated to serve as counterpoint to the government's 'inaction'. Another popular exaggeration in the rhetoric of many circles regarded the role of notorious Rasputin (who was very close to the court and reigning family), to whom all unpopular decisions were now ascribed.

Early in 1916, the government stood on perfectly firm ground, and there was no real need to resume the Duma session suspended on September 3, 1915 (in Austria, the parliament was not convened at all in 1914–1917). It could be reconvened after the war (by which time the current Duma's term would have expired, and the government could deal with a new one elected in peacetime). Yet, emperor Nicholas II was unwilling to antagonize the civil society. While he absolutely ruled out the prospect of letting the Duma form a new government, he made another concession to the Duma by replacing Prime Minister I. Goremykin (particularly maligned by the Duma) with B. Sturmer. He let the Duma resume its session on February 9, 1916.

In December of 1915, during the coordination meeting of allied general staffs in Chantilly, M. Alexeyev suggested for 1916 a joint allied strike against Hungary, with Russia attacking from the Carpathians while the allies strike north from Salonika. That would drive a wedge between Germany and its supply sources. Instead, it was decided that in the summer of 1916 the allies would launch a coordinated assault on both the western and eastern fronts. But the Germans anticipated the allies by beginning their offensive against the French fortress of Verdun in February. To help the French, on March 5–17, 1916, the Russian army undertook the offensive by Lake Naroch. While extremely gory fighting raged around Verdun (over a million soldiers perished there before the year's end), the Austrians began an offensive against Italy by advancing from the Tyrolese Alps towards the River Po (Italy joined the war on the Entente side in the summer of 1915). But on May 22, Russian army led by A. Brusilov launched a vigorous offensive along the wide segment of the South-Western Front (between Pinsk and Czernowitz). By that time, the issues with supplies shortages that so plagued the army in 1915 were completely resolved, and the troops were free to shoot as many shells as they cared to. In fact, by November 1, 1916, Russia's stockpile of artillery ordnance (7 million) even exceeded that of France (6.2 million) and Britain (3.9 million).

The 8th army (commander A. Kaledin) spearheaded the main thrust towards Lutsk. In three days, it penetrated enemy defenses to the depth of 70–80 km and reached Styr River. By early July of 1916, Russian troops took Lutsk and approached Vladimir-in-Volhynia, while to the south the 7th and 9th army seized a large territory with the cities of Buchach, Czernowitz, and Kuty. Austrian advance in Italy was blocked, and the Central Powers started redeployment of 34 divisions from Italy and the western front to the east to counter the Russian offensive. But when the German and Austrian counterstrike came (near Lutsk on June 3) it was beaten back, and on July 15 five Russian armies resumed the general offensive and took Brody, Galich, Stanislawow, and Kolomyia. By the time they reached Stokhod River, fighting became an increasingly drawn-out affair, and by early September the front stabilized along the line Stokhod River – Kisilin – Zlochev – Berezhany – Galich – Stanislawow – Delyatyn – Vorokhta – Seletin. Austrian and German casualties were about 1.5 million men and Russia's stood at 0.5 million.

This Russian victory gave the French a much-needed relief at Verdun, which helped them launch their own offensive on River Somme. As a result, by the autumn of 1916, Germany was forced to switch to the defensive on both fronts. These successes of Entente allies prompted long-vacillating Romania to declare war on Austria-Hungary (on August 14). But the Romanian invasion of Transylvania was soon trounced, and they suffered another major defeat in Dobruja where the Central Powers assembled a formidable force of German, Bulgarian, and Turkish troops. Romania lost all of Wallachia (Bucharest was evacuated on November 22), which forced Russia to stretch its front by an additional 500 km to protect what was left of Romania (and send it major arms supplies as well). This new, Romanian front was commanded by V. Sakharov. Meanwhile, on December 30, 1915, Russian troops started the offensive against Erzurum in the Caucasus front. On February 3, 1916, that key fortress was taken, and the Turks were pushed 70–100 km to the west having lost half their men and almost all artillery. The operation to seize Trebizond (January 23 to

April 5, 1916) was a success. Those two victories provided relief to British troops in Mesopotamia (earlier, at the end of 1915, the Turks dealt the British a serious defeat there). By summer, the Turks amassed a new army and tried to take Erzurum back, but failed. Moreover, the Russian counteroffensive that followed pushed them back far to the west with the loss of Erzincan. Russian troops advanced south of Lake Urmia as well. The only setback was in the south (in Persia), where the corps under Baratov had to retreat east of Hamadan.

As early as in the summer of 1916, a commission was set up to prepare for the future peace conference and to draw up Russia's wish list for such a conference. Russia expected to get eastern Galicia, northern Bukovina, and Carpathian Ruthenian area from Austria-Hungary and Constantinople with the straits and western Armenia from Turkey. Future Poland was conceived as a nation with its own army and constitution linked to Russia through a personal union. Another expectation was to create a Czechoslovak kingdom (military units made of Czechs and Slovaks taken prisoner were already being formed in Russia). The successes of Russian arms in the Caucasus led to the conclusion of agreements with Britain and France regarding postwar settlement in Turkey. Finally, Russia stood to obtain so long sought-after straits (the Bosporus and Dardanelles) and Constantinople, as well as Turkish Armenia.

By the late 1916, the effects of war began to tell on Russia, even if not so severely as on other combatant nations. Shortage of labor began to be felt in the agricultural sector, and there developed shortages of some foodstuffs. The latter was partly due to sharply reduced availability of industrial products on the market (for instance, 2/3 to 3/4 of all output of textile industry went to meet the military needs) and therefore the growing prices of goods. Unable to get as much as they wanted for their money, farmers started to hold back their own produce, rather than sell it. Even so, for wartime conditions, the reduction of agricultural output was much less than could be expected: the acreage under crops shrank by only 12%, cereal crops harvest by 20%, and sugar output by a third. But with the country being quite unused to such difficulties, many people responded by beginning to hoard staples for the rainy day. Wholesale price of bread went up by 91%, of sugar by 48%, of meat by 138%, and of butter by 145%. Even though neither the army, nor the civilian population experienced any shortages of food (much unlike Germany), the psychological effect of growing food prices made itself felt. In the summer of 1916, the attempt to recruit Central Asians for non-combat work in the army's rear (indigenous population was exempt from military draft) triggered a rebellion in Turkestan, where several thousand Russian settlers and officials were slaughtered. Martial law was imposed, and newly appointed governor A. Kuropatkin put the rebellion down before the year's end.

Overall, by the start of 1917, the situation on the Russian front was quite sound, certainly no worse than that of its allies on the western front, and there were no reasons, military or economic, to prevent Russia from holding its own till the war's end. Enemy troops never made it beyond the westernmost border-straddling governorates. Even after the worst retreats of 1915, the front line never advanced east of Pinsk or Baranovichi or caused concern that an enemy breakthrough would threaten the vital national centers (meanwhile, the western front was still dangerously close to Paris). While the northern segments of the front ran through Russian territory, in the south it ran over enemy ground (and in Trans-Caucasia it was deep in the Turkish territory). Russia held about 2 million prisoners of war (1737 thousand Austrians, 159 thousand Germans, and 65 thousand Turks).

The hardships of war were felt in Russia to a much lesser extent than in other involved nations. Also, for Russia, it was much less of an exertion of all national resources than for its foes or allies. Even though Russia fielded the biggest army of all, unlike the others it did not strain its human resources. In fact, mobilization call-up was excessive: it only increased the inevitable non-combat losses caused by illness and poor sanitation (what is known as medical losses). Besides, bloated reserve units of men torn away from their families were a receptive audience for agitation by the revolutionaries. Russia's loss of lives in combat (variously estimated from 775 to 908 thousand) was exactly the same as the added losses of Central Powers on the eastern front (about 300 thousand for Germany, 450 thousand for Austria-Hungary, and 150 thousand for Turkey). But even if one takes into account medical losses and the loss of Russian lives in captivity (the biggest medical losses actually happened at exactly the time of revolutionary turmoil and gradual collapse of the front it caused: average monthly number of frontline troops evacuated due to sickness was under 17 thousand in 1914, about 35 thousand in 1915, 52.5 thousand in 1916, and a staggering 146 thousand in 1917), the summary losses still hurt Russia much less than was the case in other countries. The percentage of men mobilized was the lowest in Russia (only 39% of all men in 15 to 49 age bracket, whereas in Germany it stood at 81%, in Austria-Hungary at 74%, in France at 79%, in Britain at 50%, and in Italy at 72%). Besides, per each 1000 of mobilized men, Russia lost 115 dead, whereas in Germany that number was 154, in Austria 122, in France 168, and in Britain 125. In terms of the effect on population at large, Russia's losses per 1000 men aged 15 to 49 stood at 45 men, Germany's 125, Austria's 90, France's 133, and Britain's 62. In terms of lives lost per 1000 of the total population, Russia lost 11, Germany 31, Austria 18, France 34, and Britain 16. Russia was just about the only combatant to have no issues with food supply. Something like the German "war bread" of 1917 vintage would have been unimaginable in Russia.

Russian industry somewhat reduced the output of civilian goods, but overall, wartime years brought a strong expansion. During the war years, the output of metalworking industry grew by 3 times, and of chemical industry by 2.5 times, while the production of armaments grew several-fold. Compared to 1914, the monthly production of rifles doubled (from 55 to 110 thousand), of machine guns grew by 6 times (from 160 to 900), of small caliber artillery guns by 9 times (from 70 to 655), of 3-inch shells for those guns by 40 times (from 50 thousand to 2 million), and of large caliber guns by 4 times. The construction of 4 dreadnoughts for the Baltic was nearing completion, and by the end of 1917 the Baltic fleet was expected to have 8 of them. The number of airplanes in the army tripled (from 263 to 716). By the spring of 1917, Russian army had 24 thousand machine guns (the French had 13.6 thousand and the British 5.2 thousand), 6957 pieces of field artillery (the French had 6588 and the British 3876), 2548 pieces of large caliber artillery (the French had 5134 and the British 2758). The bulk of all this weaponry was manufactured domestically (in 1915–1916, supplies from the overseas amounted to only 10 485 machine guns and 446 large caliber guns). The growth spurt achieved by Russian industry strongly impressed the contemporaries. Winston Churchill wrote "There were few episodes of the Great War more amazing than the revival, rearmament, and resumption of an enormous effort by Russia in 1916... By the summer of 1916, Russia, which for 18 prior months was nearly unarmed, and which survived some terrible defeats in 1915, truly managed through its own effort and the use of allies funding to field (that is to say organize, arm, and supply) 60 army corps instead of 35 that it entered the war with".

The acreage under cotton, which becomes a strategic crop during wartime, grew from 430 to 534 thousand hectares. Production of fuels was not only sustained at prewar level, but expanded: coal output went from 31.9 million tons to 34.3 million, and oil production went from 9 million tons to 9.9. Huge financial outlays required by the war (up to 39 billion rubles) were covered from domestic sources – taxation and selling of war bonds. Foreign loans played a rather minor part, they covered about 15% of all outlays (6 billion rubles). Of 16 thousand kilometers of railway track under construction when the war started, 12 thousand were completed (not counting the branch lines built behind the front to supply it). The construction of the segment of Trans-Siberian railway that followed Amur River on the Russian side of the border was completed, and the laying of the second track for the Trans-Siberian railway began. In less than two years, a 1050-kilometer long railway reaching beyond the Arctic Circle across harsh terrain was built to reach Murmansk (where a seaport was built from scratch to serve as the main entrepot for supplies brought by the allies).

Russian supreme command planned decisive offensive operations for 1917. That prospect sat poorly with those elements for whom victorious conclusion of the war would have put paid to any hope of success. The revolutionary elements exploited mental weariness brought by the war in their propaganda calling for immediate peace at any price. Meanwhile, the liberal circles gave currency to suspicions that 'forces of the right' are pressuring the government to conclude a separate peace. The Duma's 'progressive bloc' (which, unlike the revolutionary socialists, had no base of support in the general population) unleashed a barrage of criticism that only helped growing distrust of authority amongst the educated class. Every misstep of the government was misrepresented in support of widely circulated hints of 'treason in the high places'. Prior to the opening of a new Duma session on November 1, 1916, its leaders lacked any constructive program of their own, but intended to bring about the downfall of Prime Minister Sturmer's government and call for the government responsible to the Duma.

Even though the army had long lost most of its prewar cadre of professional officers (in the infantry, a regiment sometimes had only 2 to 3 professional officers; the cavalry and artillery fared better), and the absolute majority of officers (there now was 8 times more of them than at war's outbreak) were either reservists or yesterday's students, teachers, and clerks who went through an abridged course of training in military colleges or ensign schools, the order was still firmly maintained. The number of deserters was negligible and cases of refusal to follow orders extremely rare. Factory workers' milieu was a different story, especially in the capital city, where the most important defense industry plants were concentrated. That was the social group most receptive to incitement by the revolutionaries even before the war, and after years of what seemed like an endless war, such incitement bore fruit and the last vestiges of respect for the tsar's authority evaporated.

By the end of 1916 and in early 1917, there was no doubt among the politicians that the war would end with the Central Powers defeat. Those who yearned for the revolution and Russia's defeat in the war (the Bolsheviks and their closest allies among the socialists) were losing any hope. The only solution available to them was to try and take Russia out of the war before the final defeat of Austria and Germany, so that Russia would not become one of the victorious allies. In a victorious and strengthened Russia, they would have lost any influence. Those circles that did not want a revolution or Russia's defeat, but wanted to change the system of government also felt the need to make hurry. This was the moment when Russia's ability to hold back the threat from foreign enemies seemed no longer in doubt, yet the end of war did not appear imminent. Therefore, such liberal circles thought the moment propitious (if not uniquely favorable) to wrestle from the imperial authorities the concessions they could hardly hope to win in peacetime.

At the opening of Duma session on November 1, the leader of '*Kadet*' party, P. Milyukov, gave an anti-government speech with the refrain "is it foolishness or treason?" woven into it. The speech made a splash both at home and abroad. The government hastened to send the allies telegrams that allegations of a possible separate treaty are false. On November 10, Prime Minister Sturmer was replaced with A. Trepov, but on November 22 the Duma passed a resolution that demanded eradication of "the influence exerted by dark and irresponsible forces" and for a new cabinet agreeable to the Duma. The State Council passed a similar resolution. Duma session ended on December 16. The very next night, a group of right-wingers (led by V. Purishkevich and Grand Duke Dmitry Pavlovich) assassinated Rasputin, who was a discredit to the ruling family (and epitomized "the dark forces"). That did not stop the allegations of "dark forces" behind the throne though.

At the end of December of 1916, Russian troops undertook an offensive out of Riga and advanced to Mitava, but after a week of fighting the advance stopped. On December 27, Prince N. Golitsyn was named a new prime minister. On January 19, 1917, the allies gathered for their conference in Petrograd (as too 'German-sounding' Petersburg was now renamed). The French insisted on the earliest possible offensive (in early April), but that matter was left open. Russia gave France the promise to support the latter's claim to Rhineland (lands on the western bank of the Rhine). A new Duma session opened on February 14, and was marked by a direct appeal to fight the authorities from A. Kerensky (the question of putting him on trial for sedition was left in midair). By this point though, it was not the Duma speeches (those were mostly followed by the liberal-minded civil society) but the agitation of the lower classes by the agents of revolution that drove the events.

Early in 1917, Petrograd had the population of 2.5 million, but no more than 10 thousand armed men (the police, Cossack units, and boot camp units of some regiments) that the regime could rely on. At the same time, in the city and around it there were stationed about 200 thousand soldiers of reserve units (reserve battalions of regiments of the guards for the most part) who were to be sent to the front for the planned spring offensive. This mass of soldiery cooped up in cramped quarters, dying of boredom, and less than eager to go to the front was quite receptive to anti-war propaganda. They could be trouble in case of disorders. Yet, during the war such street disorders were very rare, and the danger was not given a second thought.

On February 23, 1917, the day after the emperor left for his headquarters at the front, street demonstrations broke out in Petrograd. Heavy snowdrifts delayed the trains bringing flour for baking bread into the city, and bread was temporarily in short supply. Clutches of those who were left empty-handed after standing in bread lines loudly voiced their outrage in the streets. The revolutionaries who were advocating a strike, exploited the situation. As early as February 23, there were 90 thousand striking workers, and one ward committee of the Bolsheviks decided to organize a general strike. Bread shortages were over by February 24, yet instead of ending, the demonstrations evolved into political protests under the slogans "Down with autocracy" and "Down with war". Neither the Duma, nor the government attached much importance to those demonstrations. The emperor was more concerned with attacks in the Duma than with street disorders. Upon being notified about developments in the capital on February 25, he ordered the commander of Petrograd military district, S. Khabalov to put an end to disorders.

By that time, skirmishes between the crowds and the police and Cossacks produced first casualties. On February 26, soldiers from one of the reserve battalions stationed in the city opened fire on the troops engaged in dispersing the crowds. In the morning of the 27th, the reserve battalion of Volhynia regiment mutinied and killed its commander, and reserve battalions of Pavel's and Lithuanian regiments followed suit. The whole right bank of Neva River in the city was already controlled by striking workers who now crossed to the left bank and joined forces with the mutineers. That proved to be the turning point. Khabalov and Military Minister Belyaev managed to scrape together only one thousand reliable troops, who tried to force their way to the focal area of the rebellion, but were simply swallowed by huge crowds. The mob broke into the Tauride Palace, where the Duma sat in session. The session was adjourned, and the new "Temporary committee for the restoration of order and for communication with agencies and individuals" hastily formed (chaired by Duma chairman, M. Rodzyanko). A group of revolutionaries that the mobs liberated from prison arrived at the Duma building. They and socialist members of the Duma jointly formed the first "Executive Committee of the Soviet of Workers' Deputies", which promptly sent its agents to various factories. The Soviet[27] itself first convened that same night (it was made up of representatives from mutinied units and striking factories: a total of 250 representatives, mostly Socialist-Revolutionaries and the *Menshevik* brand of Social Democrats) and elected the Executive Committee headed by N. Chheidze, M. Skobelev, and A. Kerensky. That same day, the Central Committee of Social-Democratic party issued the manifesto "To all citizens of Russia" which declared that the revolution had triumphed. Due to the hopelessness of resistance, a small detachment of loyal troops around the Winter Palace was dismissed.

From the very first days, real power in Petrograd belonged to the extreme left – the Petrograd Soviet of Deputies. On March 1, the Soviet issued its Order No1, which demanded that only the Soviet's orders be followed, that soldier committees be formed, that officers must be disarmed, and traditional forms of respect for rank be abolished. The Duma's 'Temporary Committee' in affect served as a smokescreen for the Soviet, insofar as it pretended to be the expression of "the people's will". Its reports to the army headquarters created the impression that power has passed into the hands of Duma-controlled government.

Upon learning about the military mutiny, Nicholas II sent to Petrograd a detachment of 700 Knights of the Order of St. George under General N. Ivanov and some additional army units pulled from the front. On February 28, he also left for the residence in Tsarskoye Selo. In the evening of March 1, Ivanov's troops reached Tsarskoye Selo, while the emperor's train arrived in Pskov, where Northern Front commander, General Ruzsky tried to talk the emperor into agreeing to the government responsible to the Duma. During this conversation, the emperor sent N. Ivanov the telegram instructing him to take no steps until the emperor's arrival. Early in the morning of March 2, the emperor gave his permission for Rodzyanko to form the government. When informed of that by Ruzsky, Rodzyanko replied that by then the city of Petrograd wanted the emperor's abdication. That gave events a new turn. With emperor's knowledge, Alexeyev sent all the front commanders telegrams asking for their opinion on abdication. Once Nicholas learned of the

---

[27] This Russian word that later history made known to the whole world literally means 'council'.

answers (all the commanders advised abdication) his mind was made up. When the Duma's Temporary Committee members arrived in Pskov that same evening, Nicholas II declared that he abdicates in favor of his brother, Grand Duke Mikhail Alexandrovich (and not his son and heir as was widely expected). At the same time, Prince G. Lvov was appointed Chairman of Council of Ministers, Grand Duke Nicholas Nikolaevich was made supreme commander-in-chief, and a popular general, L. Kornilov was appointed commander of Petrograd military district. The emperor also signed the appeal to the troops asking them to swear allegiance to the Provisional Government and continue the fight against foreign enemies. After the British government refused them asylum, the emperor's family stayed at Tsarskoye Selo, and on July 31 it was moved to Tobolsk in Siberia.

On March 2, 1917, the Duma's Temporary Committee was transformed into the Provisional Government. Petrograd Soviet refused to be included. It was perfectly content with the situation where it de facto replaced the ruling monarch, yet bore no responsibilities, while the legitimate Provisional Government provided it cover. Provisional Government was the government in name only, as it was fully dependent on the Soviet, which alone could wield real power.

The eight months that followed were the time of disintegration of Russian statehood. Monarchy as an institution was not abolished with the abdication of Nicholas. Even though Grand Duke Mikhail Alexandrovich did not dare accept the crown under the circumstances, the final decision on the form of government was left to the future Constituent Assembly. The machinery of Russian state continued to operate, and most laws stayed in force. Territorial integrity was maintained as well. Government bodies and agencies (except for those connected personally to the monarch, such as His Majesty's Own Chancellery or the Ministry of Court Affairs) continued to operate. Gendarme corps (political police) was abolished. Police was now known as militia. Some new ministries were spun off from the existing ones: Ministry of Labor, Ministry of Food Supply, Ministry of Social Care, Ministry of Mails and Telegraphs, Ministry of Confessions.

Local police officials were replaced with governorate, city, and *uezd* commissioners of Provisional Government. At first, those were simply chairmen of corresponding *zemstvo* boards, but later they were appointed separately. On May 21, 1917, there was introduced a new system of direct universal election to *zemstvo* bodies. The police were replaced with the militia (answerable to the *zemstvo*). Local administrative bodies of other ministries changed little. Yet, in most cases the real power was wielded by the parallel government – revolutionary *soviets*.

The first Provisional Government (where the only representative of the left was Kerensky as Minister of Justice) was short-lived. On May 5, the government added new members from the left (Socialist-Revolutionaries and *Trudoviks*). From July 24, when Kerensky became the head of government, Socialist-Revolutionaries became the majority. The Soviets were increasingly radicalized too as the Bolshevik influence within them grew. The soldiery at the war's fronts continued to be steadily corrupted by Bolshevik propaganda (with the full connivance of Kerensky and the left allied with him). Refusal to obey orders became commonplace, and there were cases of the lynching of officers.

Nevertheless, Russia stayed in the war and declared its commitment to the duties of an ally. In summer, it was decided to go on the offensive at the South-Western Front. It was doomed to failure by the degree of corruption in the troops. The offensive by the 8th, 11th, and 7th armies was launched on June 16. The 8th army managed to puncture Austrian defenses south of Stanislawow and seize Galich and Kalush. It proved impossible to press the success though, as the troops refused to risk their lives in attacks. When the enemy struck a counterblow on July 6, the troops abandoned positions and retreated with almost no resistance. At the Northern Front, the 5th army began the offensive, but soon returned to square one, and so did the 9th army at the Western Front. The offensive on the Romanian front began on July 7, but had to be rolled back by the 12th due to the dangerous situation in the north. By late July, a large territory with the cities of Zbarazh, Tarnopol, Buchach, Kolomyia, and Czernowitz was lost, and the front line rolled back to Kamenets-Podolsky.

In the spring of 1917, Lenin, who was brought back to Russia courtesy of the German High Command and amply supplied with money, was successfully spreading defeatist propaganda. On July 2–4, the Bolsheviks attempted to seize power in Petrograd, but failed, and their leaders had to go into hiding for a while. On August 12–15, a large gathering in Moscow (dubbed the Conference of State) attended by 2 thousand representatives of the army, clergy and civil society expressed its support for L. Kornilov, who was appointed commander-in-chief on July 24. Following that, Kerensky attempted to strengthen his authority against the threat from the left. In a deal with Kornilov, he promised to restore discipline in the army, while the latter began to move reliable troops towards Petrograd. Yet, in the last moment, Kerensky got scared. He had suspicions that Kornilov might want to seize power for himself and decided to betray him. On August 27, he declared Kornilov a traitor and a rebel and assumed supreme command of the army himself. In the situation, on August 28 Kornilov declared that he does not recognize Provisional Government's authority, but did nothing further, and was duly arrested. Those events, which the authorities interpreted as facing off renewed danger from the right, only helped the public's drift to the left and the growth of Bolshevik influence. Kerensky boxed himself into a position where he too could only drift to the left.

In an effort to win support of all the forces on the left, on September 1 Kerensky declared Russia to be a republic. The so-called Democratic Conference was convened on September 14 (1500 participants), and on September 21 it elected the Temporary Council of the Russian Republic (also known as pre-parliament). This Council of 555 members was to oversee the executive branch of government until the Constituent Assembly convened (elections for Constituent Assembly were scheduled for November 12). Yet, the government formed on September 25 would last only a month. In an armed coup of October 25, the Bolsheviks seized the Winter Palace and arrested the Provisional Government. The next day, they formed their own – the Council of People's Commissars. The Senate refused to recognize the Bolsheviks and was abolished, and by late November what remained of Russian Empire's laws was abrogated as well.

CPSIA information can be obtained
at www.ICGtesting.com
Printed in the USA
LVHW101044200420
654119LV00019B/1295